PRAISE FOR
THE ROAD TO COURAGE

"Roy Taylor's remarkable recall of character-forming people, events in his fifth year of life, and candor about conquering fears deliver a spellbinding story of Alaska's territorial days. I couldn't put it down.

"Our lives intersected during the late 1950s when the Taylor family homesteaded near my hometown of Ninilchik, Alaska, and helped with our fishing business."

—**LOREN LEMAN**, fisherman, engineer, legislator, and Alaska lieutenant governor

"Four-year-old Roy and five-year-old James trundle up the Alcan highway with their adventurous parents in 1954. The boys' father, a minister, has been called to a post in Valdez, Alaska, where, as it turns out, the church he was to serve is only a hole in the ground. He and his little sons set about building a log cabin church in the three months before winter sets in.

"*The Road to Courage* abounds with a lively, unforgettable cast of hardy people living in Valdez. It remains a monument to a town that would disappear in an earthquake ten years later. Roy Taylor's account of his family's faith, joy, arduous work, setbacks, strengths, and skills will lift readers' hearts. This is the most endearing memoir you will ever read."

—**LAURA KALPAKIAN**, novelist and author of *Memory into Memoir*

"*The Road to Courage* is the gentle story of a young family's survival in a cold, hostile environment. Embracing an opportunity to create a new life, the struggling Taylor family packs their meager belongings and heads north to the Alaskan frontier. Wrapped in their faith, humor, and love for each other, they confront challenges from poverty to wild beasts.

"Narrating the family's story, Roy, the youngest boy, learns to overcome fear and survive hardships through his parents' strength and his older brother's courage. In our current environment of turmoil and anxiety, *The Road to Courage* offers readers a warm hug.

—**JES HART STONE**, author of *Turbulent Waters: A Pacific Northwest Thriller,* www.jeshartstone.com

"If you've ever wondered about life in Alaska's hinterlands, you've found the perfect book to satisfy your curiosity. The story, vivid and compelling, is told with a gentle voice that ranges from soothing to heartbreaking.

"As a small child in a vast expanse teeming with danger, Roy Taylor had no say in where his family landed. Despite fighting isolation and the elements at every turn and facing truly terrifying events, the family remained steadfast in the face of the impassive Alaskan challenge.

"This elegant, deeply touching memoir will give you chills. More daring than the Ingalls clan, the Taylor family will stay in your heart forever."

—**SEÁN THOMAS DWYER**, author of *A Quest for Tears: Surviving Traumatic Brain Injury*

"Ride along with Roy as he recounts his family's epic journey along the Alcan Highway and early challenging days in Valdez, Alaska, where the saying holds true: 'What doesn't kill you only makes you stronger.'"

—**BOB DORGAN**, author of *Sea Pay*

THE ROAD TO COURAGE:

A BOY'S ADVENTURES ON AMERICA'S LAST FRONTIER

The Road to Courage:
A Boy's Adventures on America's Last Frontier

by Roy Taylor

© Copyright 2024 Roy Taylor

ISBN 979-8-88824-376-3

All rights reserved. No part of this publication may be reproduced, stored in a retrieval system, or transmitted in any form or by any means—electronic, mechanical, photocopy, recording, or any other—except for brief quotations in printed reviews, without the prior written permission of the author.

The events in this memoir are true to the best of the author's knowledge. Details of dialogue and action are intended to convey the personalities and the settings as they still live in the author's memory.

Published by

köehlerbooks™

3705 Shore Drive
Virginia Beach, VA 23455
800-435-4811
www.koehlerbooks.com

THE
ROAD TO
COURAGE

VIRGINIA BEACH
CAPE CHARLES

Perhaps the most perilous journey is back along the twisted strands woven through our family tapestry. Those who persevere may stumble upon an unsettling truth. Only by forgiving the past can we find grace to forgive ourselves.

AUTHOR'S NOTE

Despite creative dialogue and scene development, all of the characters in this memoir and their names are real, and the corresponding events and dates are true.

Roy and James at home in Cincinnati

1.
THE LETTER

The bird hurtled through our open window on the same day the letter arrived. The letter that would hurtle us into the unknown. Like a treasure map, it lured us into a world of peril and adventure and changed my life forever. Given the importance of the occasion, one might have expected a more auspicious omen. Perhaps a messenger pigeon, a mourning dove, a quail, or a pheasant. But no, it was a simple city pigeon. We ate it anyway. When you're hungry, everything looks like fair game.

Cincinnati, in the fall of 1953, was languishing through a record hot Indian summer as our family gathered around the red Formica-topped kitchen table midday on Saturday. Mom, in a blue-checked apron and floral-print dress, propped open the kitchen window. The breeze, listless and laden with scorched asphalt and diesel exhaust, scarcely cooled our sweltering, second-floor apartment but did usher in the roar of engines and the honking of horns. Tufts of brilliant fall foliage rose beyond our weathered backyard fence, a wobbly barricade against the chaos of the inner city. Within our meager haven, parched and cracked hard pack sprouted clumps of thistles and withered grass. Shards of broken beer bottles glistened, courtesy of our next-door neighbor. Though Mom always tried to cover our ears during his tirades, I once heard her whisper to Dad that she was pretty sure he was swearing in German.

As was our custom, we paused, heads bowed, for Dad's blessing on our lunch. "Our Dear Heavenly Father . . ."

Squawk! Interrupting the blessing, which turned out to be its last rites, a young pigeon skimmed the table, flapped, and darted down the hallway. Dad's chrome-legged chair clattered to the linoleum. Leaning across the table, he slammed the window shut and turned for the hall.

"Andrew!" Mom slid her chair back. "What on earth are you doing?"

"Catching that pigeon," he called. My four-year-old brother, golden eyes alight and a grin splitting his freckles, raced after Dad.

Fingertips braced on the table, Mom stood. "James, where are *you* going? You haven't been excused."

"'Scuse me. I gotta help Dad." He skidded around the corner.

Flustered but fearful of missing out, I slid off my chair and edged for the door.

"You too, huh?" Mom glowered over her wire-rim glasses. "I hoped you at least might show a smidgen of raising but go ahead, chase after that bunch of barbarians."

Good manners were important to Mom, a child of the deep South. At three and a half, I wasn't clear on the meaning of barbarian, though her tone implied I might not want to be one. Even so, I was unable to resist the ruckus.

Breaking free of her glare, I trotted down the hall to peek through the doorway of our parents' bedroom. My brother bounced on their bed shrieking and grabbing for the hysterical bird while Dad clapped and shouted encouragement. Iridescent feathers blurred as the plump pigeon ruffled my hair and whizzed into the bathroom. From the safety of the hallway, I watched Dad trap the hapless creature in the tub. With comforting coos, he returned to the kitchen, his trembling prey enfolded gently in both hands.

Arms akimbo and brown eyes blazing, Mom planted herself in the middle of the kitchen, looking a lot bigger than her five feet three inches. "*What* are you doing with that bird?"

Dad's grin revealed his crooked teeth. "We're gonna eat it."

"Are you kidding me? Whatever gets into you, Andrew?" Mom rolled her eyes. "We're no longer country folk. You've trained to be a minister. Why do you insist on acting like a hayseed?"

"Aw, hon." He sidled close around her to the kitchen sink. "God provided us with this perfectly good meal, and we don't want to seem unappreciative." He snapped the bird's neck.

I stared. Knees shaking, I wobbled to my seat. James scooted his chair to the sink and climbed up. "Can I help?" He reached for the bird.

"Of course." Dad turned to me. "How 'bout you, Roy?"

I shook my head. Dad turned, selected a paring knife from the drawer, and focused on my brother. "I'll teach you how to skin it." They set about their bloody business.

Mom sat and studied me for a moment, her dark chocolate eyes solemn. "You okay, Roy?" she murmured. "Sometimes, I simply don't know what to think about your father."

I hiccuped and squirmed. Dad liked James better. James, the first born; James the brave son.

Reading my mind, Mom hugged me, shoulder-length black curls tickling my neck. "You know your dad loves you just as much as he does James. Only, he and James somehow understand each other. Trust me, I know how it feels."

"All done." James jumped off the chair and waved the raw meat in my face before tossing it to Dad.

I screeched and nearly tumbled backward.

James caught my chair from tipping. "Sorry, Roy. I forget you're such a fraidy-cat." Bloody hands and all, he hugged me.

That evening we dined on pigeon and dumplings, which Mom insisted on calling squab. Whatever city pigeons live on—scraps of garbage, stale bakery bread, pecks of asphalt, inhaled exhaust fumes—infused an exotic flavor, far tastier than plain chicken-and-dumplings, which endures as one of the memorable meals of my life.

Swallowing her last bite, Mom smiled. "Well, at least nobody got hurt, if you don't count the pigeon. With all the excitement today, I forgot the mail." She stood. "Be right back."

She returned holding an envelope aloft. "What do you know? A letter from the Steins. Last I heard, he finished his seminary degree and was talking about planting a church. Only, this is from Alaska."

Though I couldn't remember the Steins, I knew they were friends of my parents at John Brown University, and that Mr. Stein had been best man at their wedding.

She slit the envelope, unfolded the pages, and as she read, her eyes narrowed.

"What is it, hon?" Dad eased up beside her.

"Better take a look." She handed him the letter.

"Well. Well. Well." His smile broadened with each 'well.'

"What's it say?" James hopped from toe to toe.

"The Steins are organizing a Free Methodist congregation in Valdez, Alaska," Mom said. "They're asking if we'll help them build a log church."

By now, Dad's grin was about to crack his face wide open. "What do you think, Louela?"

Lower lip trapped between her teeth, she paused. "I'm not sure what to think." She reread the letter. "*Sooo.* Alaska. The last frontier." Refolding the blue-lined sheets, she tapped them against the envelope. "Probably the last place I would ever consider living. Still, it would be good to get out of Cincinnati."

"Hooray!" My brother danced and clapped. *"Alaska!"*

My middle tightened. I looked up at Mom. The little I knew of Alaska came from Jack London's gold rush stories, tales of daring and danger that Mom had read to us. Terrifying stories of desperate men drowning while attempting to shoot Miles Canyon and the Whitehorse Rapids in homemade boats. Or people freezing to death. Or being eaten by wolves. Or both. Of course, James loved it all, but Alaska struck me as a place best experienced in books.

Mom stuffed the letter into the envelope and tossed it on the table. "Unlikely for a number of reasons, but Dad and I will discuss it." Her forehead crinkled. "I have to wonder, though, if this might be an answer to prayer. What if," she paused, "what if this is God's call to Andrew for ministry?"

Any concerns I had largely remained my own since I didn't start talking until I was four.

Why we still lived in Cincinnati a half year after Dad graduated with his theology degree from God's Bible school was unclear. Maybe my parents couldn't agree on what to do next. Perhaps they were waiting for a heavenly sign or, like many young couples in the post-war years, were simply too busy surviving to plot their future.

Cincinnati, a thriving metropolis on the Ohio River, had grown rapidly over the previous century, thanks to an influx of Irish and German immigrants, and freed slaves from Kentucky. Corporations such as Kroger and Macy's invested heavily in the architecture and culture of downtown, creating a sharp contrast to the packed slums, densest in the nation, where most of the city's residents struggled to survive on low-wage jobs. Whatever his memories may have been, though, for all his life Dad spoke fondly of Cincinnati. "Like Rome," he would say, "a city built on seven hills."

On weekdays, Dad polished his black wingtips to a mirror shine, donned a pinstripe suit that matched his gray eyes, and sold Fuller Brush and Mason shoes door-to-door. Much of that time my brother and I entertained ourselves in the back seat of our blue Plymouth sedan, and on occasion we were lucky enough to be invited inside. We watched, fascinated, as Dad scrubbed floors, couches, and dishes, anything to convince the lady of the house she couldn't live without a Fuller Brush product. Mom, meanwhile, dodged molten lead operating a Linotype machine for a newspaper, then rushed home, cooked supper, and tucked us boys in bed before Dad left to work the night shift as an orderly in a mental hospital. Work, it seemed, was easy to find, but getting ahead proved elusive.

I don't know how long we might have sustained that lifestyle if it hadn't been for the letter. The awaited sign, Dad said, the answer to their prayers. A nudge from God, Mom conceded. In the end, they both responded with a resounding *Yes!* Mom heard Dad's call to ministry. Dad heard the call of the wild.

The fourth of twelve children, Dad was raised on a hardscrabble farm in the Mississippi hills where he honed his outdoor skills before he needed to shave. His father and grandfather had been renowned for their strength, but his father's weakness for moonshine and gambling resulted in the loss of two farms at the card table. Each time, Dad's family packed their meager possessions in mule-drawn wagons and migrated farther west to start afresh. His mother was the granddaughter of a Confederate Army doctor who was murdered toward the end of the war. She ran her household with an iron hand, unwavering love, and daily prayer. Born during the influenza pandemic, Dad was not only the runt of the four boys but nearly deaf from measles as a newborn, a disability that was unrecognized until he dropped out of eleventh grade at age twenty-one to join the Army Air Corps. Tours of duty in Egypt and India during World War II stirred an inborn curiosity and awakened a dream of homesteading on a distant frontier, either in Brazil or Alaska.

Mom put her size-five foot down on moving to Brazil. But her desire for Dad to commence his career as a minister must have quelled her concerns about Alaska and his lack of ordination. In addition, the lure of ministering with Free Methodists, Mom's childhood church, was particularly appealing. A conservative branch of the Methodists, The Free Methodists had separated from the Methodist Episcopal Church in 1860, seeking freedom from slavery and pew taxes, freedom of worship, and promoting equality of women.

Mom's tangled family roots ran deep on Big Island, Louisiana, where nearly everyone was related by blood or marriage. Perhaps inbreeding was the reason her father had been born with six toes on each foot and six fingers on each hand. Extra big and extra loud, he farmed in the summer and fished trotlines in the flooded bayous during the winter. The son of a minister, he was an elder in his church, a frequent topic of conversation and family pride, while secretly nurturing a skeleton in the closet—a forbidden subject.

Mom's mother, petite and quiet, had descended from the Cajuns of south Louisiana. Her long white hair was always pulled tight in a bun, which failed to disguise the lines between her eyes that belied her soft smile. Her thoughts remained private, while she was in constant motion: farming, cooking, sewing, serving, and preserving.

My parents spent the winter of 1953-54 preparing for the arduous trek up the Alcan Highway, a newly constructed gravel road traversing the untamed Canadian wilderness. They sold their shiny new sedan and purchased a 1949 ton-and-a-half flatbed Chevy truck, which Dad transformed into our twentieth century covered wagon. He built wooden sidewalls as tall as my head and stretched army-green canvas over curved metal slats to create an enclosure high enough for him to stand upright.

Our truck's split windshield swept down to a sloping triangular hood. Horizontal grill bars resembling rows of teeth and round turn signals bulged like orange eyes from the front fenders, conjuring an image of a giant blue beetle with a green canvas back. Dad tuned the engine and relined the brakes but ran out of money before he could replace the dual tires, a decision he would regret. Haste, however, was of the essence if we were to make the journey in time to build the church before winter.

In May, when I was four and my brother was five, we drove out of Cincinnati through urban sprawl, industrial wasteland, rolling hills, and farmland toward freedom and adventure. Everything we owned was crammed under the canvas in the back: clothes, plates, glasses, silverware, sleeper couch, bureaus, chrome-legged kitchen table with matching chairs, refrigerator, Christmas ornaments, spices, all twenty-four volumes of the *Encyclopedia Britannica*, and Mom's accordion. A twin bed for us boys sat across from our parents' double bed with barely enough room between to crawl in at night.

Before heading north, we visited Dad's family in Arkansas, then said our goodbyes to Mom's parents and her six siblings in central Louisiana. No one imagined that seven years would pass before we saw them again.

Loaded up and ready to go

2.

GATEWAY TO THE NORTH

Swish-click, swish-click. The rhythm of wipers and the drumbeat of rain on the cab merged with the hiss of dual tires on wet gravel. Our truck jolted. My teeth clacked. Dad wrestled the big steering wheel, and we swerved between truck-swallowing potholes. I clutched Mom's rumpled skirt to keep from bouncing off the vinyl seat. Earlier that morning, ten days after leaving Louisiana, we drove out of Edmonton, Alberta, saying goodbye to the last pavement we would see. Now, late in the day, muck thick as gumbo slowed us to a crawl.

My brother whined, "Are we almost to Alaska?"

"Nope." Mom sighed. "But if we make it to Dawson Creek tonight, we'll be on the Alcan tomorrow. That means we're over halfway through this four-thousand-mile marathon. Unfortunately, the last fifteen hundred will be the hardest."

As we passed an abandoned car in the rain-swollen ditch, Dad's lips pursed. "I only hope the Alcan's in better shape. There's scarcely enough rock dribbled across this mud to call it a road, much less a highway." He cranked the wheel, and we lurched again. *Whumpita, whumpita.* The truck shuddered. The brakes squealed. Dad eased us to the shoulder and switched off the ignition. "Louela, can you believe it? Our second flat today." Little did he know how many times he would speak those words.

Mom's brown eyes appeared enormous through her wire-rim glasses. "Why on earth?"

"Chunks of metal break off the grader blades and poke right through these bald tires," he growled, pulling on the emergency brake.

She touched his arm. "I'm so sorry, hon. It was either new tires or gas money."

Pulling on his thick canvas coat, he stepped into ankle-deep mud and pouring rain. I stood and grabbed my jacket from behind the seatback. "I'll help!"

"Oh no, you won't! Come back here!" Mom lunged, but I scooted under the steering wheel and out the driver's door. My leather boots splatted into gray muck and sucked noisily on my way to the back of the truck.

Dad, wavy black hair damp with rain, was pulling out the heavy-duty farmer jack and a board to support it. His eyes, as gray as the overcast sky, widened. "What are you doing here?" He grinned. "Long as you're muddy, I suppose you may as well help."

The corners of my mouth quirked at the image of my older brother, green with envy, stuck on Mom's lap. I followed Dad to the right rear of the truck and squatted beside him as he knelt in the mud to position the long jack. Up and down he cranked the handle until the big dual tires hung free. The lug nuts came loose with a squeal, and he passed them to me one at a time. "Roy, please put these in the back of the truck where we won't lose them." Proud to help, I arranged each nut on the tailgate.

He hefted the oversized tire off the wheel with barely a grunt and knocked the sidewall loose from the rim with a ball-peen hammer and tire tool. The limp inner tube slithered out in his hand like a big black noodle.

"Up you go!" Lifting me and the tube onto the tailgate, he climbed up and partially inflated the inner tube before dribbling on a soapy mixture. "Watch for bubbles. They'll show us the hole. Rub around it with this abrader." He handed me the perforated cap of the patch kit. Bubbles betrayed the leak, and I roughened the surrounding area. After brushing glue around the hole, he lit it with a match. The noxious blue flare heated and cleaned the rubber. While the flame sputtered out, he cut a rubber patch with scissors, applied more glue, and pressed it firmly over the leak.

Arranging the tube on the sidewall of the tire, he tucked it where it belonged and lifted me down. "Thanks for your help, Roy, but if we have to do this too many more times, I'm not sure we'll ever make it to Alaska." Drops of rain fell from the tip of his prominent nose while he pumped up the tire. I stood back and crossed my arms. With my help, Dad could fix almost anything.

The tire on, and everything in its place, he creaked open the driver's door and lifted me to the running board, but Mom held up a hand. "Hold your horses until you pull off those muddy boots and wet jackets."

Stockinged feet crossed, I leaned back on the bench seat and smirked at my pouting brother, his lower lip protruding and gold eyes narrowed. Though nearly a year older, he was shorter and stockier than me, and his round freckled face was framed by large ears that stuck out as though pinned on as an afterthought.

A few miles later, he yipped, "Grain elevators! Are we there yet?" Like mute sentries guarding the Gateway to the North, towering grain elevators lined the highway. For a week and a half, Mom had told us exciting, danger-filled, gold rush stories about the frontier settlement of Dawson Creek. Rolling along the muddy main street between a straggle of weather-beaten cafés and false-fronted hotels, I was not impressed. It sure wasn't anything like Cincinnati.

James bounced like a bunny on Mom's lap. "Are we on the Alcan?"

"Almost." Dad pulled into a service station.

"Why's it called the Alcan?" I asked.

Mom opened her door, stepped out, and stretched. "It's short for Alaska-Canada Highway."

"And it's the only road to Alaska," Dad added, swinging us boys down. "Louela, I know it's past dinnertime, but I'd like to shop for groceries before we camp. Whitehorse is several days drive, and I hear there're hardly any stores along the way."

While the attendant filled our tank, cleaned our mud-caked windshield, and checked the radiator and oil, Mom scribbled a shopping list. At a small market, we followed her through cramped aisles where she scratched things off her list, sometimes dropping an item in the basket and sometimes returning it to a shelf. "At this rate, Andrew, we'll go broke long before we reach Alaska."

"Then I'm glad we stocked up on staples before we left home. At least we won't starve. Besides, we're over halfway to Valdez. What would be the point in turning around now?"

My brother looked up. "We aren't going back, are we?"

Mom headed for the checkout. "Of course not. We're on the home stretch."

Supplies loaded, we continued to the west end of town where James pointed ahead. "Hey, why's that sign in the middle of the street?"

Dad stopped the truck, and I stood on the seat for a better view.

"At last!" Mom said. "The sign for Mile Zero Alaska Highway."

James clapped. "Hooray! What's it say?"

"Fort St. John forty-nine miles . . . Fort Nelson three hundred . . . Whitehorse nine hundred eighteen." She gulped. "And Fairbanks, fifteen hundred and twenty-three miles."

My brother's eyes widened. "Are we almost to Valdez?"

"'Fraid not. Let me check this guidebook." She opened a thin booklet, the cover emblazoned with an orange signpost flanked by mountains, trees, and a moose beside a lake. "The clerk at the grocery store said nobody should drive the Alcan without a copy of *The Milepost*. I hope he's right, seeing as it cost a whole dollar." She thumbed through the pages. "Says here it's thirteen hundred and eighteen miles to Tok Junction, which will be our first stop in Alaska. And from there to Valdez, it's another two hundred sixty-eight miles."

"How long will that take?" James asked.

Dad laughed. "The way this trip is going, possibly forever."

That night we stayed in a public campground just past the town. Our breath was visible the next morning as we stomped around beneath a pale summer sky while downing a hasty breakfast of cold biscuits and salami. Our big tires turned north, and as they crunched across the gravel of mile one, the Alcan Highway, we clapped and cheered and blissfully ignored reality. The most challenging leg of our journey had only begun.

My brother's face lit up. "I love The Alcan."

"Ungh," I grunted. Mornings came far too early for me, unlike my up-at-dawn brother, who perched on Mom's lap, nose pressed to the window.

I was startled awake when Mom patted my shoulder. "Roy. You need to see this curved wooden bridge. I've never heard of such a thing."

I pushed up enough to squint through the windshield. Sure enough, the bridge ahead, taller than a tree, curved left as it crossed the river and threaded a gap in the hills. My head flopped against Mom's shoulder, and I dozed until she announced the Peace River.

"What milepost are we at?" James asked.

"Thirty-five."

He rocked back and forth. "Are we almost there?"

"I wish, but we've only been on the Alcan for an hour." Mom raised an eyebrow at Dad. "Thirty-five miles an hour?"

Dad grimaced. A few days earlier, while bucking a north wind in first gear across the entire Dakota plains, he had explained how underpowered the 90-horse engine was for the load it pulled.

The broad expanse of river flamed with morning sun as we thumped across the half-mile suspension bridge and left behind the last farmland we would see on our journey. When Dad geared down to climb into the mountains, I rested my head on Mom's lap.

The truck slowed, and I awoke. "Fort St. John, milepost forty-nine," Mom announced. "Take a good look. It's the last sign of civilization until we camp tonight at Fort Nelson." A peek out the window revealed odds and ends of weathered buildings strewn along the gravel.

Beyond the town, our engine growled up steep switchbacks through jack pine and poplar, the trees shrinking the nearer we approached the boundless blue sky. Though we passed parked cars at turnouts where people snapped photos of Rocky Mountain splendor, nearly everybody passed us, even the semis. Camouflaged in a blanket of gray-brown dust, our truck blended into the road.

"Hey, Mom, why are there crosses in the ditch?" my brother asked.

Mom hesitated. "The white crosses mark spots where people died in accidents."

"Did any kids die?" I asked.

"I don't know."

I studied my socks, wiggled my toes wondering what would it be like to never grow up. Mom brushed her hand through my black hair. "Roy, would you care to switch with your brother?" I nodded and climbed to the comfort of Mom's lap while James shifted to the bench seat.

After crossing the Sikanni Chief River, we ascended the gravel ribbon between ditches awash with goldenrod and yellow hawksbeard. Emerging above the tree line, we traversed Alpine meadows swathed in scarlet fireweed, studded with boulders, and daubed blue with lupine. Snowcapped peaks, jagged as a giant's broken teeth, were connected by ridges splattered white, yellow, and pink with Siberian aster, arnica, and cut-leaf anemone. I had never imagined a world so filled with beauty and yet so empty. Even during my short life in Cincinnati, I had learned to take society for granted—the structures, the interactions both common and surprising that define culture. Mom was right. We had left civilization. How could anyone live up here? How would *we* live up here?

The truck rounded a corner, and Dad slowed to a stop. Directly ahead, the gravel highway narrowed to a one-lane wooden bridge spanning a turbulent stream. Inches above the water, the crude timber frame with no side rails supported two rough planks, each just wide enough for our dual tires. Mom held her hand to her mouth. Her face blanched. "They call that a bridge?" We waited for a car to creep across from the other side. "Andrew, what are we going to do? Will it even hold us?"

"There's one way to find out." He swallowed. "I'm sure it's temporary, but it is the only way to Alaska, hon."

The clutch eased out. The tires inched forward, searching for the planks. *Whump!* A gust of mountain wind slapped the canvas on the back. The truck shuddered. James and I whimpered. Our eyes squeezed shut. Mom held us boys so tight I couldn't breathe.

Opening one eye, I stole a glance out the passenger window. My heart froze. All I could see was rushing water, not even a glimpse of the bridge. This journey was impossible. Whatever made us come here? I sucked in a breath, closed my eyes, and prayed.

The tires hit gravel, Dad shifted, and Mom wiped her forehead. "I certainly hope we don't have to do *that* again."

Even Dad was pale. "Guess we'll just take this road one mile at a time." Dad never did admit to being afraid.

We climbed into the mountains, skirting countless crystalline lakes encircled by blankets of cotton grass, bog star, and snow parsley. Streams frolicked and curtsied and dodged into gullies hidden behind palisades of trembling aspen and paper birch. An hour later, Dad parked at a turnout. "Lunchtime."

We scrambled out and gazed over the guardrail at an unbroken vista of hazy snow-crowned peaks. Mom's arm swept the northern horizon. "We're on the summit of Trutch Mountain, four thousand feet above sea level. The highest point I've been in all my twenty-eight years. You boys run around for a few minutes while I make sandwiches."

James and I scurried over lichen-roughened boulders to splash in a swift, shallow stream. The icy water was so clear that a double handful held up to the sunlight magnified the lines in my palm.

After lunch, we descended for hours through the variegated green forest, stopping briefly at a turnout for a cold dinner. I must have dozed off because Mom shook me as we crossed the long steel bridge spanning the Muskwa River, the lowest point on the Alcan at a thousand feet above sea level. "Wake up, boys. We're near Fort Nelson, where we'll spend the night."

James yawned. "What time is it?" Though the sun had set, the horizon was still visible.

Mom checked her watch. "Nine-thirty."

Dad shifted and pulled into a graveled lot. "Been a long day. No wonder we're pooped."

I peeked out the window and shrank into Mom's arms. "This place is spooky." Bathed in shadowless purple twilight, a half dozen log and rough-lumber buildings rose out of the wispy fog as dark and silent as tombs.

Mom chuckled. "Now that you mention it, Roy, I see what you mean. *The Milepost* explains this is the jumping-off point for the Land of Vanishing Men. It claims explorers who venture into this Headless Valley are never heard from again." She covered a yawn with her hand. "After jouncing across three hundred miles of gravel today, I'm afraid it will take more than a ghost to spoil my sleep."

Dad pointed. "What say we park behind that hotel for the night?" He pulled into the back lot. From the pitch-dark woods, yellow eyes glinted in our headlights.

The whites of my brother's eyes glowed, and he whispered, "What if it is haunted?" My throat tightened. Were there ghosts here? Dad switched off the headlights. James croaked, "Why aren't there any lights?"

"Probably because it's nighttime, son."

Mom opened her door. "At least there's an outhouse back here. Right now, pretty much all I need is a bathroom and my bed." She helped us boys with our pajamas, gave us a cursory tuck-in, and within moments I was drifting off, lulled by the regular breathing of my family.

A howl quavered out of the darkness. My breath caught. What kind of monster was that? A twig snapped. The forest was full of monsters. "Jesus," I whispered, "why can't I be brave like my family?" Heart pounding, I rolled toward James and pulled the quilts to my chin. His breath, a familiar balm, soothed my fears. My limbs relaxed. The last I remember, my brother snored softly beside me.

The Highway hugs another cliff

3.
IN HOT WATER

Sunshine filtered through the green canvas. The smell of bacon tempted me out of bed until I squinted between the back flaps at thin clouds framing the treetops. Mom, standing at the tailgate and flipping pancakes on the Coleman stove, smiled brightly.

Following breakfast, Dad moved the truck to the service station next door. This, along with the lodge, a half dozen houses, and a log store, comprised the entire settlement of Fort Nelson, the only break in the dense forest for three hundred miles. A scrawny man in greasy white coveralls cranked a handle up and down on the side of a tall red pipe with a transparent glass cylinder on top like an oversized bubblegum machine.

"Whatcha doin'?" James asked.

Stubbly cheeks bulging, the attendant spat a stream of brown juice through his missing front teeth. "Pumpin' gas."

"Why?"

"We'll drain gas from this here reservoir through a hose into yer tank. The numbers etched on the glass tell how many gallons we drain out, so I'll know how much to charge yer dad."

"How come you don't just pump it out the nozzle like everybody else?"

"'Cause we ain't got no 'lectricity. I hafta pump the gas up by hand, and it comes back down by gravity."

"Oh." My brother scratched his scalp. "Why don't you have electricity?"

"Just don't." The man spat again. "You sure ask a lotta questions."

"You sure spit a lot."

James scrambled into the cab. "Hey, Mom, I know why the lights are off. 'Cause, they ain't got no 'lectricity."

"*Don't have any electricity*," she corrected. Mom, a university graduate in English and secondary education, never tired of correcting her children's speech.

"My turn to ride on your lap first today," James declared.

"No fair." I ran over, grabbed a handful of skirt, and hauled myself up.

"You boys, take it easy." Mom hugged us and tousled our hair. "I think it is Roy's turn first, but I have a surprise for you both. Today we're going swimming."

I shivered. "Swimming? *Brrr!*" The mountain air nipped my skin, and every creek and lake we had seen was icy snowmelt.

"If all goes well, we should make it to Liard Hot Springs today. What do you think about that?"

"*Hooray!*" Our squabble was forgotten.

Rested, fed, and with a full gas tank, we veered west to lumber for a hundred miles over the spine of the Rockies, the truck grinding up sharp switchbacks in second gear. Like the little engine that could, we huffed over Steamboat Mountain and gathered our strength for the final push to Summit Lake, the highest point on the Alcan at over forty-two hundred feet.

Near the top, where the road clung to the face of a vertical cliff, Dad rounded a blind corner and swerved left. Mom's hand rose to her throat. *"Andrew!"*

Rocks the size of bowling balls blocked our lane. He jerked the steering wheel to the right, and the truck leaned left. Loose gravel flew into the void. The dual tires skittered along the brink of the nonexistent shoulder. Outside his window, birds circled in space.

My eyes squeezed shut.

James squeaked.

My muscles tensed. I waited for the end.

Mom's arm wrapped me. "We're okay, boys."

My breath whooshed out, and I opened my eyes. Sparse stands of pine and poplar huddled in steep-sided ravines between rounded peaks of bare stone—bald giants surveying their desolate domains. In the hazy distance, ice-scribed pinnacles marched off the edge of the earth.

Dad, a little pale, forced a smile. "Look at that. Those mountains go on forever like there's no horizon."

Mom thumbed through *The Milepost*. "Says here they go for over a hundred miles. Some of those ranges are bigger than the entire state of Connecticut. Hard to believe."

Dad nodded and geared down for the long descent. "This country does have a way of making a person feel real small. It's awe-inspiring . . . that is if it doesn't kill you."

A few miles later, the brakes squealed. Mom braced her feet on the floorboards and grabbed my shirt before I flew off the seat. The truck shuddered to a stop. James pointed from Mom's lap. "What's that!?"

I scrambled up, leaned forward, and gripped the dashboard. "Wow!" A half dozen of Santa's reindeer shuffled in the middle of the road, antlers the size of tree limbs practically scraping our front bumper.

Dad wiped a hand over his face. "Whew! That was a near miss." He turned to Mom. "I wonder how much damage one of those could do to our truck. This journey might have been over real quick." He took a deep breath and shoved the gearshift into neutral. "Well, boys, you're getting your first sighting of caribou."

"Up close," Mom added, "and not in a zoo."

James turned to her. "Can we keep one?"

Dad laughed. "They don't look much like pets to me, but I imagine one of those would dress out a nice hunk of meat. I could bag one if I'd kept a rifle."

"And if you had a license," Mom teased.

"And if they were in season." He laid on the horn. "And if it was legal to shoot them from the road." The herd ambled into the trees. He shifted into gear, eased the clutch out, and we rattled on.

"Why does the highway wander around so much?" Mom asked. Wherever the terrain flattened, for no discernible reason the road traced enormous *S* turns. "It's like every few miles, the surveyor meandered off to follow a caribou through the woods."

Dad smiled. "I think I know the answer. They built the Alcan as a military road." Dad loved to regale us with stories about his time as a GI. How he nearly died from dehydration while lost in the Egyptian desert and had cooked for General Chennault's Flying Tigers in India.

"So?"

"While stationed in India, I heard a lot of fighter pilots brag, and one thing they love is a straight road. They'll line up their sights on a column of trucks and hold the trigger down. *Rata-tat-tat*, a whole convoy blown up in seconds. Like shooting ducks in a pond."

"Oh." Mom nodded. "So that's it. They put turns in all the long straight sections to protect Army convoys?"

"Yep. Useful during the war, but now these curves are a real pain."

A short time later the truck wove through a valley along the bank of a narrow, twisting lake—a turquoise gem set between knife-edged ridges that brushed the sky. Mom flipped through her guidebook. "Muncho Lake. Says here, it goes on for nine miles, and the water is a hundred feet deep. I'm not sure I've ever seen water quite that color. Gorgeous. How about we stop here for lunch?"

Back on the road, my brother and I complained every time we slowed to let a bear cross. Or a moose. Or a caribou. Or a sheep. "Are we ever gonna get there?" James moaned. Two weeks of sponge baths had us raring for that swim Mom had promised.

"A few more minutes." Mom patted his shoulder. "The springs are right after we cross the Liard River. Who can spot the bridge first? In the meantime, I'll help you with your bathing suits." She reached behind the seatback and retrieved a sack of clothes while we stripped off jeans and flannel shirts.

Clad in trunks, we watched the mileposts creep by while clouds cloaked the sun. The truck wound out of the woods into a steep valley, and James pointed forward. "I see the bridge."

We bounced on the seat as Dad drove across the swooping suspension bridge and turned at a small wooden sign. The instant Mom opened the door, we crawled over her lap and dove to the ground in the empty parking lot.

"Whooee!" We boys raced along the quarter-mile boardwalk, only to pull up short at a steaming cauldron of bubbling water in the center of a swampy clearing. "Smells like rotten eggs." James pinched his nose. I gagged while waiting for Dad to strip to his boxers.

"You're smelling sulfur from the hot springs." He waded in. "Come on. The water's great."

James dipped in one toe. "Yow!" he yelped. "This is hot as a witch's brew!"

"Oh, don't be a sissy." Dad held out a hand. "You'll get used to it."

"No way!" I protested. "I'm not gettin' cooked."

James, meanwhile, had wandered to a larger pool a little farther down the boardwalk. "Hey, this one's just right." He splashed out to his waist.

"I'm goin' with him," I declared.

"Wait for me." Dad scrambled to the bank. "I don't know how deep that pool is, and you boys can't swim."

My brother didn't look back. "I'm okay."

I had nearly caught up to him when his head disappeared with scarcely a ripple. I stared, too frightened to move. He was right there, and just as fast, he was gone.

Dad thrashed through the turbid water to the spot where we

last saw my brother and dove beneath the surface. Now both had disappeared.

The seconds ticked. I tried to tamp down my panic, but fears loomed like buzzards circling my head.

I lurched forward. The water surged to my neck. I hadn't noticed Mom walking up behind me, soap and towels in hand.

My tongue frozen, I pointed to the placid, brown water.

Her face became ashen. The towels fell onto the boardwalk. She croaked, "*Where are Dad and James?*"

The terror on Mom's face frightened me even more. What if *she* jumped in the water? She couldn't swim, either. A scream rose from deep inside my chest. If she disappeared, I would be all alone. The cry reached my throat.

Whoosh! Dad emerged beside me, arm muscles corded as he dragged James from the water and placed him on the boardwalk where he lay limp. Dad rolled him on his side and slapped his back. My brother gasped and wheezed. Dad helped him sit up. "You okay?"

Mom raced to James. "Oh, dear Jesus!"

He coughed and spat water.

She gasped.

"Yuck." He stuck out his tongue. "That tastes horrible."

Mom wrapped him in her arms. "Oh, son, I was afraid I had lost you."

He returned her hug before struggling to his feet. "Can we go swimmin' now?"

Dad shook his head. "You could if you could swim. I hope you learned your lesson."

I certainly had. A few minutes later, we boys frolicked with Dad in the shallows until, red as lobsters, we lathered, scrubbed, shampooed, and rinsed off in the hundred-degree water.

After we toweled dry, Mom helped us don clean clothes. "My turn now," she said. "My first hot bath in two weeks. Can you boys wait in the parking lot? If anyone else shows up, run back and yell down the trail."

James hesitated. "Aren't you comin' with us, Dad?"

"I think your mother needs protection from wild animals."

She winked at Dad. "You boys will be just fine going back to the truck by yourselves."

"Yep." My brother took my hand, and we strode proudly up the boardwalk to stand guard.

Raindrops fell by the time we reached the truck, and we climbed into the cab. I drew a family of stick figures on the steamy inside of the passenger window. "James, I thought you drowned." I rubbed off one of the small images with my elbow.

He stared out the window before answering. "I did too. I was scared."

"Me too. I'm glad Dad was there." I sketched another small stick figure on the window. "He won't let anything happen to us."

My brother nodded. "He won't."

Holding hands, our parents emerged from the woods in a downpour about twenty minutes later, hair slicked down, and clothes clinging. They changed into dry clothes in the canvas-covered back and joined us in the cab.

"You boys okay?" Dad asked. We nodded, and he cranked the engine. The wipers struggled to keep up with the pouring rain. He grabbed a rag to wipe condensation off the inside of the windshield. "I still hope to make it to the first Yukon public campground today. What milepost are we looking for, Louela?"

"Six thirty-two. I figure we should be there by seven, barring another flat." Mom wiped her glasses with a handkerchief. "I'm sorry, boys, but dinner will be a little late since the beans soaking in the back will take an hour to cook after we get there." Beans, cheap and filling, were a frequent meal for our young family. Rummaging behind the seat, she pulled out a wrinkled, greasy paper sack and handed each of us a dark strip of beef jerky. "This should tide you over."

Brown juice dripping from his chin, James whined, "I'm thirsty. How much longer?"

"We just crossed Contact Creek at milepost five eighty-eight," Dad said. "So probably a little over an hour."

"That's forever," I grouched from the bench seat. "I'm tired of this trip. I wanna go home."

James crossed his arms and settled back on Mom's lap. "Where is home, anyway?"

The only road to Alaska

4.
ALCAN DREAMS

Dad turned into a gravel lot carved from the pine forest. A semi-truck filled much of the far side, and we nosed in beside several sedans, a van, and an electric-blue camper pickup parked in front of a log building. Windows flanked a door in the center of the long side, and white smoke billowed from a round, metal chimney at one end.

"Looks nice and new," Mom said.

My brother squirmed in Mom's lap. "I want out!"

"Me, too!" I tried to crawl over them. "I gotta go to the bathroom!"

Dad shoved my boots on me while Mom, with James in one arm, stepped from the passenger door to the running board and then to the ground.

Dad took my hand. "We'll meet you two in the shelter." We circled the building, which smelled of fresh linseed oil, skirted several canvas tents, and followed a double line of rough planks thrown end to end on rutted moss. The trail ended at an outhouse with a half-moon cutout on the front. He opened the door and asked, "Need help getting up?"

I poked my head inside. Rain pattered on the slanted tin roof. "No thank you."

He waited while I scrambled onto the cold wood, careful not to tumble back into the adult-sized hole. "I'm okay," I called.

While Dad took his turn, I wandered behind the outhouse to the tree line. Sharp septic odors gave way to pine resin and ancient bearded moss. Though dusk was still a couple of hours away, evening shadows stretched into darkness beneath the gray-barked evergreens. Chickadees called out songs of encouragement, and the drum roll of a woodpecker made me jump. Children's shrieks and muffled laughter drifted from the shelter.

Dad emerged into the rain. "Let's see if Mom and James need help with dinner."

Warm air spilled out the shelter door, and from one end of the room, waves of heat radiated from a crackling, cast-iron stove. Pots bubbled, and skillets sizzled on the spacious stovetop. The aroma of beans, stew, bread, and roasting meat mingled with the scent of pine smoke. Boisterous chatter from knots of adults almost drowned the staccato beat of rain on the metal roof. I spotted my brother among a half dozen children chasing one another around the picnic tables.

"Welcome!" A burly man held out a meaty hand. "There's always room for more."

"Thanks." Dad's face lit up as he shook the stranger's hand. "This place looks new. The gas attendant at Fort Nelson told us these Yukon campgrounds are free. Do you know who runs them?"

"The Canadian Dominion Government," the man replied. "They only ask that we leave 'em clean and don't sleep in the shelters."

In an empty corner of the cook-top, Mom maneuvered a Dutch oven containing cornbread batter alongside her pot of beans.

"Roy!" James sprinted across the room and grabbed my hand. "Let's go outside! Can you show me the outhouse?" He glanced back as he dragged me through the entrance. "Bye Mom."

Whatever she said was lost in the slam of the door, and we ran around the shelter through the dying drizzle. On our way back, we met Dad crossing the gravel, an empty tin pail in one hand and my brother's jacket in the other. "Mom said you might be missing this."

"Thanks." My brother tugged his coat on. "Where ya goin'? Can we come?"

Dad handed James the bucket. "Sure. You two can pump water

while I haul in a load of firewood." He motioned toward a hand pump on a concrete base not far from the shelter.

While Dad headed for a canvas-covered woodpile, James hung the bail of the bucket on the spigot. "Hey! This pump is just like the one on Grandma Smith's farm."

Unlike Cincinnati or even Grandma Taylor's place, the overgrown shack where Mom grew up had no indoor plumbing. Its unfinished wooden floors tilted and sagged, and fading wallpaper dangled from thin board walls. The surrounding farm consisted of a large garden, a chicken coop, and a weedy field on which a few cows grazed. The only thing keeping the operation afloat was the slow chug of a single-cylinder engine pumping oil from the well out back. Though as slow moving as a praying mantis, it had produced a monthly check.

I leaped and grabbed the long pump handle with both hands. Down it came with a squeal, and I jumped to push it back up. The second time down, clear, ice-cold water gushed from the spigot. I pumped until water sloshed over the rim, and we each grasped one side of the handle and staggered back to the shelter. Dad, arms heaped high with split firewood, caught up with us in time to open the door.

"Boys!" Mom waved from the back corner of the room where she had spread our blue-checked oilcloth across a picnic table. "Over here." She filled a pitcher from the bucket and threw in a scoop of powdered milk. "James, would you please stir this while I finish setting the table? Roy, could you ask Dad to check on the cornbread?"

I found Dad dropping wood into a box along the wall, pulled him down, and yelled in his ear. "Mom wants you to check the cornbread." He nodded and led me through the crowd around the stove, opened the door, and tossed in a chunk of birch. Crackling sparks escaped before he could latch the heavy door.

"Quite a cozy fire for a cool, damp evening." A young lady flashed a smile, blond braids swaying as she stirred a pot with a wooden spoon while balancing a baby on her hip. "You folks on your way to Alaska too?"

"Yes, ma'am," Dad drawled, lifting the lid from the Dutch oven.

"We're aiming for Valdez where we're supposed to help friends build a church. If we can make it up the Alcan, that is. Right now, I'm wondering if this trip will ever end."

She laughed and switched the baby to her other hip. "I know what you mean, but it'll be worth it. Free land. Free meat on the hoof. Never-ending days in the summer."

"Where are you folks headed?"

"The Matanuska Valley. They say green beans hang three feet long, and cabbages grow so big you can hardly pick them up."

"Yep." Dad set the lid back on the cornbread and stirred the beans, releasing a mouth-watering cloud of steam. "Sounds like the promised land, alright. But don't forget the frigid, never-ending winter nights, though I can hardly wait to see the northern lights."

She smiled. "True. But it never hurts to dream. Sometimes, it's the only thing that keeps you going."

Dad nodded as he picked me up. "I, too, have dreams of homesteading." He held me close. "A little clearing. A snug cabin. Just me, my family, and the wilderness." Of course, every story has two sides, but if anyone could dwell on the positives, it was Dad.

I tapped his shoulder. "I think Mom's ready."

He set me back on the wood plank floor. "Roy, go sit with James while I carry these hot kettles to the table." He turned to the woman. "God bless you and your family."

"Thank you, sir, and don't lose your dream."

Mom dished beans onto our plates alongside squares of golden cornbread with butter running down their sides. I was so hungry I forgot myself and reached for a piece. "Just a minute, Roy." She placed her hand on mine. "We haven't said grace."

Though my stomach complained, I bowed my head while Dad prayed, "Our Heavenly Father, thank You for this meal and for Your generous provision to all of us here. Thank You for safe travels today, and please watch over us all as we travel tomorrow. Bless our hopes and dreams and lead us into life everlasting."

The room had grown quiet, and I peeked around, a little embarrassed. Dad, always spoke loudly and prayed even louder, as if God might be deaf. Except for the kids, who stared wide-eyed, every head in the room was bowed, but Dad's. His face was raised toward Heaven. "In Jesus' name, amen."

Dishes rattled and conversations resumed. I blew on my steaming beans. I was famished.

"You boys slow down and chew your food." Mom frowned across the table. "People will think I raised you in a barn."

"Okay, Mom," James mumbled through a mouthful.

By the time we finished dinner, the drizzle had stopped, and orange streaked the western horizon. Fascinating stories crisscrossed the room. I was determined not to miss a moose hunter's tale. The crowd gasped as he told of stepping into a clearing, face-to-face with a bull moose. The moose had bellowed, shook his enormous rack, and pawed the ground. The hunter's gun jammed. My head jerked. Mom stroked my hair. "It's nearly nine-thirty. Sleepy?"

Shaking my head, I struggled to focus. "Huh-uh. I'm fine."

I awoke again to Dad's boots crunching across the gravel lot, my head bobbing on his shoulder. "Here, Louela." He lifted me to the back of our truck, where Mom had removed the canvas dust cover from the twin bed. She placed me beside James and tucked the quilts around us. Canvas flaps at the back gave an illusion of privacy but barely slowed the onslaught of dust and mosquitoes. Despite Mom's constant efforts, road dust permeated all of our belongings. I coughed as I lay down but was too sleepy to complain.

Mom sat on her bed and took our hands in hers.

"*Lullaby and good night, save some fun for tomorrow.*"

Her contralto warmed the crisp, rain-freshened air:

"*Say a night-night to your light,*
for your light is sleepy too.
All your toys are in bed,
they are resting and sleeping.

Close your eyes, nod your head.
Lullaby and good night."

James's shriek jolted me out of a nightmare. "Mom, I'm gettin' eaten alive!"

Across the aisle, she sat straight up, her puffy red face outlined by first light trickling through the green canvas. "Oh, James. You're so swollen, I hardly recognize you." She felt her face and glanced at Dad, who was stirring. "Good grief! Our whole family's bit up. How about you, Roy?"

"Aaagh!" I threw off the covers and hopped beside James on the narrow bed. We sparred with the voracious cloud, but no matter how hard I fought, the mosquitoes kept coming. I even breathed them in. "Augh!" I coughed.

Dad sat up. "Come on, hon. Let's get everybody in the shelter." Pulling on bathrobes and shoes, they untied the canvas and dropped to the gravel. She lifted me, he carried James, and they trotted to the safety of the building.

Inside, a white-haired man knelt by the stove's open door, blowing on glowing slivers of pine. White smoke curled into the cold room. He glanced up, and his eyes widened. "Oh, my goodness! Either you folks have been fighting all night, or you weren't prepared for these man-eating mosquitoes. I've lived with mosquitoes all my life but have never seen anything like these critters."

"Definitely the latter. Don't' scratch, Roy." Mom trapped my tender hands between hers. "We must have been truly exhausted to sleep through that." She turned to Dad. "Andrew, could you bring the calamine lotion out of the medicine kit?" The kindling crackled, and we gathered around the stove to warm our hands, although our faces felt hot enough. "The sun is up. What time is it?" Mom asked.

"Four a.m.," the man replied, slapping a stray mosquito. "I was a dairy farmer in Wisconsin and rose with the sun for so long I can't break the habit. Only it comes up a lot earlier here."

She laughed. "I grew up on a farm too, but in Louisiana the days don't change much with the seasons. It'll take some getting used to, these long summer days and, from what I hear, longer winter nights."

Dad returned with the calamine, which relieved the itching, and compresses soaked in icy well water calmed the sting.

The front door opened, and a short, round lady with a gray bun stepped in, a pale blue nightgown showing under her long coat. "Al," she scolded. "You know there aren't any cows out here that need milking." Her eyes took us in, and her brow creased. "I remember you from last night. You're the preacher. I think you forgot to pray for protection from mosquitoes." She chuckled and turned to her husband. "Al, could you look in the truck for that spare bottle of repellent and extra mosquito netting? We're not going to let these folks go through another night like this."

The man returned with a roll of fine mesh and a small flat green bottle. Dad unscrewed the lid and took a whiff. "DEET, all right, the same stuff we used in India during the war. Called it bug juice. Not an odor I'll ever forget, but it does the job. Come here, boys."

He sprinkled a few drops on his hand and rubbed our faces, necks, and wrists. The sharp chemical smell, something you'd expect in the paint section of a hardware store, bit my nose. "Yuck. This stuff stinks."

The lady laughed. "That's what the mosquitoes think, which is why it works. You'll get used to it."

Mom held out her hand. "We can't thank you enough for your kindness. What do we owe you?"

The lady shook her head. "Absolutely nothing. Only promise me you'll use it."

"No worry about that." Mom's swollen face contorted her smile into a grimace. "You're an angel."

Dad stretched. "Long as we're awake, I suppose we may as well get on with our day. You boys wait here while Mom and I go to the truck and dress. We'll be back shortly with your clothes and breakfast."

The lady sat at the table across from us boys and smiled. "How old are you?"

James spoke. "I'm five, and my brother Roy is bigger, but he's only four."

"I have a couple of grandsons about your age, but I'm not sure I would be brave enough to bring them on a trip like this. How long have you been on the road?"

"We left Louisiana two weeks ago." He yawned. "Mom says we'll be in Valdez in a few days."

"Wow!" She raised her eyebrows. "Three weeks in a truck cab with four and five-year-old boys. What are you going to do in Valdez?"

"Build a church. Dad said we're gonna make it outta logs. And we'll homestead."

"We will," I chimed in. "Soon as we get there."

She smiled. "Your parents must be very adventurous. You're from Louisiana?"

My eyes wouldn't stay open any longer, and my head dropped to the tabletop.

"Wake up, sleepyhead, you'll miss breakfast."

Arms over my head, I moaned, but Mom shook my shoulder. "Roy, wake up. You don't want to sleep through your first day in the Yukon. And, what a day it is." Mom never gave up trying to convert me into a morning person. She never succeeded, either.

Campers began to filter into the shelter, a few with puffy faces, but most rubbing sleep from their eyes. From the nearby woods, warblers, sparrows, and chickadees raised an anthem of praise. Bacon and ham sizzled alongside eggs, pancakes, and oatmeal, the aroma mingling with wood smoke. Sunlight streamed through the windows, lending the log walls a golden glow.

I slumped on the bench while Mom slipped off my pajamas and dressed me in a plaid shirt and jeans. "You boys go wash, and don't just splash a little water on your hands. I left a basin of warm, soapy water on the tailgate. You can rinse off at the water pump. Breakfast will be ready by the time you get back."

Crisp shadows stretched across the clearing where low sunlight sparkled off chips of quartz in the damp gravel. An indignant jay scolded us from atop a pine sapling, which wobbled out of the boggy moss. We splashed soapy water on our faces and took turns rinsing off under the pump spigot, the water so icy my arms ached to my shoulders.

We scurried inside where Mom waved from one of the tables, a steaming mug of coffee in her other hand. "Hey, boys."

"Mom!" I trailed James through the crowd. "I'm starving."

"Well, you're in luck." She handed us each a green Melmac plate. "I think Dad's got breakfast ready on the stove."

Dad piled our plates with pancakes, and I was drooling by the time he finished the blessing. We boys stuffed enormous forkfuls into our mouths until syrup dripped from our chins. Dad shook his head. "You two eat like lumberjacks. I don't understand how you work up such an appetite sitting in the truck all day." Our mouths were too stuffed to answer.

After breakfast, Dad checked the engine and tires while we dried and put away the dishes Mom had washed. She wiped her hands on a dishtowel and tipped my head up. "Roy, before we leave here, I want to remove those stitches from your chin. The doctor said they should come out in about ten days, and we're already overdue."

My chin tucked down. My stomach squirmed. "Do we hafta?"

"I'm afraid so. Remember, this hurts me more than it does you."

That seemed unlikely since it was my chin, but I determined to be brave. After all, the accident had been my fault. Mostly.

Two weeks earlier at Big Island, Louisiana, Grandma Smith, scarcely bigger than a leprechaun, had risen in the sultry predawn darkness, gathered eggs from the chicken coop, and fired up her wood stove. By the time we dressed, she had breakfast on the kitchen table, eggs over easy, and grits running yellow with butter that we had helped her churn the day before. We slathered flaky biscuits with butter and fig preserves she had made from the tree in the front yard.

After breakfast, while Grandma washed dishes in an enameled basin on the counter, Mom and her youngest sister lingered at the table, fingers tracing a lifetime of memories engraved in the planks. They reminisced while sipping coffee Southern style, a finger's width deep in the bottom of the cup, bitter with chicory, and strong enough to hold a spoon upright.

James and I followed Dad outside and raced in circles while he repacked the truck, his blue chambray shirt already dark with sweat. After clambering up a chrome and vinyl kitchen chair on the ground, I hauled myself to the tailgate and climbed onto another chair on the back of the truck bed. *"Cock-a-doodle-doo!"* I crowed and flapped my arms. If Grandma's squawking chickens could flap across the yard, why not me? All I needed was to want it badly enough.

Dad had smiled and resumed packing.

"I'm gonna fly. Catch me."

He mumbled something, never bothering to look up.

Bad idea, a little voice whispered in my head. I swayed. The ground seemed a long way away, but just then, the sun swelled out of the mist in the cow meadow and warmed my face. Intoxicating fragrances of honeysuckle and jasmine hitchhiked on the morning breeze. On a day such as this, anything was possible.

Before I could chicken out, I launched into space. *"Cock-a-doodle-doo!"*

"Wha—" Dad jerked around, gray eyes wide, unable to do anything but watch as I crunched chin first into hardpacked gravel. Stars flashed across a sea of black.

Only dimly aware of my father's arms scooping up my limp body, I swiped at the blood dripping from my chin as he ran to the house. In the front seat of Grandpa's car, Mom pressed a cloth from Grandma's rag bin to my chin as Dad barreled over the shimmering blacktop twenty miles to the nearest doctor's office in Alexandria.

Four stitches fixed my chin, though my faith in my father could not be so easily mended. He knew everything. He could do anything. Why had he let me down? If I couldn't even trust Dad, could I trust God?

Our departure was delayed for a day.

Most of the campers had driven away, when, with strong hands, Dad placed me on a picnic table and clasped my head as gently as an egg he was afraid might crack. Mom bit her lip, snipped the silk sutures with black-handled sewing scissors, and plucked them out with tweezers. One. Two. Three. Four. The doctor had done his job well.

From the expressions on their faces, perhaps the ordeal did hurt them more than me. Though I regretted my foolishness, I knew I wouldn't stop dreaming. Only, when I was older than four, I hoped the line between dreams and fantasy would become clearer.

Dad watching us boys on the dock

5.
TOP OF THE WORLD

After a final crossing of the Liard River, a mere trickle this high in the mountains, we began the eighty-mile push up and over the northernmost spur of the Canadian Rockies. Vistas spanned a sky so vast that our truck seemed but a speck in the world. For hundreds of miles, stunted green pine and gray muskeg closed ranks around dark bulwarks of snow-crowned peaks. Jagged purple mountain ranges extended forever before fading into the hazy horizon, like no other landscape in the world.

Dad parked at a roadside strip and turned off the ignition, the world silent but for the clicks and hisses of the overheated engine. He stretched. "I was beginning to wonder if this road would take us clear to Heaven."

"How do you get to Heaven, anyway?" I asked.

Mom chuckled as she rolled down her window. Brisk air carried the fresh scent of fireweed and heather. "We'll talk about that some other time. This sign says, 'Continental Divide.'"

James leaned out the window. "Conta what?"

"The Continental Divide. The highest mountain range running up and down North America," she explained. "Right where we're sitting, the mountains divide two large rivers. If a raindrop falls on our left," she extended her left arm, "it would run into the Yukon River and travel to the Bering Sea and maybe clear to Russia, over twenty-five hundred miles. A raindrop falling on this side," she held out her right hand, "would eventually flow down the McKenzie River into the Arctic Ocean, maybe even to the North Pole, over twenty-five hundred miles the other way."

"How far is all that?" I asked.

"From the end of one river to the end of the other? A little longer than this whole trip from Louisiana to Alaska."

I wondered if it took the water as long to travel that far as it was taking us.

James's head swiveled. "Wow!" He reached for the door handle. "I need out. I gotta go to the bathroom."

Mom opened her door.

"Me too!" I crawled over Mom's lap and ran after James for the nearby bushes.

Facing west, he unbuttoned his pants. "I'm gonna pee on Russia."

"Not me," I crowed, aiming east. "I'm gonna pee on the North Pole. Hey, Santa, surprise!"

The mile-high breeze nipped our bare skin, as did mosquitoes. In the shelter of the cab, we munched cheese-and-salami sandwiches and drank in the unfettered view of the Northern Rockies.

Dad rode the brakes down the other side, stopping for an occasional moose or Dall sheep. Three hours past the summit, he pointed forward. "Now *that* is a long lake." In the distance, a blue-green ribbon wound between steep forested slopes.

Mom thumbed through *The Milepost*. "Teslin Lake. Says here it's eighty-five miles long." The view was stunning, one I would recall five decades later while visiting our son on a Norwegian fjord.

We rumbled for a half-mile over the wooden bridge traversing the lake's eastern extension and skirted the shore for another hour. At the north end, we crossed the Teslin River and continued west. Mom turned to Dad. "We could still make it to Whitehorse today, but I don't want to visit the first real town we've seen in a week reeking like a bunch of bums. Not to mention our pink, swollen faces covered with calamine."

He glanced her way. "You have a better idea?"

"Maybe. The map shows Squanga Lake not too far ahead at milepost eight hundred fifty, and the guidebook says it's a pretty camp. We'll have time to do a little laundry yet today, and tomorrow we can show up in Whitehorse, not smelling like roadkill."

James sniffed. "I don't smell nothin'."

"*Anything*," Mom corrected.

Dad smiled. "Yeah, me neither, but that's because of olfactory fatigue. After you've smelled ripe for this long, the brain can't take it anymore and refuses to notice the stink."

"Unfortunately," she said, "I'm sure the folks in Whitehorse *would* notice."

A few minutes later, she pointed right, and Dad turned off on a narrow gravel driveway that circled through pine and alder. A dock jutted into a mile-wide lake, which wended out of sight between low rolling hills.

"There have to be some big fish in there," said Dad. "If only I'd kept a pole. At least we'll get our pick of spots." Dad pulled into a campsite near the water with a clear view of Squanga Lake. Dropping the tailgate, he retrieved a short saw with long teeth. "It appears we're on our own for firewood. Would you boys mind scrounging up dry sticks for kindling while I look for fallen trees to cut?"

"But I wanna play on the dock." James waved a hand toward the lake.

"Not without a parent, you don't," said Mom. "Have you already forgotten what happened at the hot spring?" She pulled a bag out of the back of the truck and began sorting dirty clothes. "You want to hunt for kindling or help me sort laundry?" We ran for the woods.

A fire soon blazed in a ring of stones, and we followed Dad to the dock where he filled buckets with lake water, which we helped him empty into our sizable soot-blackened kettle. Dad set it on a grate over the blaze, and while the water heated, Mom buried foil-wrapped potatoes in the coals. She moved the pot of simmering water to a flat rock and stirred in Tide.

"I'd appreciate it if you men could fetch more water from the lake to heat for rinsing." Buckets full, we returned to find Mom kneeling in her skirt on a bed of pine needles, sleeves rolled up and leaning over the steaming kettle. After rubbing each garment up and down a corrugated steel washboard, she wrung it out and tossed it in a basket.

"Can I try that?" James begged.

Brown eyes twinkling, Mom pushed damp locks from her forehead with raw, red knuckles. "Be my guest."

A couple of minutes later, my brother eyed me and grinned. "This sure is fun."

It didn't much look like fun, but he *was* older and smarter. "I wanna turn."

"Well, I don't know?" He rubbed harder. "I don't think you're old enough for this."

"Am too!" I snatched one of my dirty flannel shirts and crowded in beside him. "See!?"

"Okay." He flipped the sock he had been scrubbing into the basket and stood. "Guess maybe you are."

Sweat and steam dripped off my face by the time Mom touched my shoulder. "I think you've done your share, Roy. Thank you. I'll take over from here."

I joined James to watch Dad empty the basket of soapy clothes into a second kettle of scalding rinse water. With a stick, he stirred and retrieved each item and after it cooled, wrung it out by hand. We helped him string a cord between two trees, and soon blue jeans, black socks, white underwear, and gray, blue, red, and green shirts and skirts festooned the edge of the forest like banners at a used car lot.

James ran back to the fire. "I'm hungry. Are we ever gonna eat?"

Mom stood and arched her back. "I'm done here. I'll check on the potatoes while you men hang the last of the laundry." As we finished, a pickup camper settled in nearby, and smoke soon rose from their campfire.

Although dinner was late, the sun hovered well above the hills. Armored with bug dope, we sat on logs around the campfire, plates balanced on our laps. Chili made from yesterday's leftover beans topped baked potatoes, split and brimming with butter.

"Thank you, Father," Dad prayed, "for this food, for my family, and for the magnificence of Your creation. Amen."

The potatoes were steaming, and we took our time eating, sipping milk, joking, and laughing, our faces warmed pink by the fire, our backs chilled by mountain air. Dad told the story of the wolf and the seven kid goats, a favorite, his voice changing with each character. When the mother goat left the kids to go shopping, I shivered and hunkered closer to the flames. Then the wolf tricked them into opening the door and swallowed them whole. We boys scrambled onto Mom's lap. As always, we cheered when the mother found the wolf asleep, cut out her kids and filled the villain with heavy stones. We clapped when he tried to drink from the stream only to fall in and drown. At least in Dad's stories, a world existed in which good prevailed over evil.

Sparks popped and sailed for the evening star. The sun, a dazzling inferno, inched lower until it devoured the jagged horizon, and pale yellow seeped from behind the outline of the hills into the deepening twilight. Zephyrs caressed the lake, distorting the reflection like a cheap mirror. Wisps of unspun wool stretched across the western sky, tops black as night, undersides sopping up the last of the day's light.

"Time for bed, boys." Mom gathered our dishes. "I'll take care of these in the morning."

"Aww." I wanted this evening to never end. "Can't we stay up longer?"

"Okay, but first brush your teeth and put on your pajamas."

By the time we returned, the world, now tinged orchid, lay as silent as the pause before a hymn. Even the birds hushed their songs for a holy moment as day yielded to night. Snuggled together on the log, we wordlessly watched the sky fade to magenta, then plum, and finally to the deep purple of a northern summer night. I didn't remember being tucked into bed.

Early the next morning, as the other campers drove away, Mom called from our clothesline. "*Andrew!* The laundry froze solid last night." She held out a shirt, stiff as a board, and folded in half as though still draped over the line. "Whatever will we do now?"

"That's hilarious." His laughter died at the scowl on Mom's face. "Don't worry, hon. We'll stick the laundry down by our feet while we drive. The heater should dry it by the time we arrive in Whitehorse."

Mom turned to us boys. "I suppose your clothes from last night are clean enough for today. Get dressed and help us knock the ice out of the laundry. If we don't, water will pool on the floor of the truck."

Whap! Mom whaled with a stick on a pair of Dad's jeans. *Whap*! "So," she muttered. *Whap*! "So, the only options were Brazil or Alaska." *Whap*! Ice crystals flew as she thrashed the frozen fabric with a stick.

Dad grinned. "At least I'm pretty sure nobody in Brazil ever had to beat the ice out of their britches."

James and I bent over laughing, and even Mom covered a chuckle. While Dad packed the back of the truck, she crawled into the driver's seat, pulled out the throttle and choke knobs, and stepped on the starter pedal. *Rarr, rarr, rarr.* The starter ground. *Rarr, rarr.* She kept cranking.

"Louela, stop!" Dad dropped his load and ran for the cab. Too late. The growl of the starter tapered off. "What're you doing?"

"Trying to warm up the engine so we can thaw our laundry. Why won't it start?"

"The carburetor's flooded, and probably the battery's dead now too." After helping Mom down, he climbed in, adjusted the choke and throttle, and pressed on the starter. Nothing. Dad wiped his hand down his face, always a sign he was tired or worried. I knew he wasn't tired.

"What will we do?" Mom's voice rose. "No one else is around."

"There is a way." He dug through his tools and returned, brandishing a crank handle. "Exactly what we need. It came with the truck, and I packed it for such a time as this." He popped the hood.

"Can we watch?" James and I climbed up the bumper and stood on the fenders.

"Sure." He removed the carburetor cover and sponged inside with a rag that came out smelling of gasoline. After screwing the top back on, he picked up the hand crank. "Watch. Magician at work." The square end passed through the grill into a matching socket on the front of the motor. He rotated the handle. *Chugga, chugga.* Despite the chill in the air, sweat beaded on his face as he cranked. The engine snorted. James and I jumped down and gathered close around.

"Why won't it start, Dad?" James asked.

"It seems we need more magic." Dad panted. "Anybody know a magic word?"

Mom rolled her eyes, but my brother pointed his finger at the truck. *"Abracadabra!"*

Dad smiled, stretched, and wiped his forehead with his shirtsleeve. "I've got a *good* feeling this time." Bending over, he took a deep breath. His neck veins bulged. The crank whirled. *Kaboom!* I tumbled backward. The crank clattered to the gravel. Dad flew across the small clearing, landing with a crash in a nearby bush.

"Andrew!" Mom screamed. She ran to Dad and rolled him on his back. "Are you okay? What happened?"

Pushing aside a leafy branch, he sat up and shook his head. "Engine backfired," he mumbled. Black smoke drifted from the exhaust pipe into the trees, and a raven cawed. He struggled to his feet, rubbing his right shoulder.

"Did you break anything?" Mom put her hand on his shoulder.

He flinched. "Naw, only I'll be sore for a few days. One of the tricks I learned as a truck driver was to keep my elbow bent. Otherwise, my arm would've broken." He looked around. "Now, where did that crank end up?"

She followed him to the truck. "Andrew? Seriously? You're not trying that again, are you?"

His shrug brought a wince. "What choice do we have?" He scanned the empty campground. "We could lose a whole day waiting for someone to come along and jumpstart us." With his left hand, he recovered the crank and inserted it in the socket. "Here we go."

We all retreated several steps and held our collective breath. *Chugga, chugga, rrrr.* The engine coughed to life and purred. Dad smiled, closed the hood with his left arm, and packed his tools away. "Everybody load up, 'cause Whitehorse, here we come."

He grimaced as he wrestled the big truck out of the parking spot and onto the highway, his body twisting to move the floor-mounted gearshift.

"Andrew." Mom frowned. "Are you sure you're okay? Can you even drive?"

He bit his lip. "Yeah, I'll be fine. Shoulder's a little touchy, but we don't have far to go today."

"I'd take over if I could, but there's no way I can handle this monster." She shook her head. "You know, if you can't drive, we'll never make it to Alaska. We'd be stuck here if anything happens to you."

Stuck? In the middle of the wilderness? I scanned the forbidding forest. Would we starve to death? How long would that take? Maybe bears or wolves would eat us first.

James sat up straight on Mom's lap. "What'll happen if Dad can't take care of us?"

Mom patted his leg. "Shush. You boys needn't worry. Your father will be fine, and I can take care of you if something happens to him. Don't forget, our Heavenly Father is watching over us day and night. He led us here, and He'll take care of us."

Only, if God *was* watching over us, why did He let Dad hurt himself?

6.
WHITE HORSES AND PAINTED LADIES

Maybe God was watching over us because we had no flat tires that morning.

"Milepost nine seventeen," Mom announced. "We'll have lunch in Whitehorse."

Dad turned off the highway and descended into a broad valley. Along the far side, a river hugged a high cliff. On the near bank was the checkerboard of a town.

My brother bounced in Mom's lap. *"Whitehorse! Whitehorse!"*

"And the Yukon River," Mom said. "Remember the stories I read about the Klondike Gold Rush? How prospectors shot Miles Canyon and Whitehorse Rapids in homemade boats?"

I crowded James at the passenger window. "Yeah, and a bunch drowned. I wanna see."

"Be patient. We'll have plenty of time for sightseeing after lunch."

Cruising the dusty main street, we gawked at false-fronted hotels and gaily painted saloons. Even on a Saturday, more people strolled the boardwalks than I had seen the entire past week. While a few ladies buttoned coats over their dresses, most wore pants, something I had never seen in Cincinnati.

"There!" Mom pointed. "The Klondike Café. Let's have a real sit-down meal. After the last couple of days, I feel we deserve a treat."

"Okay, hon." Dad parked in front of a two-story lime-green

building with a full-length covered porch.

As her door latch clicked open, she frowned. "Andrew, are you sure this isn't a saloon?" Drinking alcohol was strictly forbidden by my devout mother's Free Methodist Church.

"You read the sign. It says 'café.'"

Her eyes narrowed. "It sure looks like a saloon. But then everything around here looks like a saloon." She opened her door and helped us boys down. "You two stay close."

The interior was worn but clean, and we sat around a wooden table with a red-checked tablecloth. The waitress greeted us, poured water, and set down menus. As she opened her menu, Mom's eyebrows shot up.

"The cheapest thing here," she whispered, "is a hamburger . . . for *five dollars*. In Cincinnati they cost fifteen cents. Five dollars will almost fill the gas tank. Now I'm sorry I suggested we eat out."

"But Mom?" James started.

Dad patted her hand. "It'll be all right. We deserve a treat this one time. It's been a hard trip."

She gulped. "Okay, but just this once. You boys don't mind sharing a hamburger, do you?"

"I can share." I glanced at my brother, and he nodded. I couldn't remember ever having eaten in a restaurant, and I didn't want to spoil our first chance. The burgers arrived hot, juicy, and delicious. The waitress brought us boys a double helping of French fries and a bottle of ketchup. I was hooked on restaurants.

Mom paid the bill, and we headed for the exit. James burped. She scowled. "Excuse you, young man. How will I ever turn you boys into gentlemen?"

Dad lifted us into the truck. "Knowing you, I'm sure you'll manage. Where to next?"

"I noticed a grocery store not far back. We should check our food stocks before we leave Whitehorse. Prices keep rising the farther north we go."

Dad nodded. "There was a gas station on our way into town. I'll drop you off at the grocery store to shop while I fuel up so we can hit the road without wasting time."

Mom cocked one eye at Dad. "Are you kidding me? Here we are in one of the most historic sites in Canada, and you're going to drive off without seeing anything?"

"Well, this trip has taken so long, I figure we better keep moving."

She crossed her arms. "How about this? Your shoulder's hurt, and we're so far behind it really won't matter if we take a day off to rest. Tomorrow is Sunday, after all."

"Maybe we can find a church to attend in the morning," Dad said.

Mom laughed. "From what I've seen so far, you wouldn't have any trouble finding a tavern, but a church may be harder to come by. I did spot a campground with a laundromat at the edge of town, though. Let's settle in for the night and figure out tomorrow's agenda in the morning."

"Hon, you keep reminding me why I married you. You're as smart as you are beautiful."

James and I traipsed behind Mom through the aisles of Cash and Carry. "Highway robbery," she muttered, dropping a few cans and boxes into her canvas bag. "I'll just get the things we need." She held up a giant can. "Who would've thought! Canned chicken on sale. How about jambalaya for dinner tonight?"

My brother ran ahead, eyeing glass bins behind the counter. Red and green hard candy, black licorice, and a rainbow of jellybeans called our names. Mom smiled. "Temptation everywhere. Okay, you each can pick one candy."

James immediately chose a yellow taffy square, but I studied every bin, mentally sorting the plethora of sweets. I had narrowed the possibilities down to five when Mom picked up a small red, white, and blue package. "Here, Roy. Bazooka bubblegum. It will last longer than candy, and the comic strip might keep you boys entertained for a few moments."

"Aww, Mom." But I gave in.

James popped the whole taffy in his mouth, and his left cheek bulged like a chipmunk. Back in the cab, I meticulously unwrapped and sniffed my prize. Setting aside the comic strip, I bit off precisely half of the pink rectangle and rewrapped the rest for later. Who knew when I might get bubble gum again.

At the campground, Dad stepped out of the cab, shaking his right arm. "Y'all take a gander around while I check in at the office."

Like down after a pillow fight, cottonwood fluff drifted from enormous trees in the center of the lot. *"Hallelujah!"* Mom rolled her window down. "That sign says hot showers right here for a dime. A bath in a hot spring and now a shower, all in the same week."

Dad parked the truck under a big cottonwood, lowered the tailgate, and dug out our Coleman two-burner gas stove. Mom unfolded the metal wings, pumped a knob, and struck a match on the steel bumper. As soon as she rotated a lever, the burner whooshed to life, and she set a kettle of water on the wire grate.

Dad herded us boys into the men's room, where we showered with real hot water. After toweling off, we donned clean clothes from our once-frozen laundry—slightly damp, wrinkled, and smelling like the outdoors. Our noses led us to the pot of chicken jambalaya simmering on the tailgate. When we complained that we were dying of hunger, Dad sent us to a nearby muddy playground while he kept an eye on the stove, pulled dusty sheets off the beds, and sorted dirty laundry.

He had just finished stuffing our newly muddy clothes into the laundry bag when Mom, dark eyes sparkling, strolled up smelling of lavender. Bobby pins held her wet hair in place, and her face glowed from the steaming shower.

"I'm back," she purred. Mom set her toiletries bag in the back of the truck and settled at the nearby picnic table covered with our blue-checked cloth. "Thank the Lord. They have washers and dryers here. We can do the rest of our laundry after we eat."

The next morning, I awoke to the gentle *swish, swish* of coffee percolating on the Coleman stove. The warm, nutty aroma crept beneath the quilts alongside crisp morning air, tickling my nose until I sneezed and sat up. James was gone, and I rolled off the side of our twin bed, stumbled to the canvas flaps at the back of the truck, and squinted out at the sunlight.

"Good morning, Roy." Mom looked up from flipping pancakes.

I cleared my throat. "Are we goin' to church after breakfast?"

"Your dad dearly wants to, but I almost have him convinced that he won't lose his salvation if he misses one more Sunday."

"Hon," he spoke up, "that's not what I said."

"I know," she giggled. "Only, I think God will be okay with us taking one Sunday as a real Sabbath, a day of rest. By the time we dress for church and find a place to attend, we'll be worn out again." She turned to us boys. "Who would like to see Whitehorse Rapids today?"

I raised my hand, and James pirouetted through the grass, singing, *"Whitehorse Rapids . . . Whitehorse Rapids."*

Dad smiled. "Okay, you bunch of reprobates, I'll let you win this one. We'll soon be in Valdez and back on a routine."

"Yay!" I jumped off the tailgate and hugged Dad, almost knocking him off his canvas campstool.

After breakfast, we drove downtown and parked beside the mighty Yukon River. Spray misted our faces as we stepped out of the truck. Untamed water, lashed into foam by head-high waves, raced faster than a man could run, galloping past like a herd of white horses. Mom shouted over the roar. "Now, I see why they named this Whitehorse."

Dad nodded. "Sixty years ago, gold seekers came through here in dinky little row boats." He pointed downstream where jutting rocks forced the torrent, as broad as a city block, through a funnel the width of a small house. "How would you feel about rowing through there in a boat you built yourself?" My stomach flipped. I couldn't think of anything worth that kind of risk. Not even gold.

James, wide-eyed, looked up at Dad. "People took boats through *that*? They must've been nuts!"

Mom nodded. "Most definitely. And, they were all men, which explains a lot."

"What?" Dad's innocent gray eyes widened. "Surely you're not referring to *every* man."

She rolled her eyes. "So says the man who thought it would be okay to raise his family in the Brazilian jungle with poisonous snakes and spiders."

He laughed. "Okay, you got me there."

James threw a rock in the water and pointed. "Hey, I think my pee just went by!"

I giggled, but Mom ran over and pulled us boys back from where we balanced on the frothing edge. "Enough! Let's go see Miles Canyon before one of my men does something we'll all regret."

We drove through town and parked on a plateau. As my shoes touched the ground, I gulped. The earth trembled as though shaken by an angry giant. Clinging to Mom's hand, I approached the edge and peered into the abyss. Far below, a milk-white maelstrom of whirlpools and standing waves roiled between vertical walls of corrugated stone. The rock reverberated with rolling thunder. My legs quaked.

"This is another place where hundreds of boats and many lives were lost during the gold rush," Mom said.

Dad looked back at us. "Who wants to walk with me over that bridge?" A slender footbridge made of cable and boards swayed across the canyon.

"Forget it." Mom stamped her petite foot. "Do you think I'm crazy? That wobbly contraption must be a hundred feet long. There's no way in creation I'm going out there." She glared at Dad. "Don't you ever get your fill of danger?"

"Oh, I'm sure it's perfectly safe." He held out his hands. "See, the boys will come with me." The rickety bridge moaned in the wind.

James took Dad's hand, but I shook my head and backed to safety behind Mom's skirt. At least one of my parents was making sense. Knees buckling, I watched my father and brother crab walk, hand in hand, rocking side to side over the mad waters.

Mom's lips pinched white. *"Stop this foolishness!"* she called. *"Come back here now!"*

"It's okay, hon, but we're nearly to the other side." Dad helped James to solid ground across the canyon.

"Now they have to come back." Mom shook her head. "When will my man ever grow up and start acting like an adult?"

Back on our side, Dad grinned. "How would we know what it's like out there unless we try it?"

"Lord." She lifted her face to the sky. "Give me the patience to raise my three boys." Mom pulled a bag of sandwiches and two thermoses from behind the seat. "Let's eat lunch here, and then I want to walk around Whitehorse." She handed a sandwich to Dad. "How about you?"

"Seeing as I missed church today and my shoulder's still sore, I reckon I'll go back to the campground, rest, and read my Bible. If you all want to explore the town, I'll drop you off on the way and pick you up in a couple of hours."

The sun warmed the gravel street as Mom, James, and I ambled along the dusty boardwalk past buildings as gaudy as an artist's palette. Though most businesses were closed on Sunday, clusters of tourists admired the Old West ambiance while perusing piles of trinkets in store windows.

James waited for two other kids to crawl off the iconic wooden Indian, actually the only Indian I had seen this entire trip. On tiptoes, my brother stroked the carved eagle feather headdress, painted white with red tips. "Did real Indians live here?"

Mom nodded. "I'm sure they did."

"Where are they now?"

"I don't know."

We threaded our way through walkers and gawkers another half-block down the boardwalk until James halted and leaned back in front of a large colored poster. "Wow!" Gorgeous young ladies, clad in brilliant smiles and flouncy dresses, kicked long fishnet-stockinged legs high in the air. Breathless, we boys gaped until Mom grabbed our hands and dragged us away.

"Who *are* those ladies?" my brother asked.

"Can-can dancers." She released our hands.

"What're they doin'?"

"Dancing."

"Why?"

Mom paused and took a deep breath. "Whitehorse, it seems, still has fond memories of its colorful past."

"What past?" I asked.

"The gold miners put Whitehorse on the map." She looked around, checking that no one was listening. "And painted ladies followed, furnishing entertainment."

My brother twisted his mouth sideways. "Were they painted like the Indian?"

"Um, not exactly."

"Were they real ladies?"

"I suppose you could say so."

"Why were they called painted ladies?"

"Um, I suppose because they wore makeup."

"Why don't you wear makeup?"

"Well, uh, I guess I'm not the type." She fanned her face.

"Are you hot?" James pointed. "That ice cream shop's open."

I knew she wouldn't buy ice cream on Sunday, but I tugged her skirt and begged anyway. "Can I have strawberry?"

She raised her eyes, and her head bobbed from side to side. "Just this once, why not?"

I was so astonished I froze, but my brother raced for the ice cream sign, yelling, *"Chocolate!"* I followed, and Mom jogged to catch up.

I felt sorry for Dad. Whitehorse sure was a fun town.

Alaska at last!

7.

VALDEZ OR BUST

Stroked by fronds of morning mist, black spruce spires lined the highway as we drove out of the White Horse River basin and turned west at milepost 919.

James fidgeted on the bench seat. "How much longer?" he whined. "I'm sick of the Alcan."

Mom patted his head. "If things go well, we'll reach Valdez in a couple days. Why don't you rest?"

"I'm not tired," he grumbled.

Dad, despite his injured shoulder, patched three flat tires before turning north at Haines Junction, and we ascended toward Kluane Lake.

The brakes squealed. My head jerked up from where I dozed on Mom's lap.

"Andrew!" She gasped.

Arms flung wide, I skidded across the worn vinyl. Mom snatched me back to her lap. I rose on my hands and knees and gaped. A jackknifed semi stretched across the road, the dusty white side of the trailer swelling until it filled our entire windshield. I clutched Mom's neck. She enfolded us boys in her arms.

Dad's jaw clenched. He wrestled the steering wheel. We swerved into the ditch, just clearing the rear of the semi.

Our bumper surged through brown water. Dad spun the wheel.

Tilted on two tires, we squeezed between the jackknifed semi and a roadside pond. The engine roared. We accelerated out of muddy water onto the road and up a steep hill. Halfway to the top, two cars sat crosswise on the highway, buried to their fenders in the gray morass. On either side, the shoulder dropped abruptly to dense forest. Our passage was blocked.

Dad downshifted and grunted, "Hold on."

Mom clutched us tighter. The engine bellowed. The transmission screamed. The big duals whined, but the worn tread found no purchase on the slick, gray slime. He cranked the wheel. The back of our truck pivoted closer and closer to the precipice on the left until the only thing I could see out the side window were the tips of trees. My eyes pinched shut. Bile rose in my throat.

"Andrew!" Mom shrieked. "Stop!"

The brakes squealed, but the sickening skid continued, right to the verge of the sheer drop-off. The loaded ton-and-a-half truck groaned, settled, and tipped skyward.

Too petrified to make a sound, I opened one eye. Gray clouds filled the windshield.

My older brother stared, freckles dark against his white face. "What do we do now?" he whimpered.

"Pray," Mom whispered.

I stood on the seat and looked ahead. *Rrrrr!* Far above, an enormous yellow Caterpillar clanked and puffed over the crest of the hill. Dad opened his door, stepped out, and sank in gray goo to the top of his knee boots. The windshield rose toward the clouds. I couldn't breathe. Mom's face blanched whiter than my brother's. "Andrew, you're not leaving us—"

Dad's eyes focused on the back of our truck. "Whoa!"

"What?" Her voice sounded small.

Their eyes met. "The dual outer tire is in midair, and the back of the truck bed is hangin' over a twenty-foot drop."

She made a choking sound. "What should the boys and I do?"

"Nothing! Don't move. Don't wiggle. I'll figure out something." Leaving his door ajar, Dad turned and slogged up the hill toward the idling Caterpillar. Her eyes pinched shut, Mom murmured a prayer. As my brother and I watched, Dad extended an arm toward the Cat driver who had come down as far as the two cars. Dad hollered, "Can you please help us?"

The grizzled Cat driver in knee boots and mud-caked coveralls called down. "Of course, that's why I'm here."

Dad slurped back through the muck, bent down, and looked under our front bumper. When he straightened, his face was drained of color. "The front wheels are barely touching the ground. Nobody breathe."

We teetered on the cliff longer than I could hold my breath, and despite his warning, I panted. My head was filled with visions of our family tumbling inside the cab like rag dolls, bouncing and rolling, smashing into the trees far below. Would it be my fault because I breathed? My chest tightened. I was sure my heart had stopped.

"Boys . . . sit . . . very . . . still." Mom's hoarse whisper wasn't necessary. We slowly nodded, gripping each other's hands, our knuckles white. Dad stationed himself in front of our bumper, which somehow made me feel safer, though I couldn't imagine what he could do to keep his family from tumbling to their deaths.

Time froze. So did we. Our eyes fastened on the Caterpillar. Lips moving in silent prayer, we waited while the big yellow machine deliberately winched the first car to the top. We watched the car drive over the crest and out of harm's way. Our gaze followed the Caterpillar as it circled and plodded back for the second car, which also made its way to safety. Would he ever come back? Why was he taking so long?

Clatter! Bang! Belching a blue cloud of diesel exhaust, the monster turned and clanked down the hill. Our turn, finally.

Clumps of mud flew from the tracks. The earth and our truck trembled as the driver spun the machine, backed down, and stopped a few feet from our front bumper. We rocked. My heart flipped. The driver jumped off the tracks, smiled, and gave Dad a thumbs-up. Why was he so relaxed? Why didn't he just hook us up?

The winch cable spooled out, and Dad helped him attach the hook to our truck before walking around to the driver's door. "Sit tight. I have to get in to steer." He stepped on the running board, and we bobbed like a seesaw. We leaned forward as he slid onto the seat and gripped the steering wheel. He didn't even try closing his door.

The Cat engine roared. My jaw tightened, and I willed us onward. The cable creaked. W*homp!* Our front tires slapped the mud. Inch by inch, our heavily laden truck jerked and strained through the bottomless mire. *Yes!* We were moving.

Dad's eyes trained straight ahead until all six tires found solid ground. We crested the hill. Our breath whooshed out as one. *Safe!* My grip on James's hand relaxed. Sensation tingled back into my numb fingers, now marked by my brother's fingernails.

Dad engaged the emergency brake, stepped to the hardpacked gravel, and helped the Cat driver unhook the cable. He wiped his forehead with a sleeve and held out a hand. "You saved our lives, sir. I can't thank you enough. What do we owe you?"

"Nothin'." He waved Dad away, smiling. "I'm jus' doin' my job." He explained that after the vegetation was scraped off the hill to build the highway, the permafrost melted, leaving the roadbed without support. "The road in this spot's a bog 'til winter freeze," he continued. "So, I'm stationed here ta help traffic up the hill."

"Then, God bless you, sir." Dad climbed back in and released the emergency brake. His eyes met Mom's. "Our guardian angel earned his pay today!"

Other than the rattle of the truck, we drove away in silence. This was the first time in my four-and-a-half years I had looked death in the face. What was there after you died? The tomorrow that would never come. I glanced at my brother, who asked. "Mom, remember those white crosses?"

She pulled us both to her soft lap. "Yes."

"Would they put up crosses for us if we died?"

"I'm sure they would, but we didn't die, did we?"

"Nope." He looked up at her. "If we die, will we be with Jesus?"

"I'm sure we will. Let's talk to Jesus now." Tears trickled from closed lids as she prayed. "Jesus, thank You for Your gift of eternal life. Thank You for loving James and Roy from before they were born. Thank You for being in this truck with us and for sending an angel to protect us. Please bring us safely to Valdez. Help us love and serve You all our days. Amen."

"Amen," Dad echoed.

The clouds lagged as we climbed until the only thing above the treeless landscape was an expanse of sapphire blue. To our left, a sky-high bastion of granite peaks squeezed shoulder to shoulder, a barricade between the Pacific Ocean and us.

After summiting at Bear Creek, we coasted forever until crossing a long trestle over a river of boulders, marking the old glacial moraine at the head of Kluane Lake, milepost 1054. For the next thirty miles, we meandered beside turquoise water, the smooth surface reflecting steep snowcapped mountains that dipped their feet into the far shore. Dad gazed across the water. "I wish we weren't so behind schedule. I'm sure there are enormous trout out there, and I'd love to catch one."

Mom sighed. "Is that all you think about, dear? If we don't reach Valdez soon, we're going to run out of money, and neither will there be time left to build a church before the snow falls. Remember, this trip is about you being a pastor."

"I promise, Louela, tomorrow we'll be in Alaska."

Dad filled our gas tank in Burwash Landing at the north end of the lake. Mom winced while counting bills off the scant stack remaining in her wallet. That night, we camped in another free public campground just beyond the village.

The following morning, we quickly cleared Canadian customs

at milepost 1221. A half-mile later, Dad pulled off and snapped a picture of us cheering and hooting in front of the colorful sign marking Alaska's border. Dad had kept his promise.

Mom pointed north and south. "See that clearing. *The Milepost* says the boundary between Alaska and Canada was cleared of trees for its full six-hundred-and-fifty-mile length." Straight as an arrow as far as we could see, a narrow strip, speckled purple, red, and blue with lupine, young fireweed, and forget-me-not, cleaved the somber ranks of gray-green spruce.

"Back in the truck, everyone," Dad said. "Valdez or bust!"

A hundred miles, two flat tires, one moose, and a black bear later, we pulled into a line of vehicles waiting to clear US Customs at Tok Junction. Dad rolled down his window. "Unlike leaving Canada, it looks as though this might take a while. I wonder why they didn't put both customs stations together at the border."

"I imagine because there are no towns there and no place for the customs officials to live." Mom dug in the glove compartment for the envelope with our birth certificates. "Why don't you boys go run off a little energy? Just stay in sight."

A large clearing surrounded the customs office, and a waist high shed roof in the middle of the field barely protruded above the shoulder-high grass.

"Race you!" James sprinted for the shed and reached the small building first. "Hey, a window."

"Where?" I ran to catch him, jumped to grab the edge of the roof, and missed. My foot found nothing. My chin clipped the shingles.

Whoomp!

When my eyelids cracked open, I was lying on my back, and my brother stared down through a long dark tunnel. "Roy!" he called.

I blinked. Stars spiraled.

He waved his arms over his head. "Help, Mom, Roy is dying!" He turned back toward me. "Roy, you stepped in a hole and busted your chin open on the shed roof! You're bleedin' like a stuck pig!"

My head hurt so much I didn't want to move and was too groggy to answer.

"Roy!" Mom ran up, panting. "Are you alright?" She knelt and wiped my chin with the front of my bloody shirt. "Say something!"

"Aaaah" was all I could get out.

I tried sitting up, but she pushed me back down. "That's a good sign. At least you're moving. Maybe you didn't get a concussion this time."

"What happened?" I mumbled.

"The same thing that always happens with you boys—falling or running into something or both. Now you went and broke open that same cut on your chin! It hasn't even been a week since I took out the stitches!" She scooped me up and trotted back through the long grass. "Andrew, please find our med kit." Stretching me out on the tailgate, she lifted my hand. "Talk to me, Roy."

"I'm sorry," I slurred.

She shook her head and held pressure on my cut while Dad dug through stacks of cardboard boxes for our limited first aid supplies. Unrolling gauze from a paper package, Mom wiped the blood from my chin. "Don't you boys ever tire of maiming yourselves? Now hold still while I put Merthiolate on, then I'll tape it shut again."

"No Merthiolate!" I wailed. "I'll be fine."

"Yes," she insisted. "If we don't treat it, you'll get an infection."

My brother looked on from a safe distance as Dad grasped my head with one hand and held my thrashing limbs with the other. Mom unscrewed the lid and lifted the glass rod from the bottle, a venomous orange drop dangling from the tip. The fiery potion touched my wound. I shrieked and struggled as Dad strained to hold me. We boys dreaded Merthiolate more than the pain of injury and always weighed the risk before mentioning a cut or scrape to Mom, who firmly believed in killing germs. In her opinion, nothing worked better—or from our standpoint, hurt more—than Merthiolate. I would later learn that we were both right. Merthiolate, a painful if effective antiseptic, can kill you slowly from mercury poisoning.

She smiled while taping my chin back together. "You know, Roy, this isn't what Dad meant by, 'Valdez or *bust*.'" My brother and I giggled.

After clearing customs, we found a service station. Mom stepped into the office to pay for the fuel and returned with a map that she unfolded until it covered the dash and windshield from her door to the steering wheel.

"What's that?" James stretched his neck to see over the edge.

"A map of Alaska and the Yukon." She flattened the creases. "This cost me a whole fifty cents, so be careful with it. I'll show you where we are and where we're going."

We stood on the seat while Mom's finger traced the red squiggles and tapped on a spot near the center. "We're here at Tok Junction. Next, we turn south and only have to cross one more mountain range, the Chugach Mountains, before reaching Valdez."

"How far is that?" James asked.

"I had hoped we would be there today, but between customs and patching Roy again, we won't make it 'til tomorrow." She checked *The Milepost*. "Two hundred and sixty-eight miles. About eight more hours of slow driving on gravel."

"Neat!" He smiled at Mom, who was folding the map. "Can I sit on your lap?"

She shook her head and pulled me against her chest. "I think Roy could use a little extra love right now. You can have first turn in the morning."

If my head hadn't been wrapped so tight in gauze, I would've smirked.

We drove south out of Tok Junction on a raised road built across miles of flat muskeg—immense mossy bogs of sedge and cotton grass. Spongy hummocks of creeping rhododendron and low bush blueberries thrived amid rusty red splotches of water. A sparse forest of stunted spruce emerged from the swampy ground as bent and twisted as a scene from Dr. Seuss.

We skirted shallow lakes and crossed crystal-clear streams. Mom looked up from the map. "Too bad the clouds came back. The Wrangell Mountains on our left are still live volcanoes, and there are supposed to be spectacular views along here."

"Volcanoes?" James asked. "Are they gonna blow up?"

She smiled. "No, but apparently, on a clear day, you can see smoke coming out their tops."

Dad slowed for tiny Glenallen and nodded to the right. "Anchorage is thattaway, but we'll keep straight ahead on the Richardson Highway. Valdez, here we come."

My chin ached, and I snuggled on Mom's lap. The familiar rhythm of the wipers, the hiss of big tires on wet gravel, and the sway and bang of the truck dodging potholes and frost heaves lulled me to sleep.

I awoke to Dad's voice. "I know it's late, but I'm hoping to reach Copper Center before we stop. That way, we'll arrive in Valdez early enough tomorrow to find the Steins and settle in." The Steins were the friends who wrote the letter that birthed this adventure.

"Do they know we're comin'?" I asked.

"I wrote them before we left," Mom said. "That's all I could do. There's no long-distance telephone service in Alaska."

James stopped wriggling on the floorboards, stretched, and peered over the dash. "Where's Copper Center? Why do they call it that?"

Dad put a protective hand on the floor-mounted gear shifter. "We're not going to get there at all if you knock the truck out of gear. Sit down, please."

Mom checked *The Milepost*. "Copper Center is an old Indian village on the Copper River, named for a copper mine. Keep an eye out for an Indian village."

I couldn't remember ever seeing a real Indian and was lucky enough to be sitting on Mom's lap when the settlement came into view. "Indians!" I pointed. Two men, brown faces creased with age, stood in front of a ragged collection of sod-roofed houses, log walls weathered gray. Beside each house, a small log shed had been erected on metal-wrapped posts higher than a man could reach.

"Why are those boxes way up in the air?" I asked.

"They're caches," Dad said. "I read about them. They serve as freezers. The Natives wait until after the fall freeze to kill game. Then they store their meat and fish in the caches so bears and wolverines won't eat their food." He pulled off on a narrow strip of gravel. "This looks like a spot we might be able to camp on for the night."

Following a quick supper of leftovers, Mom tucked us in, and other than the hum of mosquitoes, the night lay still. In the sub-Arctic, the summer sky never grew dark, and sleep came hard. The end of this epic journey was mere hours away. We were nearly at our new home. I felt excited and terrified at the same time.

"What do you suppose Valdez is like?" I whispered in my brother's ear.

"I dunno," he mumbled, "but Dad said the huntin' and fishin' are gonna be great. That's all I care about. I can hardly wait."

"You boys, quiet down and go to sleep," Mom murmured. "We have a big day tomorrow."

I rolled over, coughing at the familiar odors of insect repellent and dry dust. Dim twilight and crisp air leaked around the canvas flaps at the back. I pulled the stale quilts closer. Would we live in a house? Would I have my own bed? I could barely remember sleeping anywhere but in the truck. But didn't Mom say Valdez was on the gold trail? What if we found gold and struck it rich? Bought a big house. A fancy car. Why not?

Worthington Glacier, last stop before Valdez

8.
NOT QUITE FLAT BROKE

"James, Roy, wake up." Mom shook my shoulder. "It's our last day on the road, and we want an early start."

I moaned and rolled over, but she peeled back the snug covers. Shivering, I retrieved my shoes and jumped to the ground, shading my eyes against the morning sun.

Mom set the white-enameled washbasin on the tailgate. "Here's warm water. Wash up and eat your oatmeal. Dad's rarin' to head out."

The Chevy engine labored uphill for an hour out of Copper Center as we wove along the banks of silty gray rivers and past towering, glacier-clad peaks mirrored in sparkling lakes. We scrabbled over the bare backbone of the Chugach Mountains, passing so close to a glacier that it chilled us with its icy breath. Dad pulled over. "Worthington Glacier. I know we need to keep moving, but I can't resist standing on a real glacier."

A few minutes hike up a steep trail led us to a dirty river of ice fanning out from between two rocky peaks. Where the lower edge of the glacier had broken off, natural ice sculptures of swirling aquamarine adorned the verge. Mom, James, and I climbed onto a frozen ledge where Dad snapped the trip's final photo with our Brownie camera.

"I wanna go," I griped. "I'm cold. I don't like glaciers. I wanna live in a house."

Mom hugged me. "Less than an hour 'til we're there. Why don't you keep an eye out for wild animals on our walk back?"

"I'm tired of animals," I grumped.

"Speaking of wild animals, boys, check out that slope." Dad shaded his eyes. "See the white dot? That has to be a mountain goat. I can't wait to hunt one of those."

"I can hunt goats too!" James danced on his toes.

Dad laughed. "Someday."

Even squinting, I couldn't tell the goat from the boulders. All I could see were lots of steep, cold mountains.

Wending over the summit of Thompson Pass, our truck skirted washouts and crawled over frost heaves as tall as traffic barriers. Mom explained that these were from the ground freezing and thawing. We descended into the black mouth of a tunnel, which emerged into Keystone Canyon, a twisting cleft so deep and narrow that the gravel highway dwelled in eternal twilight. From waterfalls high above, streams of reflected sunlight splayed over moss-lined granite to the chasm floor to feed the turbid Lowe River on its raucous race beside our truck.

Beyond the shoulder of the foothills, the shadowed canyon gave way to a broad, sunlit plain. On the far side glittered the emerald waters of Prince William Sound. Dad pulled off the road, and we all stared, entranced by our first sight of Valdez.

All around, mile-high pinnacles thrust straight out of the sea and forested plain, linked by sheer ridges ringing natural amphitheaters—stages grand enough for the gods of old. The craggy snowcapped mountains encircled the panorama like the jaw of a prehistoric monster. Overhead, a dome of azure blue rested on the saw-tooth skyline, bounding the entire valley like an immense snow globe.

"Oh, my!" Mom's head swiveled. "Oh, my! Oh, my!"

"Is this our new home?" I breathed.

"Yes," Mom answered in a reverent tone. "This is our new home. I've heard Valdez described as 'America's Little Switzerland,' but there's nothing *little* about these mountains. It's like a Matterhorn in every direction." She pressed her palm to her chest. "I'm overwhelmed."

James stood on the seat. "Wow! Mountains everywhere. How'd we get in here?"

"It wasn't easy." Dad pointed. "Look, the town."

Halfway across the plain, a checkerboard of streets clung tenaciously between muddy tide flats and dense forest. House roofs and a pair of church steeples protruded from alder, poplar, and spruce. Two long piers jutted defiantly into the sea. Valdez measured only four blocks across and seven blocks deep and appeared tiny and vulnerable in the heart of these raw, hard mountains. Like a lovely lady, she gave no hint of her roughhouse history and certainly not of her dire future.

To our right, Valdez Glacier curled out of the mountains onto the plain like a colossal winter dragon. Gray, silty water spilled from its massive jaws and slithered to the sea, a sinuous tongue passing close enough to taste the town. I shuddered. What if the dragon awoke?

"Is it safe?" I asked.

Dad laughed. "Who said life is safe? What's the point in that?"

"Yeah, who wants safe?" James added.

I raised my hand. "Me?"

Mom put an arm around my shoulder. "I'm with Roy, but here we are, and it looks like we won't be leaving any time soon. If nothing else, I doubt life up here will be boring."

"Woo-hoo!" James pumped his arms.

"Yep," I squeaked.

Dad blasted the horn and raised a fist. "Valdez, here we come! May the adventure begin!"

Mom looked sideways at Dad. "Didn't you mean, may the church building begin? This trip has been adventure enough." Dad nodded but didn't stop grinning.

We descended into the valley and crossed a long wooden bridge over the many-fingered glacial moraine. The truck shook. W*humpita, whumpita, whumpita.* "You have got to be kidding me," Dad moaned and eased us to the shoulder, dotted with blue and yellow wildflowers. "Not another flat. Not this close to the end."

Mom dug through the glove compartment, retrieved *The Milepost*, and made a notation. "Number thirty-five, the last flat tire you're allowed on this journey, Andrew Taylor." She winked at Dad.

"I'm gonna hold you to that, hon." He stepped out. "Come on, James, and give me a hand. Let's get 'er fixed."

A half hour later, we were back on the road. Within a mile, Dad slowed to make a sharp left. "Where do the Steins live, again?" he asked.

Mom dug in her purse and pulled out a letter. "Jay said they're on Broadway, the first cross street after we drive into town, on the right side. She says to watch for a green travel trailer in their yard where we can stay until we find a place to rent."

James pointed right. "There."

We bumped through a final pothole, the tires surprisingly remaining intact. Dad pulled the truck to the side of the street and switched off the ignition. "How 'bout that, family? We're actually in Valdez."

With a grimace, Mom dug out her wallet and waved a single limp green bill. "And with five bucks to spare. I'd say after three weeks and forty-five hundred miles, we cut this trip really close."

Dad held up his hands. "Then, God must've known exactly how much we needed." His crooked teeth filled his smile. "And He blessed us with a little extra. At least we're not flat broke."

"What's flat broke?" my brother asked.

Mom put her wallet away. "It means not having any money at all, but you boys needn't worry." Still, I was thankful that James and I split that hamburger in Whitehorse. If not, we would be flat broke.

For the next few moments, nobody moved or spoke. After all the hardships of the journey, after three weeks crammed in the truck, after yearning so long to reach Valdez, the end seemed abrupt. I was relieved the trip was over. But here we were, almost flat broke and no going back. I already missed Cincinnati's tall buildings, paved streets, and traffic lights. Here were rutted gravel streets, scattered houses, and lots of forest, mountains, and mud. Sure, the view was amazing, but how would we survive in this wilderness?

The truck doors creaked open. A dog barked. A face appeared in the house's front window, followed by a tall red-haired lady in jeans rushing out to hug Mom and Dad. I peeked from behind Mom's dress.

"Jay," Mom reached back and pulled us forward, "this is James and Roy."

The lady bent and held out a hand. James took it, but I backed away, not sure about a lady in jeans with a boy's name. She smiled.

"I'm shy with strangers too, but we'll be friends soon enough. You must be worn out from the trip. Please come in. I'll put some coffee on, and there's Kool-Aid in the fridge."

We dropped our boots in the foyer and followed her into the kitchen, where a small boy sat, staring wide-eyed. Mrs. Stein busied herself at the counter. "Clovis is almost two now and quite shy." She glanced at the clock. "Wilson is working on the church, but he should be home any moment for lunch. While the coffee perks, I'll show you the trailer."

In the muddy side yard, a twelve-foot, faded-green travel trailer sagged on its tires. The ends were rounded, and the front side had two small windows and a door. Another window allowed light into the curved front, and a round metal chimney poked out at the rear.

"I'm sorry this is so stale. Should've aired it out already, but even though your letter came last week, we knew that didn't mean much when driving the Alcan."

"My, I mailed that three weeks ago from Louisiana," said Mom.

Mrs. Stein shrugged. "Welcome to Alaska."

Dad stepped inside. "Seems cozy enough."

Mrs. Stein ducked through the trailer door. "It's snug, but you won't be here long."

"Will it be safe to leave our furniture in the truck until we find a place to rent?" Dad asked.

"No problem. I don't know of anyone who even locks their door around here."

"I'm afraid I'll need a job before we can rent anything," Mom said. "This trip took a lot longer and cost way more than anticipated."

Mrs. Stein waved a hand. "Don't worry. This time of year, you won't have any trouble finding work."

I followed Mom inside, and my nose wrinkled at the musty odor. A narrow counter ran along the near side of the living space, and a dinette with benches filled the other. The short hallway led to a tiny bathroom and a bedroom crowded with a double bed. James leaped on the mattress and turned somersaults.

"James, hop off there!" Mom scolded. "You know better than that."

"After three weeks in that truck cab," Mrs. Stein said, "you must all be stir-crazy. We can walk downtown after lunch and show you around while the trailer airs out. We'd love to have you join us for dinner tonight, and tomorrow you can grocery shop."

Mom's eyes met Dad's. "Dinner tonight would be wonderful. We have enough staples to get by for a while after that."

We emerged to Mr. Stein's greeting. "You're here! Thank the Lord." He hugged Mom and Dad. "We were praying you would make it before we leave for Missouri." A head taller than Dad with receding brown hair and an unquenchable smile, he bent to shake our hands. "You must be James and Roy. Welcome to Valdez, boys." He motioned for us to follow him into the house.

Clovis couldn't resist Dad's charms for long, and by the time we finished eating and set off on our walk, he rode on Dad's shoulders. The unpaved streets were deserted, and I chased James the half-block to Alaska Avenue. "Hey, a sidewalk!" My brother darted for the boardwalk. *Whack!* The loose end of a board flew up and smacked him on the forehead. With a grunt, he staggered back and sat on the gravel.

All four adults came running, and Mom scooped him up. "Son, you okay?"

He nodded. "Uh-huh, but I'm walkin' in the street after this."

"Sorry about that," Mr. Stein said. "Until you know where the loose boards are, you're probably safer in the middle of the street than on these old boardwalks."

Dad looked around. "Where's the church?"

"Well." Mr. Stein cleared his throat. "Actually—" He smoothed his hair and adjusted his glasses. "The church is still a pile of logs and a big hole in the ground back that-a-way." He pointed over his shoulder. "We'll stop by on our way home. Coming up on our right is the hospital though a new one is being built down Hobart Street."

Mom paused. "I'm impressed you have a hospital in a town this small."

"We've not had an easy time keeping a doctor here," Mrs. Stein replied. "Most of the credit goes to our town commissioner, Margaret Keenan Harris, who is the closest thing we have to a mayor. Oh, by the way, Louela, I noticed an ad on the bulletin board in the post office about Dr. Spencer needing a receptionist. You might inquire."

"I will," said Mom, "but did I hear you, right? Your town commissioner is a woman?"

"Yep, and not just any woman. An eighty-two-year-old force of nature. Without her, our nearest doctor would be in Anchorage, a long day's drive, and sometimes in winter, you can't get there at all."

"Hey, neat!" James sprinted for a muddy playground between a small, two-story clapboard building and a modern, one-story structure covering a quarter of the block.

"James, come back here," Mom called.

"It's okay," Mrs. Stein said. "Those are the old and new elementary schools, right next to the sheriff's office and jail." She waved a hand at a two-story building with a green false front.

"That looks like something from the Old West," Mom remarked.

"It is." Mrs. Stein nodded. "Much of Valdez was built during the 1890's gold rush when this truly was the Old West."

"Alaska Avenue continues on to the dock," said Mr. Stein, sounding like a tour guide as we dodged mud puddles and stepped aside for the occasional car. "But we'll save that for another day. Let's work our way back to the church site through the business district."

He turned right along the waterfront, and we continued past colorful wooden storefronts. What he called the business district turned out to be two unpaved blocks long. Arms outstretched to the rugged horizon, Mom twirled in the middle of the pocked gravel street. "All this natural beauty. How does anyone get any work done around here?"

Mrs. Stein laughed. "Probably explains why God gives us so many cloudy days. You were lucky to show up when the sun is shining, which is maybe a third of the time."

Mr. Stein pointed. "If you keep going out McKinley Street, you'll pass the airport."

"You have an airport?" Mom asked.

"Alaska has more airports than roads," he answered. "From here, we'll circle back to the church site. On our right is the Children's Home, which we'll visit soon."

Mr. Stein rounded the corner to Fifth Street. "Last stop!" His hand swept out with a flourish. "Welcome to the Valdez Free Methodist Church." James raced across the gravel and scrambled up unpeeled logs stacked higher than a man's head in the only clearing along the entire forested block. Other than the logs and a giant mudhole beside the potholed street, we could have been in the wilderness.

Dad held his chin while sizing up the log pile and the nearby hole brimming with muddy water. "Wilson, I'm guessing this excavation is about twenty-four feet square. I assume it's for the foundation?"

"Good eye, Andy. Twenty-four feet on a side and three feet deep. We bought the logs last fall and dug the foundation pit using the town Caterpillar, but the freeze set in early, and we couldn't go any further."

Dad raised an eyebrow. "That's when you sent the letter."

Mr. Stein nodded. "You have no idea how much I've looked forward to you joining me on this project."

"I think maybe I do. Especially since I also don't see a single power line on this street." Dad wiped his hand down his face. "We'll need to start right away to have a chance of beating the snow. I'll be here in the morning."

"That's what I love about you, Andy. You never see obstacles, only challenges."

That evening, it felt odd eating around a table in a room with painted walls and a ceiling. Mom excused us early to unpack enough clothes and utensils to live in the trailer until we found a permanent home. I wandered over a few feet to where she was making the bed.

"Where am I gonna sleep?" I rubbed one eye.

"With James on the dinette benches. Tired?" She followed me back to the dinette and unfolded sheets and quilts, spreading them across the narrow green vinyl seats. "Time for pajamas, boys."

Standing on a stool, brushing my teeth at the miniature sink, I frowned at the rusty chrome fixtures and peeling wallpaper. On the other hand, it was a real bathroom, and we had a warm place to sleep. Best of all, no mosquitoes.

After Mom sang a lullaby and kissed us on our foreheads, we said our prayers. "You boys like it here? What do you think about Valdez?"

"Love it," my brother answered. "I can't wait to start homesteading."

I focused on the sagging vinyl ceiling. "It's not like Cincinnati," I mumbled. "Glad the trip is over, but I don't want any more adventures for a long, long time."

Cheek pressed against the cool, cracked vinyl seatback, I pulled the warm quilts tight and curled up. Even if we *were* almost flat broke, I was grateful for a real roof. But as I drifted off, one question spun in my head; *What surprise will Valdez spring on me tomorrow?*

9.

CHEECHAKOS

A shrill whistle jarred me awake. I stretched stiff limbs and forced open reluctant eyelids. Sunbeams streamed through faded gauze curtains and cracked green vinyl tickled my nose. I sneezed.

"Good morning, Roy. Ready for your first day in Valdez?" Mom, a hissing teakettle in her hand, smiled from the kitchenette. So that was the whistle. I was in the trailer. The long journey was over.

"Um," I croaked, "are we in Valdez?"

"Yep," she replied. "Really, truly. No more sleeping in the truck. You can wash in the bathroom while I dish your oatmeal."

I stumbled to the bathroom, rose on tiptoes, and turned the sink faucet on, off, on, off, on, off. Neat.

"Don't waste water," Mom called.

She spooned brown sugar into my bowl of cinnamon oatmeal with raisins, a staple for our frugal family, and handed me a slice of buttered toast. I stirred lazy brown swirls in the steaming raisin-dotted oatmeal. "Where's Dad and James?"

"They left early with Mr. Stein to look over the building project. Soon as you finish breakfast, we'll join them."

Turning to the narrow green counter, she ran water into the small sink, warmed it with boiling teakettle water, and dropped dishes into the suds. "What luxury! An actual sink and counter! I don't think we appreciate how much we have 'til we give it up." She chatted as she washed dishes and stacked them on a drying rack. "Now brush your teeth, get your clothes on, and let's go. The air's chilly even though it's sunny."

I trotted beside Mom around the corner to Fifth Street, the crisp air tangy with wood smoke and redolent from lush summer foliage. Stands of soaring white birch, twisting alder, spreading cottonwood, and second-growth spruce populated the street. Sun-dappled mats of creeping dogwood carpeted breaks in the forest, pointy leaves fanning out like guards around delicate white blossoms. Shallow ditches sprouted sparse clumps of lanky grass and horsetail, yellow with dust. The surrounding snowcapped pinnacles seemed but steps away, because, technically speaking, they were.

We stopped at the hole in the ground that marked the foundation of the future church. On one side rose the stack of spruce logs destined to become walls. Each one had been squared off on three sides at a sawmill, the fourth side still covered in rough bark. Life-sized Lincoln Logs.

"Hey, Roy!" James yelled from atop the logs. *"Come see what I'm doin'!"* He waved a foot-long blade with a handle sticking out on each end. Sunlight glinted from its wicked edge. *"I'm skinnin' logs!"*

I sprinted for the pile, but Mom flew by me, lifted her long skirt, and began climbing. "James, put that thing down right now! You'll cut your hand off!"

Dad sidled out from behind the stack. "It's okay, hon. That's just a drawknife."

"It is *not* okay!" Mom grasped the knife and aimed the blade at Dad like a courtroom exhibit. "Don't you know anything? Five-year-olds do not play with sharp blades! And you're not even watching him!"

Mr. Stein edged around the pile. "Sorry, Louela. Andy and I were so busy going over the project I guess we forgot to pay attention."

Dad held out his hands, palms up. "How were we supposed to know he would pick that thing up?"

"This frontier is dangerous enough without sharp blades in the mix. How will I ever leave the boys with you and go to work? And if I don't work, how will you build a church to pastor?"

Mr. Stein's smile shriveled, and he retreated around the pile. Dad forced a grin and scratched his temple. "Well, at some point, we have to teach the boys common sense so that they can think for themselves."

Hand on her hip, she glowered down at Dad. "Until then, Andrew Taylor, how about showing a little common sense yourself? You *are* the adult here." She studied the drawknife. "How does this thingamajig work, anyway?"

Dad's face relaxed. "How about if I show you, and you can teach the boys. With everyone pitching in, this project will go a whole lot faster. Need help getting down?"

"Thank you! I'll be just fine. Follow me, James." Lifting her skirt with one hand, she clambered off the logs and thrust the peeler at Dad. "Maybe we'll try it tomorrow. Jay volunteered to watch the boys this afternoon while I apply for the receptionist job. Come along, boys." We jogged to keep up as she stalked away.

Mom unpacked her clothes after lunch and used Mrs. Stein's iron on her light blue dress with fitted bodice. She showered in their bathroom, dressed, and tied her dark hair back with a blue ribbon.

James glanced up from playing on the floor with one of Clovis' trucks. "Wow, Mom! You sure look nice."

Her face glowed. "Pray this interview goes well. We certainly need a paycheck." I couldn't help wondering why anyone had to dress up for a job in this town.

James, Clovis, and I walked together behind Mom and Mrs. Stein two blocks down Alaska Avenue to the old clinic. "Good luck, Louela," Mrs. Stein said. "While you're inside, I'll show the boys around downtown, but we should be back before you're done. Come, boys, let's check out Gilson's Mercantile."

We followed her along the McKinley Street boardwalk. James paused and stared at a tall sign. "What's that?"

She herded us into Gilson's. "It seems you can't even get to a grocery store here without going past a bar." To my surprise, Mrs. Stein stopped in front of the candy counter. "Here, boys, after that long trip, you deserve a little treat. Each of you can pick one candy." We made our choices. She paid at the counter and led us around the block and back to the clinic.

The waiting room was nearly deserted as I climbed onto a hard-backed chair, swung my legs, and rolled a root beer barrel over my tongue. My brother's contortions had us all laughing as he struggled to fit his teeth around an enormous jawbreaker. Mom came out smiling. "Say hello to Valdez's new medical receptionist. I start next week."

James mumbled around the jawbreaker, *"Hooway!* We won't be fwat bwoke anymore." The middle-aged lady behind the desk peered over her glasses. Mom blushed and hurried us out the door.

Mrs. Stein wiped pink jellybean drool off Clovis' chin before hugging Mom. "Congratulations."

"Does this mean we can live in a real house?" I asked.

"Yes, but I won't get a paycheck right away, so we'll be in the trailer a while longer."

"How long?"

"Three weeks, the same amount of time we were on the road, but at least we'll stay in one place and have a roof over our heads."

At the church site, we shared the news with Dad, who grabbed Mom by the waist and swung her around. "Wonderful!"

"Andrew!" She stepped away and brushed off her dress. "Look at your clothes. They're filthy."

"Sorry. I'm just so happy. I knew I could count on you, hon."

"You know I'll do whatever it takes to see your ministry succeed. Only pray it's enough. My salary seems high, but so are prices."

I frowned. "If you work, who's gonna take care of James and me?"

She bent and hugged me. "Dad will."

"You said he would let us hurt ourselves."

She sighed, squatted, and held me at arm's length until our brown eyes locked. "I'm sorry I said that. I was upset. Your father loves you more than anything, and he will keep you safe, but to be sure, he and I will talk."

Dad gave a wry grin. "Thanks for the vote of confidence."

"Well." Mom lifted me in her arms. "Your brothers told me stories of how you grew up chasing each other with Roman candles on horseback and staging battles across fields at night with live ammunition. Don't think for a second, you're going to raise *my* boys like that!"

His gray eyes focused somewhere far away. "I know I've done some crazy things in the past, but trust me, hon, I love my sons way too much to see them harmed." He turned to her. "For now, please try to be patient. I will learn to be a good father." He sighed. "I only wish I knew what that looked like."

Mom set me down and clasped her hands behind Dad's neck. "You *are* a good father and a good man, Andrew Taylor, which is why I married you." They kissed long enough for us boys to scurry up the log pile.

The next afternoon, we crowded into the Steins' sedan for the trip across town to El Nathan Children's Home. "If I remember my Hebrew," Dad commented, "El Nathan means God-given. What's the story here?"

"The story is one Valdez is quite proud of." Mr. Stein turned left on Nizina Avenue. "The orphanage started twenty years ago when a missionary woman took in a Native child found abandoned on the old Valdez Trail. Over time, more orphans were dropped at her doorstep until she launched the Children's Home with nothing but faith that God would supply their needs. The following year someone donated the main house, really a mansion, which they're still using. Over the years, citizens gave them several nearby homes, and their headcount soared to over a hundred."

Mom exclaimed, "Wow! That's a lot of kids to keep track of."

"It was, but seven years ago, the big hospital fire spread to the orphanage buildings, and they lost all but the main house. Fortunately, no one was hurt, and they transferred most of the children to Lazy Mountain Children's Home in Palmer. Now, El Nathan has a dozen kids."

We parked in the driveway beside a two-story colonial-style house atop a low knoll and backed by woods. With dormer windows and an enclosed porch across the front, it was the grandest house I had seen in Valdez. White paint curled off the siding, but welcoming smoke rose from a round metal chimney. Mr. Stein mounted the steps and knocked on the door. A brown face peeked through the window and disappeared.

Moments later, a lady pulled open the door. Her frizzy red hair and sturdy build filled the doorway; twinkling blue eyes and a broad smile warmed the entire street. "Welcome! Welcome!" She looked right past Mr. Stein. "You must be Andrew and Louela. I'm Esther Peterson, but everybody calls me Aunt Pedo. I'm thrilled to finally meet you. Wilson, what took you so long bringing the Taylors around?" I had never met anyone like her who radiated so much good cheer. I hoped I could call her Aunt.

She waved us up the steps and through the porch into an enormous kitchen where a tall, thin lady stood. Gray hair pulled up in a tight bun, her lips curled up in a smile as though it were hard work. Aunt Pedo beamed. "Taylors, please meet Louise Segerquist. If it weren't for Aunt Louise," she laughed, "this outfit would have run off the rails a long time ago."

Several children, ranging from my age to late teens, wandered into the kitchen, all with straight black hair and warm brown skin. They smiled shyly as Aunt Pedo swept her hand across the room. "These precious children are our family. Come, kids, meet the Taylors. Mr. Taylor will be our new pastor."

I shrank behind Mom. My brother's freckled face slipped into a grin. "Hi, I'm James."

One girl snickered, but a tall skinny boy a little older than my brother stepped forward, buck teeth exposed by a broad smile, brown eyes huge behind thick glasses. "I'm Eddie. Wanna see my room?"

James turned to Mom. "Can we?"

"Sure. Just don't break anything."

We trailed Eddie up the stairs, along a hallway, into a room with four bunk beds and a desk. "This is one of the boys' rooms," he informed us. "The girls sleep at the other end of the hall, and Aunt Pedo and Aunt Louise's bedrooms are downstairs."

James scanned the room. "Neat. How many live here?"

"Only eight of us kids. Aunt Louise said there used to be a bunch more."

"How come you live here? Where're your moms?"

Eddie's smile faded. "Don't know. Probably died from TB. If Aunt Pedo and Aunt Louise didn't take care of us, who knows where we'd be." He shivered as though to shed the thought.

My jaw sagged. No mom or dad? I couldn't even imagine.

James ran a finger along Eddie's arm. "How'd you get so brown?"

"I'm Indian, but most of the kids here are Aleut, and some are part Polish too."

James's forehead creased. "But Eskimos live in Alaska. I never heard of Aleuts."

"They're from the Aleutian Islands," he explained. "The Eskimos live up north."

"Can we play now?" I asked.

Eddie smiled. "Sure. Let's go outside."

We thundered downstairs and through the living room.

"Slow down and show a few manners." Aunt Louise frowned.

"Go run off some energy!" encouraged Aunt Pedo.

After playing tetherball in the muddy side yard, I nearly fell off a scary tire swing behind the house. Eddie brushed me off and led us back inside.

The adults were sipping coffee and nibbling raisin oatmeal cookies. "Have a seat." Aunt Louise nodded toward the long benches, started a plate of cookies around the table, and resumed the conversation. "Aside from Eskimos, Aleuts, and Indians, there are only two classes of people in Alaska: Cheechakos and Sourdoughs."

"*Cheechakos* and *Sourdoughs*?" Mom repeated.

"No matter where you came from or what you did, everyone starts out a Cheechako, an Indian word for a newcomer. And you'll stay a Cheechako until you've survived at least a few winters here. If you stick it out long enough, you might ripen into a Sourdough."

Mom adjusted her skirt. "Why are they called Sourdoughs? I've read that term somewhere."

"It comes from the tradition of old-timers protecting their sourdough starter during the coldest months by keeping it close to their bodies."

"Oh." Mom crossed her legs. "We have a lot to learn."

"And Louela." Aunt Pedo shook her head. "The skirts have to go."

"But I only wear skirts and dresses," Mom protested.

Aunt Pedo laughed. "When I arrived, I felt the same way. Then I took a trip by dogsled to a Native village. As I climbed on top of the loaded sled in my dress, the Eskimo musher sputtered, 'White lady not modest.' I was so embarrassed. As soon as I reached home, I ordered several pairs of pants from Sears and Roebuck."

"We'll see." Mom straightened the pleats on her skirt. "I'm not convinced that Sourdough has to mean uncivilized."

Aunt Pedo snickered. "I'll give you a week."

Anna Bortel, Mom, Jay and Wilson Stein in front of the blood red House

10.
THE BLOOD-RED HOUSE

Arriving at the building site the next morning, Mom kicked out a denim-clad leg, the pants rolled up about five inches.

"Well, aren't you lovely?" Dad, who had come earlier with James, knelt beside the water-filled excavation. His grin widened, and he ran a hand through his hair. "You're going to have to grow into those jeans, though."

She laughed. "I won't complain since Jay was kind enough to loan them to me. What can Roy and I do? If we're going to get this finished before winter, we all need to kick in."

"You can peel logs." He stepped into a small shed and came out with two tools and a pair of gloves that he held out for Mom. Raising an implement resembling a straightened hoe with a six-inch-wide blade, he explained, "This peeling spud works just the opposite of a garden hoe. You push it along the log to take off the rough bark." He handed me the other tool, the one Mom had confiscated from James. "And this one is a drawknife. Be careful, Roy! This blade is very sharp. You hold it by both handles and pull it toward yourself to remove the inner bark. The log must be bare wood because any bark you leave behind can harbor insects and cause rot."

"I wanna peel!" My brother grabbed the free handle of my drawknife.

"No, mine!" I tugged back.

Mom gripped his arm. "You boys, stop that! This isn't a game, and you can seriously hurt yourselves. James, you stay with Dad while I work with Roy." James kicked a clod of mud and slouched behind Dad to the foundation.

Hair tied back with a bandanna, Mom drew on gloves like gauntlets, turned, and faced the enormous stack of logs, twice her height and twenty feet across. One hand gripping the peeler, the other on her hip, she gulped. "Well, I guess we'll tackle this the same way you'd eat an elephant, one bite at a time." Hand in hand, we climbed atop the pile where she balanced on one of the logs, gripped the long handle with both hands, set the edge against the bark, and pushed. Nothing happened.

"What're ya doin', Mom?" I swung the drawknife around and around by a handle.

"Put that thing down before you hurt yourself!" she barked. Teeth bared, she leaned forward and growled, *"Arrr!"* The knife-edge bit deep, and a long strip of thin, scaly, gray-brown bark curled up with a soft *shush*. Mom rammed the tool again, and a peel stripped off, all the way to the end. Hoisting the peeler, she brandished it above her head with both hands. "Ha!" she crowed. "I can do this." I gaped as she worked her way across the top of the log. Whose mom was this? It must have been the jeans.

"Now, Roy," she panted, leaning on the handle of her peeler, "your turn." I scrambled up beside her, and she helped me sit on the log, grip the drawknife by both handles and pull the blade slowly toward myself. "Not too deep." She tipped my hands up. "You don't want to gouge the wood. Just keep scraping 'til the inner bark is all gone."

She moved to another log while I worked the drawknife back and forth, back and forth, long strips of reddish-brown bark dropping away. Before long, my arms quivered, but I was too proud to quit before Mom did. Finally, she leaned on the peeler handle and wiped her face with a handkerchief. "Andrew," she called, "what do we do now? All the logs on top are peeled."

He straightened. "Impressive! You two have been busy. Come on down while I grab a peavey and roll the finished logs off the pile." Stepping into the shed, he came out holding a stout wooden shaft as long as he was tall with a spike at the bottom end. A foot from the sharp tip, a C-shaped metal arm was attached by a hinge. He climbed up the stack, rammed the articulating arm into the side of a log, and rotated the peavey until the spike gripped the wood. "You boys go stand in the street with your Mom. I'm not completely sure where these logs might end up."

We retreated to the safety of the street as Dad heaved on the long peavey handle until the log rolled off the backside of the heap with a thump. "Just stay where you are," he instructed. "I'm building a new pile of peeled logs." After rolling all the finished logs off the top, he climbed down. "Let's break for lunch."

We joined Dad on a log, and Mom tugged her gloves off and massaged her fingers before digging in a paper sack and handing out sandwiches. Dad looked at Mom. "I can't go any further on the foundation until we haul gravel from the riverbank. Only I can't do that until we empty the truck, and we can't empty the truck until we find a place to live."

Mom handed him a thermos of coffee and poured milk from another for us boys. "I saw an ad in the post office for a rental on Alaska Avenue and walked by it yesterday. I haven't mentioned it because the outside's uglier than sin, but it's affordable."

Dad shrugged. "We might have to take what we can get."

"If it's still available in a couple weeks when I get paid, we can check it out."

After lunch, Mom stretched and gingerly pulled her gloves back on. "I don't know about you all, but I could use a little toughening up." She flexed her biceps. "One thing's for sure, Alaska will make us strong if it doesn't kill us first."

Dad laughed and found another peeling spud in the shed. "I can't take a chance on you getting any tougher than me." He winked at Mom.

We wore blisters on our hands and then wore the blisters off before we broke for the day. James and I bit our lips and tried not to squirm while Mom dripped Merthiolate on our raw palms and covered them with Band-Aids. "I'm sorry, my little men. You worked so hard today. Dad and I are proud of you."

I was proud of us too.

A few days later, we saw the Steins off on their trip to Missouri. The following week Anna Bortel arrived from Ohio with her friend Dorothy Fisher to help with the project. Miss Fisher had volunteered to assist her on the drive up the Alcan but planned to fly back home in a few weeks. A member of the small congregation had given us a fresh-caught salmon, and Mom invited the two young ladies to the trailer for a baked salmon dinner.

Easily the tallest woman I had ever seen, Miss Bortel peered down at us boys through thick lenses, which made her laughing brown eyes enormous. Short dark hair framed her elongated face, and lots of teeth showed when she smiled, which was most of the time. I liked her.

She was a schoolteacher, she explained, but after reading an article in a church newsletter about the Valdez project, she wrote the Steins with an offer to help. "Now that I've made it up the Alcan," she said, "I need to find a job."

"Are you flat broke?" I asked. "We're almost flat broke."

"Roy!" Mom's face flushed.

Miss Bortel laughed. "Actually, you're not far from the truth. I wrote ahead and applied for a teaching position, but in the meantime, I'll need to find something that pays."

"I understand you're renting the Steins' house while they're gone," Dad said.

She nodded.

"Then I hope you don't mind us living in your side yard for the moment. I assume the church group can still meet in your living room on Sundays?"

"Of course."

"Any chance you could help teach the children in Sunday school?"

Miss Bortel glanced at Miss Fisher who nodded. "Dot and I would love to. We are teachers."

"You're hired!" Dad stuck out his hand. "The pay is nonexistent, but the rewards are beyond measure."

She laughed and shook his hand across the table. "A deal."

Curly-haired Miss Fisher, a foot shorter than Miss Bortel and a bit rounder, asked, "What kind of help do you need on the church?"

"It just so happens," Dad answered, "that we're hiring log peelers."

Miss Fisher laughed. "If it pays as well as teaching Sunday school, I'm in, although I'm afraid I'm a complete greenhorn."

Mom smiled. "The term up here is Cheechako, and from what I'm told, we all fit the description."

"Well then," Miss Bortel said, winking at us boys, "I'll be in good company."

Before the meal was over, we had made two new friends.

That Sunday, twenty people, including the entire orphanage, crowded into the Steins' living room, adults on the couch and chairs around the walls. Children sprawled on the linoleum. Dad stood in the middle of the squirming mass and smiled. "I don't know how this usually goes, but we're here to encourage one another to love God and to love others. Louela, can you start us out with a song?"

Mom opened the case at her feet and pulled out her full-sized accordion while Dad retrieved a harmonica from his pocket.

Aunt Pedo laughed aloud. "You've got to be kidding! No more a cappella? Where did you learn to play those?"

Mom unclipped the fasteners on her accordion, slipped her arms through the straps, and ran a scale. "I played and sang in a ladies gospel trio while attending John Brown University."

Aunt Pedo nodded. "Andy, what's the story behind your harmonica?

That's an unusual instrument in church."

Dad tilted his head. "Well, I'm not so sure looking back that it's something I'm proud of, but as a teenager in the thirties, I played in a minstrel theater troupe. We painted our faces black and our lips red, dressed up in black suits with white gloves and shoes, and performed at fairs and talent shows. We sang, danced, and did acrobatics. Since I couldn't sing, I learned to dance and play the harmonica." Though I never knew Dad to be overtly racist, neither did he apologize for his time as a minstrel. I suspect it was one of the few highlights of his youth.

Aunt Pedo raised her eyebrows. "Do you still play the minstrel songs?"

Dad warbled a run on his harmonica. "No way. They're part of the past I left behind. Everything changed when Jesus found me. I was a GI stationed in Bakersfield and living such a rough life that one of my buddies told me if I ever stepped in a church, it would probably fall on my head. Instead, Jesus gave me a new life. Now, everything I do, I do for Him, even playing this harmonica." He turned to Mom. "So, what hymn are we singing?"

The bellows expanded on Mom's accordion, and the opening notes of "All for Jesus" blasted through the small room. Dad's harmonica wailed and trilled around the breathy march of the accordion. Even though dancing was frowned on in Free Methodist churches, every foot tapped the rhythm as we belted out the first verse.

"All for Jesus, all for Jesus!
All my being's ransomed powers;
all my thoughts and words and doings,
all my days and all my hours."

For the next two weeks, while Mom was at work, Dad, James, and I peeled logs with help from Miss Bortel and Miss Fisher. The Friday Mom arrived home with her first paycheck, our family walked downtown and found the landlord, who handed over the key. Mom led us three blocks back up Alaska Avenue and stopped between Fourth and Fifth Streets.

James stared. "This is it?"

A short muddy path led through a yard tufted with gray grass and spiny weeds to a narrow, two-story house. There was a gable window below the steeply peaked roof, a picture window beside the porch, and a single window on the right side. Asphalt shingles encrusted the front, and ragged tarpaper wrapped the rest, including a lean-to clinging to the rear. Red paint, dark as dried blood, coated the entire thing.

While we guys gaped in horror, Mom pulled out the key, strode to the door, and turned the lock. "Perhaps the inside isn't quite so hideous," she said. "Let's take a look."

"Do we hafta?" I asked.

Mom chuckled and crooked a finger. "Come along, Roy."

The door creaked on its hinges, and we disappeared inside. I tried to swallow, but my mouth was too dry. Was it haunted? It sure looked like a witch's house. I shifted and swayed. I had to do this. Squaring my shoulders, I tiptoed across the threshold, slithered past coat hooks and shelves, and crept down a short hallway.

A doorway on the right opened into a good-sized living room. Opposite this was a bedroom, followed by a stairway, and then a tiny bathroom with a clawfoot tub. I scooted to join my family in the small kitchen behind the living room. Along the back wall, an electric washing machine and oil cookstove/heater flanked a sink and counter, leaving just enough room for the refrigerator still stowed in our truck. A single window on my right let in light, and a door in the other corner accessed the low-ceilinged lean-to. I followed the others up the steep, narrow stairway between the bedroom and bath to an attic bedroom. Red and gray paisley linoleum ran through the entire house.

Arms flung wide, James asked, "Can Roy and I sleep up here? Please? I love it."

Mom laughed. "This may not be the most attractive house, but it meets our needs and is affordable. What do you think, Andrew?"

He didn't hesitate. "It's perfect! And yes, James, this will make a great boys' room."

I sighed.

James grabbed Mom's arm. "Can we unload the truck now?"

"Tomorrow. First, I have to pay the rent."

The next morning, we unloaded boxes of clothes, furniture, household items, and books. Gray-brown Alcan dust coated everything. A friend of the Steins helped Dad lift our refrigerator off the truck bed and set it beside the sink. They arranged our red Formica-topped table and red-and-white striped, padded vinyl chairs in the kitchen.

Chin in hand, Mom studied the room. "You might have known, with all the reds in this house, not a single one matches our dinette set."

Our couch and coffee table filled the living room wall opposite the front window. Dad's dark green overstuffed chair barely squeezed in by the door, and Mom's floral upholstered chair backed against the far wall. The first-floor bedroom was filled by the double bed and a bureau.

James and I helped Dad carry the twin bed we shared upstairs, placing it with the head end beside the window that overlooked the street. Our bureau stood on the other side of the window. Near the foot of the bed, on the short wall under the slanted ceiling, a miniature door accessed attic storage space.

We boys darted back and forth from the truck to the bedrooms and the kitchen while Mom scrubbed the refrigerator, stove, sink, and cabinets and washed every dish. Straightening, she brushed damp strands of hair from her face. "Why don't you see if Dad needs some help."

We charged outside and tangled with Dad's legs as he carried in the last load of boxes. The empty truck beckoned. Hoisting ourselves onto the tailgate, we peered into the back, now just green canvas stretched above rough floorboards. Only days ago, this had been our home. Now it felt so empty, so forlorn. What made a home, anyway? I turned to study the blood-red house. Would that ever feel like home?

James and I trundled back inside, where Mom was pulling wet sheets from the washing machine. "Andrew, would you mind hanging these on the line out back? They won't dry by bedtime, but I can't stand to breath Alcan dust one more day." She handed him a bag of clothespins and retrieved another set of bed sheets from a box on the kitchen floor. "Can you boys make your own bed?"

"Yep!" I snatched our bedding out of her hand and raced James up the steps. Wow! A real bedroom. *Our* bedroom. I spread the sheets on the mattress.

"Hey, look here!" my brother called, his head poking in the small door in the short wall.

"What?" I asked, working to flatten a sheet.

"There's a huge space in here, and it's really dark. Neat."

"What's in it?"

"Nothin'." He pulled his head out and grinned. "'Cept maybe a ghost."

"There is not!" I turned to Mom who had just come up the stairs. "James is pretending there's a ghost in the attic."

Mom retrieved James, sat on the bed, and lifted us to her lap. "God made you two with something special in mind. So, try and think of one another instead of yourselves. Now, let me help you get these sheets on so we can eat."

After lunch, my brother and I explored our new yard, mostly scattered tufts of long grass poking out of the mud between rocks and weeds. The narrow backyard merged into thick cottonwood and alder. Scraps of boards stacked beside the house served as bulldozers and trucks, and I was lost to time when James stood and sniffed. "Dinner."

The aroma hit me, and my mouth watered. Our highway project abandoned, we followed our noses into the kitchen where Mom glanced up from sliding a tray of cornbread muffins out of the oven. "What's for dinner?" James hopped on one foot. "I'm starving."

She smiled. "Good, because tonight will be special, our first dinner at our own table in six weeks. Go wash up."

We returned to a magical space. On the table, white candles suffused the room with flickering golden shadows. Our chartreuse plates were covered by colorful mosaics of fresh salmon, mountains of mashed potatoes brimming with lakes of butter, creamed peas lumpy with spring onions, and cornbread muffins. Dad bowed his head. "Our Heavenly Father, thank You for our new home and Your gracious provision. Amen."

"Remember your manners." Mom slipped into her cultured voice. "One hand on your lap, no elbows on the table."

After dinner, I dragged myself up the stairs and pulled on blue-striped flannel pajamas. Mom tucked us under the quilts, said prayers, and sang a lullaby.

I was drifting off when I jolted awake. The haunted attic! I raised my head. Valdez had no streetlights, but long summer twilight filled the window enough to outline the attic door at the foot of the bed. The doorway to the unknown. What terror lay in wait behind that flimsy plywood? My heart hammered. Was my brother right? Was our new home haunted?

"James?" I whispered.

Nothing.

How could he be sleeping? What evil lurked, waiting to pounce? To drag me from my bed. Would anyone even find my body?

A grunting moan wavered out of the darkness. I pulled the covers over my head and froze. Terrified. Unable to breathe.

Silence hovered.

I waited.

The house lay as still as a cemetery.

Courage flickered. I peeked from beneath the quilt, my eyes glued to the sinister plywood square. What was that noise? Scratching? Clawing? Would the monster come smashing into our bedroom?

A wavering moan rose from right beside me.

The ghost!

Heart thumping, I sat straight up.

Then James snored. I let out my breath. So, he was the monster.

I sighed and squeezed Pluto, my faithful stuffed dog, his scraggly fur worn gray from a lifetime of hugging.

"Jesus," I whispered, "help me not to be such a fraidy-cat. Please make me brave like James. Like real homesteaders. Amen."

11.

FOURTH OF JULY

James twirled like a top on the kitchen floor. The heavy petroleum fragrance of floor wax filled the room. "Why can't we watch fireworks? We watched fireworks in Cincinnati."

Her hair secured by a blue paisley kerchief, Mom leaned back on her knees, taking a break from buffing the linoleum with a rag. "This isn't Cincinnati. In Alaska, the summer sky doesn't get dark enough to see fireworks, so the town is sponsoring a street carnival this afternoon instead."

"Can we go?" I asked.

"Of course. I hear that people drive clear from Anchorage to see it, so it must be good."

James frowned. "I still want fireworks."

"Well, there aren't any, so you may as well stop griping." Mom stood, wiped her face with a handkerchief, and stretched. "Dr. Spencer lent us their ice cream maker. If you boys will help me with this floor, we'll have time to buy ice cream fixings before the carnival starts."

James skated across the room on stockinged feet. "I'll help. What do I do?"

"Polish 'til the linoleum shines." She tossed us each a rag and disappeared into her bedroom.

We dropped to our knees and rubbed and rubbed until the red paisley glowed. She came out wearing a print dress with tiny flowers, her narrow waist encircled with a thin, black patent leather belt, and her black hair tied back with a pink ribbon. "The floor looks great. Thanks, boys. Let's go shopping."

McKinley Street, the major thoroughfare along the waterfront, bustled in preparation for the festivities. Hammers rang as carnival booths and plywood tables took shape on the boardwalks along both sides of the graveled street. Yesterday's puddles dried in the sun, and shop doors were propped open. We ducked into Bill Egan's Valdez Supply. James and I stopped in the entryway to eye a row of glass candy canisters behind the counter. The proprietor looked up from bagging groceries.

"Hello, Mrs. Taylor. Give me a minute, and I'll be with you." The sleeves of his chambray shirt were rolled up to his elbows. Keys clacked on the tall black cash register, and numbers whirred in the little window at the top. *Thunk*. The drawer slid open, and he counted change to a customer before turning his attention to Mom.

"Mr. Egan! I'm surprised you remembered my name. We're so new."

"I make it my business to remember names. I'm considering a run for public office. What can I do for you today?" Mr. Eagan was of average height with straight dark hair receding from a high forehead. His eyes were intense, his jaw was square, but his generous smile lit up his entire face. I trusted him.

Mom held out her empty shopping bag. "We're looking for ingredients to make ice cream."

"Canned milk is at the end of aisle two, and sugar is nearby." He nodded toward the back of the small store. Frosted glass globes dangled from a high ceiling. Between four rows of grocery shelves, yellow light glinted off waxed linoleum. I wondered if he polished his own floor. "Have you ever made ice cream from canned milk?"

She shook her head. "I was a farm girl. We always had fresh milk and cream."

"We Alaskans make do with what we have," Mr. Egan said, "and not many of us have a cow. But I'll let you in on a little secret." He leaned forward, and his eyes twinkled. "You're about to make the best ice cream ever!"

Mom tilted her head. "Without fresh ingredients?"

"The secret? Sweetened condensed milk. Make a vanilla custard with sweetened condensed milk, evaporated milk, egg yolks, sugar, and vanilla. Strain it and let it cool a few hours before churning." He tapped the counter and stepped back. "You'll be amazed at the flavor."

"Intriguing. Do you sell ice?"

He shook his head. "On most days you might talk the cannery out of a bucketful, but they're closed for the holiday. Try driving out to the old railroad tunnel. Most years, you can find snow in there 'til late summer."

She tilted her head. "Railroad tunnel? I haven't seen or heard a train around here."

"That's because there aren't any," he said. "The tunnel is one of the quirks in our town's colorful past. Almost fifty years ago, a local company blasted most of the way through the mountain to build a railroad to the Kennecott Copper Mines. But, before they could finish, a competing company blockaded the entrance, which ended in a shootout."

Mom's eyebrows shot up. "A gunfight? In Valdez?"

"Yep. The Keystone Canyon Gun Battle. Left several Valdez residents dead, and the project abandoned. Now we have a tunnel to nowhere."

"How do we find this infamous site?"

"Easy. Take the highway out to Mile 15. The entrance is on the right. People call it the bear cave."

"Much appreciated. Come on, boys." She led us down aisle two.

Bear cave! Please, God, help us find ice somewhere else. Anywhere, but in a bear cave.

We hurried home with a bulging grocery bag, and the aroma of custard soon overlay the lingering odor of floor wax. Mom rested her stirring spoon on the counter. "You two run over to the building site and ask Dad if he's ready to come home. I feel rich since I cashed my paycheck, and I'd like to splurge on lunch at the carnival."

By noon, our family had joined the pilgrimage downtown. When we reached McKinley Street, Dad lifted me to his shoulders. The crowd stretched for three blocks. The entire population of Valdez, maybe fourteen hundred in the summer, must have been there, plus several hundred weekend visitors. Ladies dazzled like spring flowers in shirtwaist dresses, flouncy skirts, and high heels. Teenagers flirted in bobby socks and saddle shoes. Men strutted in slacks and plaid shirts, a few with sweaters or even sport coats. Olive-drab knots of soldiers on leave from the base in Anchorage chatted and smoked as they cruised the carnival. I couldn't recall seeing this many people in one place since Dad took us to a Reds game in Cincinnati.

Carnival booths and tables strung with red, white, and blue bunting lined the boardwalks. Mr. Egan waved at us from the first table. "Andrew and Louela, can I talk you into signing a petition for Alaska to become a state?"

Before Dad could answer, tempting aromas wafted past. Across the street, a fifty-five-gallon barrel, cut in half and hinged along the back, lay sideways on a stand, and white smoke boiled from its short chimney. A Native man, long black braids draped down the front of his red plaid shirt, lifted the lid and brushed melted butter on glistening salmon fillets.

Mr. Egan held up a clipboard and waved his free hand toward an American flag pinned on the wall behind him. "This flag looks lonely with only forty-eight stars. We need to make it forty-nine. More importantly, if you're up here to stay, you've written off your right to representation. Alaskans deserve a voice in Congress like every other American."

"C'mon, Dad!" I bounced on his shoulders.

Two tables past the salmon smoker, hamburgers sizzled on a stout iron grate. A beefy, bearded man whose muscles strained his T-shirt flipped patties with a long-handled spatula. Grease dripped and flared like volcanoes on the glowing coals, while on the back of the grate, plump sausages swelled and split. Behind the next table, two giant cast-iron cauldrons simmered and steamed.

A cacophony of voices barked.

"Fresh salmon, just caught, grilled on alder!"

"Moose burgers, caribou sausages . . . come and get 'em!"

"Moose stew and the best chili in Alaska, two bits a bowl!"

My head spun. Not even in Cincinnati had I experienced so many sights, aromas, and sounds jostling in one street.

Mr. Egan held out a fountain pen. "What do you think?"

Mom smiled. "I hope you understand. We're so new here we haven't had time to think about statehood, and the boys are overdue for lunch."

Hands raised in surrender, he laughed. "Any politician knows empty stomachs don't listen to speeches. I'll catch you another time."

"You know," she called back as we walked away, "I'm still impressed that you remembered our names. If Alaska does become the forty-ninth state, it wouldn't surprise me if you are elected to office."

Minutes later, we dodged through the crowd, James and I blowing on steaming caribou sausages while Mom bit into grilled salmon. Dad attacked a moose burger the size of a salad plate and thick with sliced onion and leaf lettuce. He had to spread his jaws as wide as a hippopotamus to get around the toasted bun. Not since that burger in Whitehorse, purchased with the dregs of our dwindling resources, had we eaten out. Then, it was hard to share my parents' optimism. Now, we were settled in a house, and Mom had a steady paycheck. Though only four, I knew better than to think we were done with hardships, but perhaps the worst was over. Maybe we *would* settle down. Live the American Dream. That day, as we celebrated the birthday of the greatest, most prosperous country in the world, even I felt a stirring of hope for the future.

Mom let go of my hand and pointed down the street. "Looks like Aunt Pedo and the kids are signing up for games. You boys interested?"

"I am!" James, his face a mural of mustard and ketchup, jumped, trying to see through the crowd.

"What kinda games?" I asked as we reached the table.

She perused the lists. "Bike races, foot races, three-legged races, and gunnysack races. Then there's a pie-eating contest, an egg-throwing contest, and apple bobbing." She turned to Aunt Pedo. "What do you think the boys would like?"

"Jimmy and Eddie signed up for the three-legged race and the gunnysack race," said Aunt Pedo. "Why don't you boys join them?"

I was baffled. "What do we gotta do?"

"*Have to do*." Mom corrected while scrubbing a napkin across James's face. "The three-legged race is for two people. They tie one of your legs to your partner's leg, which means that unless you work together, you'll fall flat on your face. Care to try?"

James studied me with pursed lips until the lady behind the table explained, "Everyone wins a prize. At least twenty-five cents. It's what we do with the money we don't spend on fireworks."

My brother grabbed my arm and tugged. "C'mon Roy. You jus' have to be in the race, and you'll win a whole quarter."

I hesitated, but the lure of so much wealth won me over, and I nodded. "Sure."

Mom added our names to the sheet. "How about the gunnysack race? You hop with your legs in a gunnysack."

I turned to Dad. "I'll do it if you will."

He laughed. "Why not? I can't let you kids make all the big bucks."

"After this lunch," Mom said, "you could all benefit from exercise, especially since we're making ice cream later." She added our names to the list. "Anyone interested in pie-eating and apple-bobbing?"

James raised his hand, and I said, "Okay, if James'll do it, so will I."

Contestants had gathered on the street for the foot races, and behind them, riders balanced fat-tired bicycles while awaiting their turn. We fidgeted in the line for the three-legged race. When a lady tied our ankles together with a short length of rope, my anxiety shot up. We staggered into a ragged row across the street. She held up her hand. "Ready, set, go!" Her hand dropped, and a dozen pairs of kids took an awkward step with their free legs and tumbled to the gravel. The crowd roared with laughter as each duo struggled back up to balance on three feet.

James circled my waist with his arm. "Roy, put your arm around me. I'll count. Step with your left foot on one, then your right foot on two. Got it?"

"Okay." I gripped him tight.

He chanted, "One, two, one, two." Miraculously, we were on our way, and I risked a look around. Most teams still thrashed on the ground. Only two pairs stayed ahead of us. He stepped up the beat, and I focused on matching the cadence. We picked up our pace until, little by little, we overtook two older girls and moved into second place. Eddie and Jimmy hopped frantically to hold their lead.

"One, two, one, two." James panted, and we were on their heels.

Dad whooped and clapped, and Mom screamed above the cheering crowd, *"James, Roy, quicker. You can do it!"* But with a final surge, the bigger boys hobbled across the finish line first. Mom hugged us and untied the rope. "Second place. I'm so proud of you." She squatted down and fixed us with her gaze. "Try to remember how much more you can accomplish by working as a team." The crisp dollar bill the lady pressed into each of our hands reinforced Mom's wisdom. I loved feeling rich. It beat flat broke, for sure.

Dad, wiry and quick, won the gunnysack race for adults and collected his two dollars and fifty cents. I went down on the second hop in the kid's gunnysack race and was flailing with my face in the dirt as the winners were announced.

A man's voice rose above the crowd. "Nobody signed up for the ladies' nail driving contest. Any volunteers?"

Dad turned to Mom, who shook her head. Gangly Miss Bortel walked over and laid a hand on Mom's arm. "Louela, let's do this together."

Mom pulled back, but Dad urged, "Go have a good time, hon. What's to lose?"

"My dignity!" she shot back, clutching her purse.

"Ladies, last chance," the man called.

Mom frowned. Giggling, Miss Bortel grasped her elbow and raised their hands in the air. "We'll do it!"

Two other brave ladies passed handbags to their husbands. "So will we!"

A crowd gathered. Mom's lips stretched into a tight smile.

"Step on up, ladies." The man stood beside a thick plank across two sawhorses. "The nails are already started, so you simply need to drive yours in. The first one down wins." He handed them each a heavy claw hammer.

In full skirts and heels, the ladies sorted themselves into a line of blue, green, and pink florals and red with white polka dots. Four hammers came up in wobbling, one-handed grips. Mom brushed a curl behind one ear and pushed her glasses up.

"Ready, set, go!" the man barked.

In unison, the hammers made four dainty smacks on the board, completely missing the nails. Up and down, they flew, but the big nails refused to budge.

Jeers volleyed across the street.

"Whatsa matter? 'Fraid you'll break a fingernail?"

"Takes more muscle than fryin' an egg, don't it?"

"Don't worry. It ain't gonna smear your lipstick!"

Mom's cheeks flushed bright red.

"Louela," Dad hollered, "grab the handle with both hands and hit that nail like it didja wrong."

She wrapped her fingers around the leather grip, raised her hammer above her head, and *whap*! The nail sank halfway through the board. "Go, Louela!" Dad pumped his fist. James and I shrieked and danced in circles. *Whap! Wham!* Mom's nail sank flush. The crowd applauded while pounding continued in a race for second place. Miss Bortel walked away with the twenty-five-cent consolation prize. Even in a dress, my mother was the strongest lady in Valdez. It must have been from peeling those logs.

Mom beamed and waved her two dollars and two quarters over her head. "This," she boasted to Dad, "is my money to spend on whatever I want. Now, onto apple bobbing."

A carpet of red apples floated in two galvanized tubs, one for boys and one for girls. "Put your hands behind your backs and try coming up with an apple in your teeth," a lady instructed. "Get ready, set, go!"

Water churned and sloshed as the half dozen small boys chased apples too large for their mouths. Bending at the waist with hands behind my back, I bobbed for an apple. It ducked beneath the frigid water. Down to the bottom I pursued my elusive quarry and came up choking. Like a dog, James shook his hair, sucked in a deep breath, and stuck his head completely under. Up he came, a dripping apple between his teeth, and walked away with two dollars and two quarters. All I got was wet hair, a headache, and a measly twenty-five cents.

Our family skipped the egg-throwing contest. Dad explained, "We toss balls, not food." At our house, wasting food was akin to sin.

Next up was the pie-eating competition for kids. Paper plates heaped with generous slices of blueberry pie, the plump berries oozing from flaky, golden crusts, circled a makeshift table of plywood atop sawhorses. James and I lined up straight across from each other and, as instructed, tucked our hands behind our backs. Knowing how much it annoyed me, my brother wiggled his ears and smirked. "You ain't got a chance."

I was searching for a witty comeback when the lady said, "Go!" We plunged our faces into the crisp, woven crust and, abandoning all pride, feverishly gobbled sweet, sticky filling. The task proved impossible without the gooey blue mess going up your nose, in your eyes, and through your hair. As far as I could tell, James never even came up for air.

"Done!" he snorted, blue goo shooting out his nostrils.

I was still working my way through the crust. I burped and examined his plate, licked clean but for a few stray crumbs. "You cheated!" Of course, they didn't count against him the pie coating his head where only the whites of his eyes showed through the blue morass. He grinned purple and pocketed his two dollars and fifty cents. I crammed another puny quarter into my pocket, and Mom led us back to the deserted apple-bobbing tub to wash the pie off.

"Anyone want dessert?" asked Dad as we shook the water out of our hair.

We groaned.

"Well, I have a hankerin' for pie, and I believe I just spotted my favorite."

Mom smiled. "Coconut cream?"

"You guessed it."

We trailed him through the crowd to an array of homemade pies spread across a red-checked tablecloth. Behind the table, ready to take his order, stood an enormous lady with long, straight blond hair. When she moved, her body jiggled like Jell-O.

Dad eyed a mountain of golden meringue. "Coconut cream, I hope?"

The lady, her bulk barely contained by a green sleeveless dress and blue gingham apron, flashed him a toothy smile. "Ya. Two bits a slice. Vant some?"

"Oh," Mom asked, "are you from Scandinavia?"

The lady's eyes twinkled. "Actually, my grandparents immigrated from Sveden, but dis is how ve talked in Visconsin." She turned to Dad. "Coconut for you?"

He reached in his pocket for a quarter. "Please, one piece."

Grasping a long butcher knife in her sausage fingers, she carved an enormous triangle of pie. She slipped the wicked blade beneath the crust, lifted a wedge of creamy custard, woolly with shredded coconut and topped with glistening meringue, and slid the masterpiece onto a paper plate. As stuffed as I felt, my mouth watered until she raised the blade again, and her pink tongue slithered out between thick lips. Avoiding the sharp edge, she licked one side and then the other before setting the knife back on the table.

We gasped.

Dad took a step back, the quarter clenched in his hand. His gaze shifted from the lady to the knife, then to his pie, and back to the lady. His lips moved, but nothing came out. Focusing on the irresistible meringue, he sighed, stepped forward, and slapped his coin on the table. "Thank you." He was committed.

With a resolute breath, he picked up the plate, forked in a hearty bite, and chewed as though it was the best dessert he had ever eaten. Maybe it was. He ate the whole thing.

Walking away, James crinkled his nose and stuck out his tongue. "Yuck, Dad! How could you eat that?"

He shrugged. "Some things in life aren't worth fussing over. Besides, if we never take a risk, we'll never know what we're missing."

Mom shook her head. "Sooner or later, Andrew Taylor, you're going to find yourself in a real pickle with that attitude of yours."

"I'm sure you're right, as usual," he grinned, "but that *was* the best coconut cream pie I ever tasted."

"Speaking of dessert," said Mom, "we better think about churning ice cream."

Dad wiped meringue off his lips. "Where do you suppose we can find ice?"

"Bill Egan told me we could find snow in the railroad tunnel at Mile 15. If you three want to check it out, I need to get supper going."

Dad nodded. "I've heard of it. People call it the bear cave."

My stomach lurched. So, there really *was* a bear cave.

Dad squinted at the sun, circling toward the western peaks, and checked his wristwatch before shaking it. "This poor old thing must've stopped again, but if we head home now, we should make it back from the tunnel by dinner time."

Mom glanced at her wrist. "Four o'clock. Let's go so I can start dinner."

As we worked our way through the crowd back to Alaska Avenue, my chest tightened. "I'll stay and help Mom," I volunteered.

She shook her head. "Not today. All the Taylor men are going to the bear cave while Mom gets a few minutes to herself." Too shocked to reply, I could only stare. What kind of mother would literally throw her children to the bears to gain a little time for herself?

Dad tossed tin buckets in the back, and I dragged myself into the truck cab beside James. Mom waved cheerily from the door. "Have fun, boys."

We drove to our doom. *Thump, thump, thump. Thump, thump, thump.* The bald tires beat an ominous rhythm across the plank bridge spanning the broad glacial moraine. At the far end, Dad pointed to our right. "Look, the cemetery."

"Hey!" James stood on the seat for a better view out the passenger window. "I wonder if that's where they buried the guys that got shot."

"What guys?" Dad asked.

"The men that died in the bear cave fighting the railroad battle. Mr. Egan told us about it."

"I haven't heard that story." He downshifted as we climbed into the canyon. "Here's hoping we don't find any bodies in the cave."

"Bodies?" I shivered, and even my brother blanched.

Dad chuckled. "Just teasing."

What if there were bodies in the cave? Would they be skeletons by now?

Minutes later, we passed Horsetail Falls, and James pointed up the mountainside. "Look, Roy, a bear!"

My shoulders hunched. "There is not." I pouted. "You made that up."

Dad parked on the shoulder. "James, enough teasing. Everybody out, and let's hunt some snow."

My brother opened the cab door. "There it is! The bear cave!"

Directly across a shallow stream at the base of a high cliff, a soot-black portal pierced the mountain, rough granite teeth gaping wide enough to devour a locomotive. The creek burbled. A jay called from nearby spruce. Like the sighs of dead men, cheerless groans escaped the yawning mouth of the cave.

"Did you hear that?" I whispered to James.

"What?"

I motioned toward the cave. "Ghosts."

He twirled a finger by his temple. "You're crazy. It's just the wind. Don't be such a chicken."

Dad handed us each a two-gallon bucket and strode across the shallow creek on steppingstones. James hopped from stone to stone while I lagged, my breath coming in short gasps.

"I brought a flashlight since any snow will be a ways in." Dad glanced over his shoulder. "Both of you stay with me, although I'm sure there won't be any bears in the cave this time of year."

How could he be so sure? He had never been in the cave before. He should have at least brought a gun instead of a lousy flashlight. Several times he had pointed out black bears on the mountainsides, so he knew they were around. Maybe we hadn't seen any today because they were all in the cave.

I wavered near the entrance, where darkness snuffed out the light. Moans swelled from unseen depths. Warning us? Or luring us to a gruesome fate?

"Come on, Roy." James gestured from the monstrous maw. "You better stay with us."

"Okay," I quavered. My brother was right. What if a bear came home and found me standing alone at the entrance? A boy my size would make a tasty lunch. With a deep breath, I stole forward, determined not to let them out of my sight. Step by trembling step, I forced myself a half dozen paces into the dreaded shadows, life-giving sunlight falling farther and farther behind, the jagged burden of ancient rock looming above. Straight as an arrow, the tunnel bored deep into the roots of the mountain. James and Dad faded into the gloom.

"Wait." My croak was lost among ominous groans. Seized by terror, I ran to catch up, tripped, and fell in an icy puddle. I scrambled to my feet, dripping and shivering. Spine-chilling echoes reverberated from every direction.

Drip, drip.

Gurgle.

Moan.

Splash.

How could this mountain make so much noise unless something really did live here? The temperature dropped. I crept forward. "Da-ad!" The blackness swallowed my wail.

"Yesss, Royyy?" echoed all around.

My eyes struggled to adjust to the near darkness. I teetered on the verge of panic. "Where are you?"

"Right here." A click brought a blinding yellow beam. "Come on," Dad called. "We found lots of snow."

I ran to the light where they scooped handfuls of wet, granular snow from hardpacked drifts at the back of the cave, topping their buckets off. "Here you go, Roy." Dad handed me a bucket piled high with snow, trading it for my empty one.

"Brrr." James blew on his hands. "I'm cold. Can we go home now and make ice cream?"

"Yep. This didn't take long at all."

Dad's flashlight showed the way, and I hurried for the safety of the sunlight. Outside, I paused and filled my lungs with warm earthy air. We hopped across the steppingstones, dropped the buckets in the back of the truck, and climbed on the bench seat for the drive home.

"Mom!" James ran into the house, holding out a bucket of snow. "Look what we got!"

"Nice." She smiled and glanced my way. "Did everyone go in the cave?"

"Yep. Roy helped, too, and the cave was so cool, except we didn't see a single bear."

"I'm sure that's just as well." She took the buckets and set them on the kitchen floor. "If you *had* seen any bears, though, I know Dad could count on you boys to be brave."

We nodded gravely. I had been brave. Really brave. Well, to be honest, despite being terrified out of my mind, I walked into the bear cave. Was that bravery, or just stupidity?

"Somethin' smells yummy." James hopped on one foot. "I'm hungry."

"I'm cooking potato chowder for dinner. Go wash up while I prepare the churn. We'll make ice cream first so it will have time to harden in the freezer while we eat."

When we returned, the ice cream churn's green wooden bucket rested in a washbasin on the kitchen floor. Mom stood at the counter, pouring vanilla custard into the metal canister. Inserting the dasher and securing the lid, she placed it in the bucket and latched the crank on top. We helped her pack layers of snow and rock salt around the canister.

Dad settled at the table with his Bible and a pad of paper. "I'll put finishing touches on tomorrow's sermon while you boys churn."

"Can I go first?" my brother begged.

"Of course." Mom got a short stool. "Just sit here and crank the handle 'round and 'round."

"I want a turn," I grumbled.

She smiled. "Don't worry. I'm sure James will be more than willing to share the fun."

James cranked and cranked while I hopped from foot to foot. "James," I whined, "my turn now."

To my surprise, he stood. "Okay."

Aha! I shoved him out of the way and pushed the long crank up, over, and back around again and again and again until my arm felt like rubber. "James, your turn now."

He sat in the corner, building a cabin with Lincoln Logs, and didn't even look up. "I already had my turn. I'm busy."

"Mom!" I complained. "Make James take his turn."

Glancing up from stirring the pot of soup, she asked, "Who wants ice cream?"

Two hands shot up. Dad leaned back in his chair and raised his hand too.

Mom focused on James. "If you want ice cream, then you need to do your part."

"What about Dad?" James whined. "Why doesn't he have to help?"

Dad spoke up. "Don't worry. I'll get my chance when the ice cream is too hard for you to crank. Please take turns spelling each other."

We traded back and forth while Mom added snow, and water drained through a hole near the top of the bucket. When his five-year-old arms could no longer move the handle, James stood. "Mom! The ice cream's too hard."

"Good, that means we're nearly finished. Now, Dad can take over."

Dad cranked until even he grunted. "Done. We'd better get the dasher out before the ice cream hardens too much." Unlatching the crank, he removed the lid and pulled out the long paddle. Like magic, velvety white ice cream dangled from the blades. "Who wants to scrape the dasher?"

"I do!"

"I do!"

We leaped in circles until Mom handed us each a spoon. I scraped the paddle and slipped the spoon in my mouth. Mmm! Never had I eaten ice cream like this—so rich, so creamy, so sweet. But there was something more. What *was* that flavor? The edge of danger? A hint of courage? I smacked my lips. It must have been the bear cave snow. Would I ever taste ice cream like that again?

Mom reclaimed our spoons and took a lick from the beater. "Amazing! Who would have thought you could make ice cream this good with canned milk?" She nodded toward the table. "Soup's ready."

During dinner, Dad asked, "What are you boys going to do with your prize money?"

"Buy a gun," James blurted.

Mom rolled her eyes. "Fat chance. How about you, Roy?"

"I'm gonna save mine. That way, I'll never be flat broke."

"That's my boy." She patted my hand. "I'll dish up ice cream."

Scraping the last smudge of vanilla goodness from my dessert bowl, I licked the spoon clean and sat back. My eyelids drooped despite the late evening sunlight.

"You boys have had a big day, and it's after eight o'clock." Mom stacked dishes in the sink. "Brush your teeth and scoot on up to bed. I'll be there in a minute."

We dragged ourselves up the steep stairs, and Mom joined us. After tucking a quilt around our shoulders, she sat on the side of the bed, sang a lullaby, and said a prayer. "So." She stroked our heads. "Did anyone miss fireworks today?"

"Naw," James mumbled, glancing at his prize money piled high on the bureau. "Who needs 'em?"

"Me neither." I yawned. "The Fourth of July was neat, but the best part was bear-cave ice cream."

She kissed us each on the forehead. "Life can surprise us. Sleep well, my brave little men."

Dad dip netting salmon from the Copper River

12.
FISHING LESSONS

James and I shivered on the open flatbed between Miss Bortel and Miss Fisher as our truck lumbered over deserted streets to the Children's Home. The sun may have been up, but gray clouds resting on rooftops wrapped us in a chill mist. Miss Fisher tugged her wool cap with a gloved hand. "Feels wrong wearing long johns in July."

Miss Bortel shifted closer to us boys. "I'm sure glad I wore mine."

Sockeye salmon were running up the Copper River. Aunt Pedo wanted to catch enough to can for the orphanage and had offered to teach the grownups how to fish with dip nets. Tall and solid as a tree trunk, she waved from the driveway of the orphanage. Her Army surplus jacket was buttoned over a shapeless dress, and her feet were clad in leather work boots. Beside her slouched Jimmy, a lanky teen with a round face and crew cut. Three dark-eyed teenage girls in jeans and sweatshirts huddled nearby.

"Good morning, Andy," Aunt Pedo greeted Dad. "I managed to borrow a half dozen dip nets and filled a cooler with ice for the fish."

Dad hefted one of the nets, its weathered handle twice as long as he was tall. "Wow! This is one serious net." James and I together could have fit inside the twine mesh webbing. The nets clattered on the flatbed, and we all scooted as far away as possible to escape the stench of old fish. Jimmy and the girls squeezed in beside us.

"Where's Eddie?" I asked Jimmy.

"In bed. He's too young to fish the Copper."

"But he's older than James and me."

Jimmy shrugged, his expression unreadable as usual.

Aunt Louise had invited James and me to play at the Children's Home for the day, explaining that the river was too dangerous for children. Dad insisted that his boys couldn't miss out on such an authentic Alaskan adventure, and Mom caved in. Now here we were, the only little kids in the bunch.

To my surprise, Dad looked our way. "This does sound dangerous, and I'm having second thoughts, boys. I wonder if maybe you should take Aunt Louise up on her offer to keep you today."

I glanced at James, but he shook his head, and his smug expression told me he wasn't budging. If he could do this, so could I. "I'm going," I said.

Dad shrugged, Mom grimaced, and they slid onto the bench seats. Aunt Pedo joined them while the rest of us hunkered behind the meager windbreak of the cab. The overcast lightened as we drove out of town on the Richardson Highway and crawled out of the valley into shadowy Keystone Canyon. Damp wind swept over the low wooden sides, penetrating my jacket as though it were gauze, and I shivered too hard to sleep.

We jounced along the gravel highway, up and over the pass within spitting distance of the fog-cloaked glacier before following the skyline north. After two hours, Dad turned right on the Chitina cutoff and wound downhill between veiled peaks. We barely slowed for Chitina, now nearly abandoned. A relic of the Kennecott Copper Mine, its splintered boardwalks and dozen false-fronted buildings could have been a scene from a Wild West ghost town.

For another hour, we jolted between vertical walls of dense rock before descending to cross a bridge spanning a cascade of low waterfalls. Dad pulled over, and the adults climbed out. "O'Brien Creek," announced Aunt Pedo. "Last chance for a bathroom break." Half-hidden in the woods were a couple of outhouses made of unpainted boards warped and weathered, and roofs green with moss. They smelled no better than they looked.

Back in the truck, we lurched and ground up a sharp rise to an old railroad bed. The rails were long gone, but our wheels bounced over stretches of wooden ties. I could have touched the wet rock wall on our right while on our left was nothing but clouds. My heart stopped. The rocky passage traversed a slope that plummeted to the rushing river and was so eroded in places I was sure one dual wheel hung out over the precipice. Back pressed against the cab, I curled into a queasy ball and squeezed my eyes shut until Dad finally turned off the engine.

Aunt Pedo grabbed dip nets. "Everybody off! Time to go fishin'."

The teenagers vaulted to the muddy ground and caught James and me as Miss Bortel lifted us over the tailgate. My limbs were so stiff I wobbled as I swiveled my head, but the flat light failed to reveal a river anywhere. A low rocky rise blocked our way forward. Behind us, colossal pyramids, flanks cloaked by spruce and alder and slashed by avalanche scars of purple-pink fireweed, ascended into the featureless gray sky. Salmonberry blossoms and bluebells dotted the edge of the clearing where we parked alongside patches of feathery green horsetail, stinging nettles, and spiny-stemmed devil's club. Fragrant wild roses perfumed the still air.

Too late, I felt a prick and slapped my neck. My hand came away bloody. "I'm gettin' eaten alive."

Aunt Pedo pulled an army-green bottle from her jacket pocket. "Everybody line up for DEET before we head out."

Dad handed a short wooden club to my brother. "This is the official salmon killer. Don't lose it." He hitched a knapsack over his shoulders and gathered up two nets while the women each carried one. The teenagers divvied up coils of rope, and he turned to Aunt Pedo. "All right, fearless leader, show us the way."

She lifted her hand toward the rise. "Up and over, soldiers, although I must warn you, the far side may test your courage."

Courage? This was supposed to be a fishing trip. I could conjure faint memories of fishing on a lazy bayou in Louisiana. The worst thing that happened was hooking a bluegill and flipping it over my head into tree branches. After that, I pretty much lost interest and played in the mud until Mom asked me where my pole was. *Oh boy!* Deep breath. *Here we go, another Alaskan adventure.*

Dad took James's hand, I took Mom's, and we scrambled behind the troops. At the crest of the low rise, Mom clutched my fingers and froze. A mile-wide, steep-walled canyon stretched from horizon to horizon. Etched along the mud and gravel bottom, a broad river twined through multi-fingered channels. At our toes, the ground plunged for half a city block to disappear into the swirling, churning river, which dashed along the jagged shore as fast as a man could run. My stomach dropped to my boots. I should have stayed with Eddie.

"This way." Aunt Pedo swung her net to the left where a rocky footpath, no more than a game trail, had been worn across the steep bank by the intrepid feet of countless fishermen. "Be careful," she warned, setting out on the treacherous traverse, her wild red curls blazing the way. "The rocks are slippery, and if you lose your footing, you'll make a speedy one-way trip into the river."

Gaze locked on my boot laces, I tried not to sway.

One by one, we gathered our courage and fell into a single file. Step by cautious step, we edged along the dew-slickened rock. Mom's face blanched, and her lips pinched. She towed me behind her with a grip so tight I couldn't feel my fingers.

A few terrifying minutes later, Aunt Pedo stopped and studied the pitch leading to the churning water far below. "We fish down there!" she shouted.

Between us and the river, wet gray slate angled down to the raging torrent in fractured layers. Gargantuan boulders jutted into the water, creating whirlpools and standing waves. The rock we stood on amplified the deep rumble of rushing water.

Without hesitation, Aunt Pedo and the teenagers worked their way down the incline. This was obviously not their first trip. *Sourdoughs.*

Dad looked back at Mom and lifted an eyebrow. "You and Roy okay?" Though she gave a tight nod, the whites of her eyes betrayed her terror. *Cheechakos.* He started down, gripping the nets with one hand and James with the other.

Mom turned to me and grimaced. "Ready?" Petrified, I managed to nod, and she pulled me over the precipice. I squeezed my eyes shut. All I could think of was the deep icy water at the bottom. My toe caught, and my eyelids flew open. I focused on the crevices in the stone. My body trembled. "We're almost there, Roy, just a few more steps. Let's count. One, two, three . . ." Mom never released her grip until, at last, we stood with the others on a broad slate shelf at the river's edge. Legs like Jell-O, I collapsed to the rock.

Back up the hill, Miss Fisher gripped a boulder with one hand. A few feet above her, Miss Bortel—her rump high in the air—crawled backward on all fours. Dad cupped his hands to be heard over the growl of the water. "You two okay?"

Miss Fisher giggled. "We'll be fine, won't we, Anna? Only a half dozen more steps, girl."

A few minutes later, a white-faced Miss Bortel crawled out on the ledge where we waited, straightened up, and ran a hand through her hair. "I hate heights. I always have."

Aunt Pedo smiled. "Well then, I'm proud of you for doing this." She lifted her net. "Now listen up, all of you. This water is glacial melt, barely above freezing. So, fishing lesson number one—don't fall in. If you do, you'll be paralyzed by the cold and most certainly will die."

Mom turned a shade paler. My legs quivered.

Aunt Pedo continued, "Lesson number two—since we can't see the fish in this silty water, you'll have to dip your net by blind faith, and the more your net is in the water, the more salmon you'll catch. This takes us to lesson number three—your net can only trap salmon if they swim into it. Since the fish swim upstream, you need to make your mesh go upstream as well."

She dipped her hoop partway in the water and swung it downstream. The mesh trailed upstream. "This is one way—passing your hoop downstream through the water, then picking it up and doing it over and over again." When the net came even with her body, the handle jerked. She chortled, hoisted a thrashing silvery salmon, and whirled the hoop to the rock. With practiced motions, the teenagers secured the net. *"Whooee!"* She glanced around. "Who's got the club?"

James let go of Dad's hand and brandished the weapon above his head. "Me! Can I kill it?" He sprang forward, his shoes slipped, and he shot, feet first, toward the edge of the rock.

Mom shrieked, "James!"

Dad's nets clattered to the rock, and he threw himself flat, catching James's coat with one hand and hauling him back to safety. I was too shocked to move. Dad held James close. "Son." He took a deep breath. "I could never bear it if I lost you. Now, give Aunt Pedo the club, and she'll show us how to kill salmon."

White-faced and trembling, James offered the club to Aunt Pedo without letting go of Dad's hand. *Thunk. Thunk.* She smacked the fish on the head and picked it out of the net. "We need to bleed it to preserve the flesh." She slipped a knife out of a sheath on her belt and sliced out the gills. Blood ran red across the rock as she passed a small rope through the gill opening and out the mouth and tossed the limp body back into the water. "The salmon stay fresher if we keep them in the cold water on a stringer."

Features stern, she turned back to us. "Before we move on to lesson number four, who can repeat lesson one?"

"Don't fall in the river!" the teenagers chanted in unison.

Aunt Pedo nodded. "Now, lesson four—rather than waving a net through the water all day, smart people find an eddy. Who knows what an eddy is?"

Miss Fisher raised her net. "A whirlpool in the water behind a rock."

Aunt Pedo smiled. "Right. It makes the water run upriver for a bit, and that opens your mesh upstream.

Mom asked, "How do we find these eddies?" Which made me think of Eddie, enjoying a lazy breakfast in a warm kitchen. If only I were there.

"It's not hard," Aunt Pedo replied. "Find a big boulder or an outcropping of rock and check just downstream. Let me show you." She braced herself on the downstream edge of the shelf and dipped her hoop halfway in the water. The mesh drifted back toward the rock. "It turns out that salmon like eddies, too, because they can rest and get a boost up the river." She lowered the hoop farther into the water, and seconds later, pulled it out with another thrashing sockeye.

Dad could stand it no longer. "Louela, you and the boys come with me to that next point." He indicated a sharp bend where the rocky shore formed a long spine into the white torrent. Rough boulders and scraggly bushes littered the steep slope.

"Go ahead," Aunt Pedo called. "Keep a close eye on those boys. The rest of us will stay here."

Although I would have been content to remain on the flat solid rock, Dad was already working his way along the bank with James in tow. "Come on! I found a great eddy behind this outcropping." We caught up, and he passed my brother to Mom. "Here, Louela, you keep an eye on the boys while I give this a shot."

Mom worked her way a few feet around the point and stopped behind a large boulder. Releasing our hands, she pointed to a stout shrub sticking out of the rocks above our heads and glared. "See that?" She dropped into her command voice, low and slow. "You so much as think about coming out from behind this safe spot, I am going to tie you to that bush." She paused. "Understood?"

We both nodded. I sure wouldn't take a chance on falling into that icy water and drowning.

"Got one!" Dad whooped and hauled his net out of the swift current. "No, I got two!" He leaned against the load and flung the catch onto the rocky bank. A pair of glittering salmon flipped and slapped the hard ground. "Looks like we left the fish killer with the others. Louela, can you knock them on the head with a rock?"

Her eyes narrowed. "You remember what I said about leaving this safe place?" We both nodded, though my brother's attention was on the thrashing net.

"Hurry up, hon!" Dad waved at Mom. "The fish are calling!"

She took James's hand and placed it in mine. Her brown eyes pinned me. "Roy, can I trust you not to let go of your big brother?"

I gripped James's hand and nodded. "Sure, Mom."

She found a fist-sized rock, worked her way over to Dad, and smashed each fish on the head until they lay still. He cut out their gills, strung them on a rope, and wasted no time plunging his net back in with the exuberance of a prospector who just struck gold.

An hour and four salmon later, he asked Mom, "You wanna try?"

My brother piped up, "Yeah. I'm bored. It's my turn."

Dad laughed. "Ladies first. Besides, this spot is way too dangerous for kids. We'll hunt for a safer perch after a bit. Now, hon, put your net in here." He indicated a swirl in the water.

With tiny steps, she maneuvered down the angled rock. I couldn't bear to watch but couldn't look away, either. What if she fell in? Life without Mom was, well, not even possible.

White knuckled, she clenched the long handle and dipped the hoop into the current. Smiling, she turned. "This isn't hard. See, the eddy holds it in place. I could do this one-handed." She held one hand out to her side. The net whirled. She stumbled. Dad seized her jacket, and she grasped the handle with both hands.

"Whoa, hon, pull it up."

Grunting, she levered back until the dripping hoop rose out of the water. The net circled to shore, and Mom broke into a grin. Three salmon flipped in the mesh. James strained against my grip.

Dad secured the webbing and bashed the fish heads. "Woo-hoo! Look at you go! Three in one scoop. Maybe I should let you do all the fishing. But after this, please keep both hands on the handle."

"I learned my lesson. Let's move on and find a place where the boys can have a turn."

He picked up the net, retrieved the fish-laden stringer, and led the way. A boy attached to each hand, Mom followed along the mossy slope.

Around the next corner, Dad raised the net. "There we go! A fishing platform." Someone had built a square deck out over the roiling river. The algae-slimed wood, still wet from the night's rain, shook continuously despite support pilings angling out from the bank. The flat surface was about as high above the water as I was tall, had no railings around the edges, and didn't look a bit safe, but Dad submerged his stringer of fish and walked out on the rough planks. He bounced a couple of times, and the whole thing lurched. As did my stomach. He smiled. "See, the platform is completely safe. Come on out."

Despite Dad's attempt to reassure us, my brother and I took baby steps as Mom guided us onto the wobbly planks, which trembled with the power of the river. Dad held out the long-handled net. "Who wants to go first?"

My heart crept to my throat, but James grabbed the handle, now slippery with fish slime. "Me!" Face flushed, he hopped from one foot to the other. "What do I do!? What do I do!?" He swung the long net past my head, and I fell to all fours, clinging to the slick deck with my fingernails. Why couldn't my brother ever be afraid? Was there something wrong with him, or me?

Dad took the net in one hand and clutched the back of James's jacket with the other. "Lower the hoop into the water. They built this platform at an eddy, so it shouldn't be hard to hold the net in place."

James tipped the hoop into the turbulent flow and squinted at the turbid surface. "Come on, fishy," he coaxed. "Come on, fishy," The handle jerked. His eyes widened.

"You got one. You got one!" Dad, still clutching James's jacket, practically bounced. "Now, pull!"

James heaved on the handle, and the hoop flew out of the water. He whirled it around, and the hysterical salmon landed in my face. Blinded by spray, I backed away. My feet reached the edge of the platform. Mom jerked me up by my belt and hoisted me to shore.

James flailed the net. Dad clung to him while attempting to grab a small rock from the bank to bash the fish. Giving up, he tucked my brother under one arm and carried boy, net, and fish to solid ground.

"Well!" Mom fanned her face with her free hand. "That was exciting. But let's skip the drama from now on."

Dad bled the limp salmon and fastened it on the stringer. "I couldn't agree more. Only two people on the platform at a time. So, Roy, are you ready for your turn?"

I shuddered. My legs wobbled. The steep bank spun. Everything in Alaska was scary. But, if I didn't try, would I always be sorry? My throat tightened. "Okay," I squeaked.

Dad squatted. "You don't have to do this if you don't want to."

I cleared my throat and reached out a shaky hand. "Yes! I want to fish!"

He passed me the net and steadied me while I shuffled across the swaying platform. "Don't worry. I'll hang on to you no matter what happens. Just grip the handle with both hands. If you feel a bump, raise it." He seized my coat with one hand and the end of the pole with the other while I lowered the net into the murky water. Dad had made it look easy, but I discovered I needed to continually twist and lever the handle to keep the hoop lined up. My heart banged. My breath came in quick gasps. *Bam*! The handle jerked, and the net weighed a ton.

"Got one!" I yelled, looking up to see Dad grinning.

He eased me away from the edge. "Pull hard, Roy. Heave 'im out of the water." I leaned back and strained until the river released its bounty, two salmon dancing in a rainbow of spray. The net swung to the bank where Mom stood ready, rock in hand, and moments later, my gleaming trophies lay still.

"I did it!" If I could do this, I could do anything.

James hopped and waved his arms from behind a boulder. "Yay, Roy!"

"Nicely done, son." Dad bled the fish and added them to the stringer while Mom hugged me and led me safely to shore.

"You make me proud," she whispered in my ear.

I blushed. "Thanks." I could tell Dad was proud of me, too.

He retrieved the net. "I'd rather keep fishing while the sockeyes are running, but maybe we better grab some lunch."

We gathered behind a boulder, and Mom pulled biscuits, salami, and jerky out of the canvas knapsack along with a thermos of milk. Over the next few hours, we took turns fishing, and the stringers of fish grew.

Aunt Pedo appeared around the point. "Hey, guys! How's it going?"

Dad hefted both stringers, a dozen salmon on each. "I'd say all right."

"We've done well, too," she said. "Maybe we'd better start back."

"What time is it?" Mom asked. "Neither of us has a watch, and you can't see the sun through these thick clouds."

Aunt Pedo smiled. "Welcome to summertime in the Far North. My watch says almost seven."

Mom's jaw dropped. "No wonder the boys are complaining they're hungry. Why didn't you get us sooner?"

"In Alaska, when the fish are running, we fish. Besides, we were having too much fun."

We followed the riverbank back to the rock ledge. Miss Bortel held our hands as James and I scrabbled up, and we traversed the sheer slope to the road. The other adults struggled to the top, dragging long stringers, while the teenagers carried the nets. Dad wrestled two bulging gunnysacks up the incline.

"How many fish do you s'pose we ended up with?" he grunted, heaving another load onto the truck bed, now almost covered with plump gunnysacks.

Aunt Pedo tossed the nets beside the sacks. "We'll know in a few minutes when we stop to clean 'em at the creek."

Dad lifted me onto the flatbed, and I crawled to the front, where we huddled for the treacherous ride across the hillside.

By the time we reached O'Brien Creek, I was in a daze. Gray clouds shed just enough light to reveal adults and teens gutting fish in the ripples. Gulls wheeled and swooped, clamoring for the bounteous feast of heads and guts drifting through clear, burbling water. Dad rinsed his bloody knife in the stream. "Can you boys stuff the cleaned fish in the gunnysacks with some ice? Good chance to practice counting while you're at it."

"Sure!" James hefted a headless carcass and nodded toward a pile of gunny sacks. "Roy, you hold the sack open." I swayed to my feet. If my brother could do this, so could I. While I held the sack, he slid the salmon in, followed by a couple of double handfuls of ice from the bright red cooler. "One," he began the count.

An hour later, Dad slammed the back gate shut and looked our way. "How many?"

"Sixty-five sockeyes!" James gloated.

On the three-hour journey home, we slumped on the flatbed, a dog pile of misery, reeking of fish, and clinging together for warmth in the only space not covered by sacks of iced salmon. The sky grew dark, and I slept fitfully. Tires bounced and slammed through potholes as the truck crawled over the pass and down into Valdez.

Lighted windows welcomed us when we pulled up at midnight in front of the Children's Home. Untangling stiff joints and aching limbs, we shuffled into the warm, white kitchen, rich with the savory aroma of moose stew.

Aunt Louise set bowls on the table. "I made a big pot of stew, but nobody eats until you wash off that fish slime." While we waited our turn for the bathrooms, the younger children, who had stayed home, wandered down from their beds. "How'd it go with the young boys?" Aunt Louise asked, her mouth a featureless straight lint.

"Terrifying," Mom answered. "At least nobody got hurt but the fish."

Dad caught Aunt Pedo's gaze before replying, "Fishing lesson number five—don't take preschoolers to the Copper River."

By the time we mopped out our bowls, my head was bobbing.

Dad folded his napkin. "Those fish won't be as fresh in the morning. We really should can them yet tonight."

Moans circled the room, but Mom stood. "Andrew's right, and if we work together, this shouldn't take too long."

Aunt Pedo nodded. "Louela, I like your style. You know anything about canning fish?"

"I grew up preserving my dad's catch," Mom explained. "He's a fisherman in the swamps of Louisiana. Carp and catfish instead of salmon, but the process must be the same. I'm just not sure how long it will take us to get all the bones out."

"Don't worry about the bones." Aunt Pedo pushed her bulk off the bench. "We leave salmon bones in because the heat softens them. Okay, then. Andy, if you will haul the fish inside, the youngsters can wash and scale them in the sinks." She handed paring knives to the teenagers and table knives to us smaller children. Sliding chairs up to the big double sink, she filled both basins with cold water and added vinegar, which she explained would help remove the slime.

Dad carried in a gunnysack bulging with salmon and emptied it into the sink. "Who knows how to scale?" To my surprise, all the orphans, even the smallest, raised their hands. How come they knew so much? Were they born Sourdoughs?

Jimmy turned to James and me. "I'll show you." He reached into the water, grasped a fish by the tail, and ran his knife under the scales from tail to head. He scraped until the side of the fish was dull red, and the sink glittered with silvery scales.

We scaled and scaled until James shook the water from his hands and slid down off the chair. "My hands are gonna freeze and fall off," he whimpered.

The girls snickered, but Mom said, "It's okay. You've had a long day." She dried his hands with a towel. "Why don't you go rest on the couch?" He trundled into the living room.

I was so tired that every part of my body ached. But everyone else kept working, and I refused to quit. Besides, the process fascinated me.

As we finished scaling each fish, the teenage girls plopped it on a cutting board and sliced off fins and tail using razor-sharp fillet knives. As Mom sectioned the meat into cylinders, Miss Fisher and Miss Bortel packed them into one-pound cans, adding a spoonful each of salt. Aunt Louise placed the full cans in shallow boiling water in a roasting pan on the stove.

"Why do you put them in hot water without lids?" Miss Bortel asked.

Aunt Louise stuck a thermometer in a can. "We heat them until they steam, which displaces air. Oxygen ruins the flavor and might cause the salmon to spoil." She turned to Aunt Pedo. "These are ready. We need to get the lids on while they're still steaming."

Aunt Pedo retrieved a hot can with a tong-like lifter and wiped the rim. I took a break from scaling to follow the action. She set it in the canning machine, secured to the kitchen table with a thumbscrew. The apparatus stood about a foot high with a crank handle on one side and a lever on the other. I watched as she placed a lid on a can. It was a little larger than the can's flared top, and around the rim was a gasket of rubber-like material. She pressed down hard on the lever.

"What does that do?" I asked.

"This lever brings the head of the sealer down on the can. It pinches the rim against two rollers on the outside." She picked me up with one arm and turned the handle. "As we crank, the first roller bends the lid over the can and back under the edge in a hook. It creates five layers of metal around the rim, two layers from the can, and three from the lid."

She showed me the other side of the canner. "This second roller squeezes the seam together, and the rubber seals it airtight." She touched a number on the front of the machine. "See this? When the needle hits zero, the can is sealed."

She cranked the handle until I called, "Zero."

The lever came up, and she held the can out for my inspection. "What do you think?"

"Wow!" The golden can looked like the ones in the store. "It's like magic!"

She smiled and set the sealed can in one of three large pressure cookers. "A lot of things are like magic until you understand them."

Dad came in, swinging four salmon by the tails. "Great news! The last of the catch! How about we scale these to eat fresh? Anna and Dot can take one, we'll take one, and two will stay here."

No one had the energy to celebrate. As Aunt Louise said goodnight to the little ones and sent them up the stairs, I climbed on a chair and helped scale the last fish. All that was left was a bucket of tails and fins and a golden pyramid of cans waiting their turn in the pressure cooker.

On cue, the weights atop the pressure cookers jiggled, and Aunt Louise checked the wall clock. "Two a.m. Since I stayed home all day, I'll stay up and keep the canners going. The rest of you better find your beds while you can. I'll clean up."

Mom surveyed the carnage. Blood and fish scales coated the counters and tabletop, and muddy tracks crisscrossed the linoleum. "Are you sure?"

"Absolutely. With nearly three hundred pints to go, I'll have plenty of time." Aunt Louise glanced out the window and let slip a rare smile. "The sky is already showing light. You'd best hurry if you want to beat the sunrise."

Dad stepped into the living room and returned with James sound asleep on his shoulder. "Good night, all. See you at Steins' house for church at ten?"

Aunt Pedo smiled. "No promises, but we'll try." She beamed at the teens. "Off to bed, you wonderful kids. I'm so proud of you." As they disappeared up the stairs, she turned to Dad. "I hope you learned something today about the dangers up here."

He hugged James. "I did. It's hard being a parent."

Miss Fisher and Miss Bortel climbed to the flatbed, and Mom placed me on the bench seat beside my brother. The cracked vinyl cooled my cheek, and I closed my eyes, knowing this day, the longest day of my life, would stay with me forever. The wilderness had tested us, and we had survived. There was hope. We might make Alaskans after all.

13.
LAYING THE FOUNDATION

A cobalt dome outlined the rugged bowl of snowcapped peaks cradling Valdez. Rays of sunlight leaked over purple-cloaked mountains across the bay. The crisp green line of dawn crept across the valley floor, though fog still shrouded the ravines.

Our truck doors creaked, and Dad, James, and I stepped down to the broad bank of the Lowe River, the gravel still dark with dew. A raven croaked. Seagulls bickered and mewed. Stretching, I followed my brother to the river's edge, where silty gray water gurgled over a bed of glacier-rounded rock. Sunbeams skipped off ripples. I zipped my insulated jacket higher against Alaska's midsummer chill. James heaved a stone into the river, and iridescent droplets scattered.

"Hey, boys," Dad called, "we're loading the truck over here."

We shuffled back to the truck where he rhythmically shoveled river rock onto a pile atop the wooden flatbed, working his rusty blade through the coarse gravel with his boot.

My brother frowned. "What're we s'posed to do?"

Dad flung another shovelful. "Just start throwin' rocks in the back," he grunted. "We all need to pitch in if we expect to get the church built before the snow falls."

"But Dad," James complained, "the hole for the foundation is humongous. No way we can fill that."

Dad tossed another shovel of gravel. "I'll admit it's a big job, but we only have to cover the bottom. Let's see how fast we can finish this load." We boys pitched stones the size of our fists, and Dad's shovel never slowed.

By midmorning, James was at the water's edge inspecting a sun-bleached log while I kept throwing rocks. High above, an invisible thermal bore a pair of bald eagles. One swooped, splashed, and flapped away, a squirming trout impaled on its razor-sharp talons. Dad glanced at the sun. "Time to unload. This rig's sittin' low on the springs." Tossing his shovel into the back, he boosted us into the cab. We inched our way across the shallow ditch to the gravel highway, the heavily laden truck squatting and swaying at every turn.

We parked at the church site, and Dad swung us to the flatbed. We threw rocks into a wheelbarrow while he shoveled. When it was full, he jumped down and dumped the load into the excavation. We worked until, with a splash, the last wheelbarrow load vanished beneath the muddy water.

James walked to the edge of the abyss. "Where's all this stuff goin'? The water just swallows it up!" He flung his hands out and wailed, "This will take forever!"

Dad leaned on his shovel and sighed. "It does seem to go all the way to China, but this is only our first load, and we have at least forty to go. Let's drive by the house for a bite before we make another run."

After lunch, Dad shoveled, and I threw rocks. James meandered along the riverbank. "Hey!" I hollered. "What're ya doin'? You're s'posed to be helpin'." He waved and smiled. It wasn't fair. My arms quivered, and my fingers ached. "Dad, aren't you gonna make him help?"

Dad didn't pause. "He's probably tired, but I do appreciate how hard you're working, Roy." His shovel crunched, followed by a thump and skitter, and the pile grew in the back of the truck. As annoyed as I felt, I kept throwing rocks. I couldn't let Dad down.

After we emptied our second load, Dad checked his wristwatch. "This thing stopped again. I have no idea what time it is, but the sky is light, so it can't be too late. You boys up for another run?" I nodded.

By the time we returned with our third load, the sun dawdled along the western peaks, the eastern horizon mottled as purple as an old bruise. I grasped a rock, and my fingers stung. "Dad! Somethin's wrong with my hands."

He stuck his shovel in the pile of gravel and stooped to inspect. In the dim light, my fingertips resembled raw hamburger. His eyebrows shot up. "Roy! What did you do?"

"I dunno. I was throwin' rocks." Tears welled as a deep fire ran from my fingertips to my elbows. I sobbed, "I wanna go home. I want Mom."

"Oh, son, I'm so sorry." He picked me up. "Come along, James, time to go." We left the half-empty truck sitting where it was. I whimpered on Dad's shoulder while my brother trotted to keep up. From the dark woods, an owl hooted mournful consolation.

We found Mom reclining on the couch in her pink satin dressing gown. Looking up, she set her book on the coffee table and pulled on her glasses. "Well, look who decided to come home. Do you men have any idea what time it is?"

Dad shook his head. "My wristwatch stopped, but the sky's still light."

She uncurled off the couch. "It's nine-thirty at night. Dinner was supposed to be hours ago. I don't suppose you or the boys had anything to eat? What were you—" she shifted midsentence. "Roy, what's wrong? Why are you crying? You're hurt."

Dad grimaced. "I'm sorry. We were making such good progress I didn't want to quit. You better look at Roy's fingers."

A quick check of my hands and her eyes flashed lightning. "These fingers are a bloody mess. What were you doing?"

"I was helpin' Dad throw rocks on the truck," I choked. "I'm sorry."

"Don't you be upset. You're not the one in trouble." She glared at Dad. "What in the world were you thinking, or would that be asking too much?" Her voice could have frozen a river. Scooping me from Dad's arms, she turned for the bathroom.

He started to follow. "Need help?"

"We're just fine," Mom threw over her shoulder. "Maybe you can at least warm up the stew, so these poor boys don't have to go to bed hungry."

I whined and panted as she washed sand from my wounds, applied Merthiolate, and wrapped my fingers with gauze. While we ate, I sniffled and lifted my spoon clumsily to my mouth with bandaged hands, hoping to inspire guilt in James for his laziness. He ignored me. By the time we finished dinner, I was too tired to care and fell straight into bed.

The next day, Dad shoveled gravel while we boys played by the river. He quit on time, and we had dinner ready before Mom came in the door.

After the meal, she excused herself and returned a few minutes later, hands behind her back and a smug expression on her face. "Surprise!" She presented Dad with a small, gift-wrapped package. "I planned on giving you this for Christmas, but I think it won't wait."

He shook the box and smiled sheepishly. "I have a fair idea of what this is. And, yes, I could sure use it now."

James grabbed the package. "Open it!"

Dad laughed, untied the ribbon, and tore off the paper. Inside lay a shiny, stainless-steel wristwatch. His mouth fell open. "You're kidding! A self-winding Timex." Holding it out, he admired the white face and gold hands before fastening the black leather strap on his wrist. "And the time is already set."

"You've used up your last excuse for coming home late. Merry midsummer Christmas, dear." They hugged so long that James and I grew bored and stepped out into the calm evening to play.

The next morning Dad drained the excavation with a gas-powered pump, revealing thin topsoil overlying silty sand. Day after day, we hauled gravel until we covered the base with a thick layer of rocks for the crawlspace. I wore black cotton work gloves while my fingers healed, and my hands toughened. Wielding picks and shovels, we helped Dad dig a trench around the perimeter deeper than he was tall for the concrete footings.

James squinted into the opening. "Why do we need such a deep ditch if we're just gonna fill it up?"

"Frost heaves," Dad said. "The ground around here freezes about three feet deep in the winter and thaws in the summer. This makes it swell and shrink. Remember getting stuck on that hill on the Alcan? The time the Caterpillar rescued us?"

Wide-eyed, we nodded.

"If we don't dig the footings deeper than the frost, when the frozen soil melts to mud, this building will settle, and the floor and walls will crack. We don't want that to happen to the church, do we?"

I shook my head. "No way!"

My brother kicked a loose pebble into the ditch. "I s'pose. But this'll pro'bly take us the rest of our lives."

Dad retrieved the shovel. "I've read you the story Jesus told about the wise and foolish men building their houses."

"I know!" James waved. "The wolf blew down the one made out of sand."

"*Uhh.*" Dad scratched his head. "You're getting your stories mixed up. At any rate, like the wise man, we want to build God's house on the rock so it will stand through any storm. Come on, let's get another load of gravel. By the time we finish, this foundation should survive an earthquake."

James's prediction that it would take forever turned out to be close to the truth. We hauled gravel for all of July and into August until we had lined the entire bottom of the pit. Next, we built gargantuan piles of rock and sand, higher than my head, beside the trench.

"These," Dad explained, "are for mixing with cement to make concrete for the footings and foundation. The footings go deep, and the foundation wall sits on top of it, like our legs are supported by our feet."

That Saturday, Dad shook us awake.

"Get up, boys. The sky is cloudy without rain, perfect for pouring concrete."

I moaned and pulled the pillow over my head, but James pranced down to the kitchen. "Can we help?"

"Of course," Dad answered. "Today is all-hands-on-deck."

Blinking sleep from my eyes, I swayed at the kitchen door and mumbled," What does that mean, anyway?"

"It's a sailing term. It means that we need all the help we can get—every man on the ship's crew. Thank the Lord, Mr. Stein is back. We'll pick him up on our way to the dock."

Now I was confused. "Is that why we hafta go to the dock? To get on a boat."

Dad sighed. "No, to load the cement we ordered from Seattle."

Dad backed up our flatbed to a weathered one-story warehouse adjacent to the dock, and Mr. Stein hopped out and opened a giant garage door. Along one wall rose a towering stack of brown paper sacks, liberally sprinkled with fine gray grit. "You boys stay out of the way while we load these bags on the truck," Dad said. "They weigh almost a hundred pounds apiece, and I don't want you getting hurt."

We made four roundtrips with the truck before the cement was all stacked at the building site and covered with a tarp. Later that morning, four volunteers, all friends of the Steins, arrived. The biggest man, head shaved and muscles bulging the sleeves of his T-shirt, unhooked a two-wheel trailer from the back of his pickup and pushed it to the edge of the foundation. Atop the trailer was a big barrel, slanted sideways with a gas motor attached at one end. Arms crossed, he scrutinized the piles. "Sure that's enough gravel and sand? Don't wanna run out in the middle of the job."

"Should be," Dad replied. "By my calculations, we have nearly thirty tons of gravel and twenty of sand."

At four years old, I couldn't say what a ton was, but Dad, James, and

I had shoveled every pound of that gravel and sand twice, and it had to be a lot. I helped dig this trench and line the base with rock. Leaning back, I crossed my arms, and new muscles bulged my shirtsleeves.

The big man nodded. "Let's git 'er goin'." He yanked the starter rope. The mixer engine coughed to life in a cloud of black smoke, and the barrel revolved. My brother and I sat on a log to observe.

Awkwardly at first and then with smooth efficiency, the team loaded the drum with gravel, sand, cement, and water. The small engine thrummed, and the rocks murmured inside the metal drum. Every few minutes, the man tipped the drum, and concrete poured into wheelbarrows, which others dumped into the wooden forms crisscrossed with rebar at the bottom of the ditch. As the gray mud slid in, one of the men would jump down and smooth it with a board.

Mom and Mrs. Stein brought ham and cheese sandwiches and coffee in metal thermoses for lunch. The crew sat on the logs and ate in shifts, but the mixer never paused until the job was finished in the late afternoon.

Dad slumped at the dinner table that evening. "Tomorrow is Sunday and a day off from work. That'll give the footings a chance to cure before we pour the foundation." He yawned. "I don't know about you all, but I'm heading for bed. Thank the Lord, my sermon's ready."

Our small congregation, a dozen adults and twice as many kids, half from the orphanage, gathered at the Steins' the next morning. Mom ran her arms through her accordion straps and released the bellows. "Thanks to the Steins for bringing these new hymnals back from the States." She smiled. "Or, as Alaskans call it, 'The Lower 48.' I think we need a pick me up." Her smile widened. "Our opening hymn is on page three-forty."

Her accordion blasted out the beat, and by the time we reached the chorus—*"Hallelujah! Thine the glory, hallelujah! Amen."* Everyone smiled and tapped their feet.

His leather-bound Bible draped over calloused hands, Dad, in a dark striped suit and tie, stood near the door. "Our Scripture for today comes from Paul's first letter to the Corinthians. 'For other foundation can no man lay than that which is laid, Jesus Christ.'" His gaze swept the room. "Yesterday was a historic day for this congregation. We poured footings for the foundation of our new church. We dug them deep, beneath heaving frost and shifting sand. We laid them with the intent that this church will stand firm for generations to come. As proud as I am of the efforts and skills many of you brought to this project, this foundation and even this building will not be our real accomplishment here."

He paused, and I squirmed on the hard linoleum, puzzled. What did he mean? Our work was building this church. That's the reason our family came north.

"For, however well we build, a fire, a flood, or an earthquake may devour everything. Our only accomplishments of lasting value are those that remain after all else has been destroyed. As followers of Jesus, He calls us to share His love with others, and no better foundation can we lay than the love of Jesus Christ, our Rock, and our Cornerstone. His love never fails."

One parishioner lifted a hand. "Amen!"

Mom stood, the bellows of her accordion expanded, and rich chords swelled. The congregation joined her alto voice in four-part harmony.

"How firm a foundation, ye Saints of the Lord
Is laid for your faith in His excellent word!

The room trembled to the bass beat of her instrument as we sang out.

For I am thy God and will still give thee aid.
I'll strengthen thee, help thee, and cause thee to stand,
upheld by My gracious omnipotent hand."

My heart soared like an eagle on the wind.

Walking home through the misty rain, our family detoured to check the new concrete. I leaned over the ditch and peered with pride at the sturdy footings that reached far into the earth.

"Mom?" I looked up and took her hand. "This looks awful strong to me. Why did Dad say this isn't the foundation we came to build?"

She smiled and hitched me up in her arms. "It is strong, and I'm proud of the hard work you boys and Dad have done. But nothing we make of wood or concrete will stand forever. We did come to Alaska to build this church, but what truly matters is that we build our lives on the foundation of Jesus' love." She kissed my cheek and set me down. "Now, let's get along home and have some lunch."

14.

WILLIWAW!

On Friday morning, Dad turned left instead of right after stepping out of our door.

"Where we goin'?" James stopped and pointed behind us. "The church is thattaway."

"You're right," Dad said. "But all work and no play makes Jack a dull boy. Let's go to the dock today. I want to see if we can fish off it."

"Last one there's a rotten egg!" My brother took off. I chased him down the gravel street with Dad jogging behind.

The pier at the terminus of Alaska Avenue was as wide as the street and stretched for over three city blocks into Valdez Bay. Used only when freighters or other large ships unloaded, it was now empty. Gulls wheeled and cried in the brisk onshore breeze, ripe with nose-nipping essence of fish cannery, decomposing seaweed, and creosote. I peeked over the edge. It was a long drop to the ocean. "Boys, come back here and hold my hands," Dad ordered. "That's at least thirty feet down to the water."

A man in a brown canvas jacket, stained and worn yellow at the seams, leaned over the railing, gaze fixed across the bay. At the sound of our voices, he swiveled. A grizzled crew cut topped his head, and his weather-beaten cheeks sprouted bristle like gray moss on a rock. After a moment's perusal, he drawled, "You folks new heah?"

"Yep," Dad said. "Moved here this summer. Wondering if the fishing is any good off the pier."

"Y'all like fishin'?" He cleared his throat and spat. Phlegm sailed downwind to the waves far below.

Dad stepped back. "We love fishing. Can we catch anything from here?"

"You might," the man said. "Mebbe pull out a few flounder and bullheads." He paused and took a step closer. "What would y'all think about goin' bottom fishin' 'cross the bay? I got a boat."

"What kinda boat?"

He shrugged. "Nothin' special, a sixteen-foot runabout. But she'll take ya there an' back on a good day. Name's Jim, by the way." He extended a grubby hand.

Dad took it. "I'm Andy, and this is James and Roy. Yes, we would be interested in going out. What would it cost?"

"Not a thang." He hacked and spat again. "How 'bout t'morrah?"

Dad grinned. "Tomorrow it is. What time, and what do we need to bring?"

"Be heah by eight," he said. "Just yer lunch and warm clothes. The wind gits cold out on the bay. See ya then." He turned and walked away.

James, eyes round, pulled on Dad's hand. "We really goin' fishin'?"

"Why not?" Dad led us farther out the long pier. "What do we have to lose?"

That evening, while Dad helped Mom prepare dinner, he mentioned, "By the way, the boys and I are going fishing on the bay tomorrow with someone we met on the dock."

Her knife paused from chopping onion. "Who?"

"A gentleman by the name of Jim."

"You know anything about this Jim?"

"He seemed nice."

"What about his boat? What's it like? Some of those derelicts down at the harbor are on the verge of sinking."

"Umm." Dad snaked an arm around her shoulders. "To be honest, I'm not sure."

She stepped away, head cocked and hands on her waist. "I've hardly seen you all week, and now you and the boys are going to leave me here alone while you go fishing with a total stranger in a vessel that may not even be seaworthy?"

Dad scratched his temple. "Umm. I guess you could look at it that way. But what a terrific opportunity for the boys to experience Alaska."

Mom crossed her arms. "Yeah, like the *last* great opportunity to experience Alaska, nearly getting us all drowned in the Copper River."

He pulled her in. "Oh, hon, how could we know that was no place for young kids?"

"Maybe because no other young kids were there? I doubt there will be any other young kids on that boat tomorrow, either."

"I'm sure fishing from a boat won't be anything like that, and I would hate for the boys to miss this."

"You mean you don't want to miss this."

James tugged on her apron. "Please, Mom. I wanna go. Please, with sugar on top?"

I kept quiet. The memories of Copper River and the bear cave stirred mixed emotions in me, and I waited to see how this would play out.

"What about your sermon?" she asked.

"Not to worry. I've got some ideas."

"Care to share them with me? I need to pick hymns to go with the message."

"Umm, we'll talk about it after we get back."

"I don't understand you, Andrew. I thought pastoring was your primary motivation in life."

"You know it is, but when will we get an opportunity like this again?"

She took a deep breath and bit her lip. "Okay, then. I suppose that's the way things are. Adventure. Always adventure." He reached out, but she slipped away. "Fine." Her voice was harsh. "You just promise me you won't take any chances with my boys."

"Yay!" James grabbed my hands, and we jigged around the kitchen table.

The next morning, we downed our oatmeal and zipped on warm jackets while Mom packed bologna sandwiches and a thermos of milk. At eight sharp, we huddled on the dock, the planks still damp from the night's rain. Clouds, wispy as cotton candy, floated in a blue sky, and the water lay so calm the mountains reflected from the far side of the bay.

"Hey!" James pointed. "Here he comes."

The boat sidling up to the pier appeared puny and was entirely open except for a small plywood triangle at the bow. The outboard muttered to a stop, and Jim wrapped an arm around a piling. He smiled and waved. "We certainly picked a perfect day. Come on down."

I craned my neck over the edge of the creosoted beam. My eyes ran down the slimy wooden ladder between us and Jim's runabout—an impossibly far distance. There were more rickety steps than I could count. No way would I go down there.

"One minute, please," Dad called over the mewling of gulls. He squatted and looked us in the eyes. "You boys okay going down there?"

James nodded, but I shook my head.

"You'll be fine," Dad reassured me. "I'll go first, and you can climb down together inside my arms. Even if you slip, I'll have you." He slung the knapsack containing our lunch on his back and disappeared over the edge. "C'mon," he called.

James dropped face down on the dock and backed his legs over the brink. With a grin, he dropped out of sight. Either I had to follow or walk home—and I wasn't doing that if James didn't. Spread-eagled on the splintery planks, I eased my leather boots out. For a long moment, all I felt was nothing.

Something grabbed one foot, and I jerked. "I got you, Roy." Dad's calm voice rose from below. "Just a little farther, and I'll set your foot on the first step." Stomach fluttering, I inched backward until Dad pulled my boot down and rested it on the rung. I breathed out.

"Only thirty more steps." He gripped me tightly. "You can do this."

Jim waited at the bottom until we stepped into the bobbing boat. "Sorry 'bout the long climb, but we managed ta hit low tide. The dock is so high 'cause the supply ships tie up heah to unload."

With a pull on the starter cord, the outboard purred to life. He rotated the handle, and we swung toward the bay. "Jus' take a seat and hold on. It'll take us fifteen minutes ta get theah." He nodded toward a plank fastened across the midsection, and James and I plunked down on either side of Dad.

I ducked my head under Dad's arm to escape the blast of cold air as the runabout screamed for the far side of the bay. By the time the engine shut off, I was stiff as an icicle and had to stretch to straighten up. The boat swayed in the shadow of a cliff so close I could almost touch the sheer granite that soared for hundreds of feet straight out of the cerulean sea. A broad band of blue-black mussels and pimply white barnacles clung to the wall around the lapping water like a Baroque picture frame.

Jim pulled out two beefy bamboo rods with reels as big as my hands and white with corrosion. He knotted leaders to the stout braided fishing line and attached brass swivels. To these, he fastened long minnow-shaped lead weights painted blue with green yarn skirts. Next, he tied sharp treble hooks to the end.

"Heah ya go, Andy." He handed one of the rigs to Dad and extended the other rod's tip over the side. "Even this close ta the cliffs, the water's over two hunnerd feet deep. Release the brake and let the weight freefall ta the bottom." He flipped a lever on his reel, and the spool hummed. The green line ran out in a blur then slackened. "Soon as it hits the seafloor, reel a cuppla yards back in and start jiggin'." Flicking the brake lever on, he turned his crank a few times and waved the pole up and down. Within seconds, the tip bent, and his smile revealed gaps between yellow teeth.

"You got one," Dad said, standing so fast he almost tipped over the side.

"Yep." Jim cranked and cranked. I thought nothing would happen until, in a spray of water, a bright orange fish the length of Dad's forearm thumped into the bilge and lay limp. The chunky body, armored with large scales and spiny fins, sloped down to a generous mouth. Like bubblegum, a translucent white sphere ballooned out of the mouth, and on each side of the head yellow eyes bulged in astonishment.

I backed away, but James poked the bubble. "What's that?"

Jim pricked it with a knife, and the orb whooshed and collapsed. "Technic'ly, this is a yelloweye rockfish, but we mos'ly call 'em red snappers. The balloon comin' out its mouth is the air bladder. We pulled it up so fast it ditten have time ta decompress. By the time they git t' the surface, they're purdy much dead." He retrieved a pair of rusty pliers from his tackle box and disengaged the hook. With his pocketknife, he cut out the gills and bled it overboard.

James hefted the snapper with a grunt. "This's a whale."

Jim dropped his hook back in. "Yep. A few more o' these ten-pounders and we'll have ourselves a mess."

Before Jim's weight hit bottom, Dad's rod bent almost double. He cranked and cranked. "It sure takes a lot of reeling just to catch one fish," he grunted. From his grin, I knew it wasn't a complaint.

Jim jigged his pole up and down. "Mebbe, but wait'll ya eat one o' these thangs. Best fish ya ever et. One o' ya boys wanna try?"

"Me!" James leaped over the tackle box.

Jim steadied him by the coat. "If yer not careful, you'll be fish bait yerself. Heah, take hold o' this rig and wave it up and down, real slow. I'll hang on t' you and the butt end."

Dad reeled his prize over the side. He worked the hook out of the giant red snapper with pliers and passed his rod my way. "Roy, you ready to give it a try?"

My stomach squirmed. My chest tightened. I had to do this. With a stiff nod, I gripped the cork handle. The tackle proved heavier than expected, and Dad steadied the butt end behind my hands as he reached over my shoulder. "Just flip this brake off, son, and let your line out." I clicked the lever forward, and the spool whirred. The colorful lure plunked into the smooth water. Green-braided line streaked through corroded eyes until, without warning, everything stopped, and the line fell slack. "Now, Roy," Dad instructed, "flip the brake back on, crank the handle a few times, and start jigging it up and down."

"Got one!" James arched his short, stout body against the tug of the rod, the tip touching the water. "What do I do!?"

Jim steadied him. "Jus' reel 'er in."

While my brother retrieved his line, I raised my hook off the bottom enough to start jigging, which meant waving my whole body back and forth. *Thunk*! The rig jerked like it had snagged a locomotive. The star drag clicked a few times. I hauled back, but the tip of the rod still made circles in the water. "Reel 'im in, Roy," Dad encouraged. "You've got a live one."

I cranked and cranked and cranked. My shoulder ached, my arm grew numb, and still nothing showed. The braided line ran through dripping metal eyes and scurried back and forth across the drum.

"I got 'im!" James fell backward in the bilge, his monstrous prize flopping on top of him. Yellow eyes bulged, and the air bladder ballooned from its mouth. Jim pulled out the hook while my brother hugged the ugly critter to his chest. "My beautiful fish!"

Dad chuckled and asked, "You okay, Roy? Want some help?"

My reel had slowed to a crawl, but I shook my head. "I'm okay." If my brother could do this, so could I.

With a splash, my monster rose from the water. It must have weighed a ton, and I lurched forward. Dad held me tight as I swung my trophy around, and it slithered over the gunwale and into the boat. What a beauty!

We took turns fishing, Jim removing hooks and tossing snappers into the bilge as we caught them. A cloud of gulls screamed in frustration. "The gulls expect us ta feed 'em scraps," Jim explained, "but the fish'll be easier ta fillet if we don't gut 'em."

By midmorning, I lay back against the gunwale, relaxing in the warm sunshine. Eyes half-closed, I admired our haul, now covering most of the bottom of the boat. A sudden chill brought a shiver, and I raised my head. Above the nearby mountains, black clouds glowered down like bearded giants. One puffed, and a ripple danced across the mirrored ocean, which over the morning had evolved from blue to vibrant green, but now lay as sullen and dark as jade.

Jim looked up. "Time ta go. Andy, reel in yer line. Williwaw comin'."

"*Williwaw?*" Dad asked.

"Yep." Jim scurried to secure gear. "Yer fixin' ta meet a real nightmare, the nastiest blast of icy air ya can imagine." His voice rose. "Rushes down the mountainside like a hurricane. We gotta go."

Dad furiously reeled in two hundred feet of line, but by the time everything was stowed, wind frisked across the rain-pocked water, and waves slapped the wooden strakes. Jim yanked on the starter cord until his face flushed, but the outboard wouldn't so much as cough. "Dang! What a time fer this stupid motor ta act up." He squeezed the gas bulb, checked the choke, and pulled the rope. Nothing!

Dad frowned. "Mind if I give it a try?" Opening the throttle all the way, he cranked a couple of times, turned it back down to idle, and tried again. *Rrrrr*. He stepped back.

Jim flipped the shifter into gear and turned toward port. "Thanks, Andy. Now hold on. The water's gonna be rough before we're back. You boys had better scoot up under that shelter." He indicated the triangle of plywood covering the bow.

Dad helped us duck under the cover, barely high enough for two small boys to sit upright. We clutched the wooden ribs on the sides for support. Nose to nose, we stared at each other. The engine roared, and the boat raced for home.

"Hang on, Andy," Jim shouted above the squall. "We'll hit some bad water, but I don't dare slow down."

Like a bucking horse, the bow bolted for the sky then dropped like a rock. My stomach stayed in my throat. *Wham!* The plywood whacked my head—a sledgehammer blow. Stars exploded. The hull slammed the next wave. We shot skyward, and, again, the cover smacked my skull. Across from me, two Jameses, eyes squeezed shut, gripped the ribs with white knuckles.

"I gotta get out!" I crawled from under our refuge, only to choke as a freezing sluice of bay water slapped me in the face. I gasped for breath. Dad pushed me back under the plywood, where I grabbed the ribs and held on.

He bailed nonstop with a rusty three-pound coffee can. Jim knelt at the stern and held the tiller with one hand and the gunwale with the other. Wiping salt spray from his eyes, he guided us through driving rain and frothing chop higher than my head.

Up and slam! Up and slam! My head bashed the unyielding plywood. I clenched my teeth to keep from biting my tongue. Over the shriek of the wind and the roar of the waves, I could hear the steady scrape of Dad bailing.

Wave after wave, my head pounded the hard wood. Minute by minute, the agony wore on. I recalled sermons about everlasting punishment. If hell was anything like this, I fervently resolved not to go there. With no options, I pinched my eyes shut and hung tight. Nothing, I promised myself, goes on forever.

I don't know how long the three-mile ride lasted, but the fading roar of the engine brought profound relief. The bow settled, and I opened my eyes. Both Jameses stared back, rubbing their heads in perfect synchrony. I gingerly massaged my tender scalp, now knobby as a pomegranate.

Dad tossed a final can of bilge water over the side and ducked his head under the shelter. "Come on out, boys. We're fine now."

Gulls hovered like kites, the wind whistled, and rain angled across the bay. Though whitecaps roiled outside the small boat harbor, behind the enormous logs guarding the marina entrance the water seemed as calm as a bathtub. Jim steered us to a wooden float beside the boat ramp a block from the main pier where we had loaded, now only vaguely visible through the storm.

"Thank goodness we made it back safe. I hope y'all don't mind helpin' me git the boat loaded on the trailer. It would be insanity ta try unloadin' at the big dock. The waves'd pound us ta pieces 'gainst the pilings."

Dad nodded. "Sure. But, what a storm. I wasn't sure we were going to make it."

Jim tilted the outboard up. "That's Alaska fer ya." He jumped to the float and pulled us forward. "She's a jealous lover. One mistake and yer a goner. But, boy, when she smiles, can she eva' make ya feel like a champ."

Dad lifted us out of the boat, and we swayed before collapsing to the rain-washed deck. He frowned. "You boys alright?"

James grimaced. "Yeah. Wobbly. Head hurts, but okay."

While the men secured the runabout onto the trailer, we staggered through the rain to Jim's rusty orange pickup. Dad slid in beside us and laughed aloud. "During the war, I traveled clear around the globe, but I've never seen a place like this that will feed you like the gods one minute, then eat you alive and spit you out the next. I love it!"

James and I glanced at each other. My brother shook his head.

"What's Mom gonna say when she sees us?" I asked.

Dad winked. "Leave the talking to me. She'll be happy we're safe, and that we have all these fish."

The wind moaned through the treetops as Jim pulled up in front of our house. Stepping out, he handed each of us boys a snapper and unloaded a dozen more onto the ground. "Enjoy. Y'all worked hard fer these. Mebbe we'll do it ag'in some time."

"Maybe." Dad waved. "Thank you, and God bless you."

The door flew open, and Mom rushed out. "You're back. You weren't fishing in the middle of this gale, were you?"

Dad hugged her. "Nothing to worry about. We started right back, soon as the wind picked up. What do you think about all these snappers?"

She glared suspiciously at him before fastening her gaze on us boys. "Thank God, you're safe." James and I pinned our hands to our sides, determined to keep our tender scalps a secret.

She scanned our catch. "That is a nice mess of fish, though. I hope they taste better than they look."

Dad's face relaxed. "Jim said they're some of the best fish he's ever eaten, and we'll have plenty to share with the Children's Home. Come on, boys. Help me carry these beauties to the backyard so we can wash them."

After washing the fish, Dad carried our catch to the kitchen in five-gallon buckets. Mom pointed down the hall. "You boys go scrub off that fishy smell and change into dry clothes before you touch anything."

We returned downstairs to the rhythmic sigh of a blade drawn across a whetstone. Dad paused, dripped a little oil on the dark stone, then resumed sliding his hunting knife up and down the hone, leading with the sharp edge. After a while, he stopped and touched the blade to the back of his hand, leaving a small hairless patch. "Gettin' there. James, can you bring me a sheet of paper, please?"

James brought a *Saturday Evening Post* from the living room. Dad drew the knife down a single page. An inch-wide strip of thin paper fluttered to the floor. "That'll do." He wiped the blade on his jeans, reached into the bucket, and slapped a ten-pound snapper on the cutting board. "I've never filleted one of these, but it can't be much different than a catfish." Grasping the head with his left hand, he sliced behind the gills, sliding the blade along the backbone to the tail, leaving the rib cage behind. After flipping the fish over, he repeated the maneuver on the other side. He stood back. "You skin a catfish then fillet it, but I think I can skin these like a carp."

With a fillet skin-side down, he pressed on it with his left hand while running the knife blade between the skin and the flesh. "I know what I want for lunch." He placed the pale pink, skinless, boneless two-pound fillet on a plate. "Louela, would you mind heating the skillet and breading this in cornmeal and flour while I finish up here? I'll bury the carcasses in the backyard. They make good compost if the neighbor's cat doesn't dig them up."

"Sure." She set our cast-iron skillet on the stove and dropped in two dollops of Crisco. Turning, she caught James rubbing his scalp. "You boys didn't get hurt, did you? Come here and let me take a look."

He backed into the hallway, and I followed. "We're goin' to our bedroom to play. Can you call us for lunch?" We escaped up the stairs.

"How's your head?" my brother asked.

I fingered the tender knobs. "Hurts."

Massaging his scalp, he winced. "Yeah, mine too, but we were brave." He sniffed. The aroma of frying fish drifted up the stairwell. "Those fish are gonna be so worth it."

And they were. Sweet, flakey, succulent.

Jay, Dorothy, Anna, and our family bidding Dorothy farewell at the airport

15.

RAISING THE WALLS

The air crackled. Tension rose like the August thunderheads towering over the peaks across the bay. James and I leaned back in open-mouthed astonishment, heads swiveling like dashboard dolls from Dad to Mr. Stein and back again. The four of us stood between the concrete foundation and the enormous pile of peeled logs.

Mr. Stein's pallid face was flushed pink all the way to his receding hairline. He shook his head. "That's not a proper way to build with logs. I've never seen such a thing, and I can't imagine how it would even hold together."

Dad took a slow breath. "I'm telling you, Wilson, I know how to construct a log house, and the saddle-notch method will take way too long. If we have to scribe and notch every log we'll still be stacking them a year from now. Besides, that isn't as strong as the butt-and-pass technique."

A head taller than Dad, Mr. Stein glared down. "And I'm telling you, Andy, if you don't lock the logs together, the first little earth tremor that comes along—and we get plenty of those—will shake the walls down like pick-up sticks. I've seen a lot of log construction up here, and there must be a reason why people stick with tradition."

Dad's jaw clenched. "Wilson, I'll admit notching's more common, but that doesn't mean it's best. And there's more than one tradition."

"What are you talking about?"

Dad crossed his arms. "My ancestors were using the butt-and-pass method in the Carolina wilderness before the Revolutionary War. When they migrated across the Smoky Mountains, they brought that tradition with them. We still built that way when I was a kid, for the simple reason that it proved fast and durable.

Mr. Stein ran a hand through his hair and studied the ground. "You're asking a lot of me, Andy. Before today, I'd never even heard of butt-and-pass, and we'll only get one chance to do this right."

Dad pointed at the white-topped mountains. "Look out there. How long 'til the snow flies?"

"Maybe two months."

"The only chance we have to get this buttoned up by then is to do it my way."

I held my breath. Why would the two kindest men I knew argue like this? Dad was right, of course. He always was. Except, maybe, when disagreeing with Mom. Lips pinched and arms crossed, he waited.

Finally, Mr. Stein raised his eyes, and his expression softened. Sighing, he offered his hand. "Andy, you know a ton more about construction than I do, so for now, let's go with your idea and see how it works out. My apologies for losing my temper."

They clasped hands and gripped each other's arms. Like a receding tide, the tension ebbed away. Eyes closed, Dad lifted his face toward Heaven. "Father, thank You that even when we disagree, we can learn from each other as iron sharpens iron. Teach us to love one another and to appreciate our differences. Now, grant us strength and wisdom for the task ahead. Amen."

Mr. Stein stepped back, hooked a thumb in his overall strap, and eyeballed the stack of logs. "So, where do we start?"

Dad's mouth twisted as he squinted at the pile. "Those brutes weigh four to eight hundred pounds each." His eyes traced the foundation, a gravel square enclosed by low concrete walls spiked by rebar. "If we had four men, we could stack the first few runs by picking up the logs one end at a time. Since there are only two of us and we don't have a crane, we'll need to set up lifting-posts."

"How does that work?"

"We'll dig a posthole inside each corner of the foundation and erect a thick pole taller than the walls. Then we can attach a block-and-tackle to the top of two poles at a time for hoisting logs onto the wall. Do you know anyone who might loan us a couple sets of block-and-tackle?"

"I think so."

Block and tackle? I was bewildered. How did grownups know all these things?

"If you can start digging postholes at each corner, I'll take the boys out to Mile 13, and we'll scrounge up some posts. Aunt Louise said we could cut trees there. Mind if we borrow your chainsaw?"

Mr. Stein picked up a shovel and nodded toward the trunk of his car. "Help yourself, Andy. I'll try to have the holes ready by the time you get back."

We boys crawled into the truck, and Dad took the highway to Keystone Canyon, turning left at Mile 13. The steep driveway curved up to a two-story, clapboard house fronted by a full airy porch. A dense spruce forest ascended the foothills of the mountains directly behind the house. On our left, scattered trees opened on an expansive meadow.

James turned to Dad. "What is this place?"

He lifted us from the high bench seat to the gravel driveway. "A house someone donated to the Children's Home. Aunt Louise told me they bring the kids out here to hike in the summer or snowshoe and ski in winter." He lowered the tailgate and retrieved a double-bit ax and the chainsaw.

"See that pile over there?" He pointed beside the house to a canvas-covered stack as high as his head. "Aunt Louise is donating all that lumber, at least three hundred dollars' worth. We'll come back for it when we're ready to build the roof and interior walls. Now, let's find four straight trees, big around as your heads."

We climbed the wooded slope behind the house and scanned for the perfect trees. "Those will do." Dad indicated several young spruce, their tips reaching for the meager shafts of sunlight that leaked through the dense old-growth forest, their trunks straight and bare of limbs higher than a man could touch. "You boys stay behind this big tree while I drop 'em."

James and I fidgeted in the ankle-deep moss behind a gnarled tree, sneaking peeks at Dad. He leaned the double-bit ax against a trunk and cranked the chainsaw. The engine roared and belched acrid gray smoke. Squirrels chittered, and birds took flight. The whirring chain touched the base of a small spruce, and within moments, the tree crashed down. He felled three more just as quickly. James started to come out, but Dad waved him back. Pacing nine long steps beside each downed tree, he cut off the tops and stripped the limbs with the saw. When the roaring stopped, we ran out.

He exchanged the saw for his ax. "Stay where you are while I finish limbing." The blade swung in a smooth rhythm as he sliced off the remaining small limbs. *Whack!* The edge bit into a fresh, resinous stump, and Dad reached back and stretched. "Nice poles. Can you boys help me drag them to the truck?"

"Yeah!" James sprinted for the nearest fallen tree, and I followed, but between us, we strained to wiggle the small end. "How're we s'posed to get these to the truck?"

"Gravity," Dad explained, gesturing to the slope we'd just climbed. "Together, the three of us should be able to drag these down that steep slope." He hefted the base of the first log and gripped it against his waist while James and I clung to the trunk right behind him. "Off we go!" Dad set out at a trot down the hillside, dodging trees and boulders while we leaped and stumbled and hung on for dear life. If our fingers hadn't been stuck to the sap, we would have dropped off like beetles. Hands still glued to the bark, I staggered to a halt behind the truck.

"You two alright?"

We nodded, and he extricated our digits from the sticky bark. "You boys remind me of Br'er Rabbit after he punched the tar baby.

Now, think you can push while I lift the heavy end to the truck bed?"

James and I grabbed the log.

"Ready? Heave!" He swung the trunk to his shoulder and placed it on the flatbed. We shoved. When the base of the pole reached the cab, the small end flipped up, jerking our feet off the ground. Dad laughed as he caught us each by one arm and lowered us to the gravel.

"Ugh!" My fingers stuck together, and even my arms were tacky. I wished I had worn gloves and long sleeves like Dad.

After three more trips, he tethered the poles to the flatbed with rope, more than half their length hanging in midair. "Time to see if Wilson has those holes dug."

I crawled into the cab. Spruce needles prickled my arms, and the legs of my jeans clung together. We hadn't even started building the walls, and I was sticky, dirty, and tuckered out. Would this whole job be so hard? Why couldn't kids up here just play? I sure missed Cincinnati.

At the job site, Mr. Stein waved from the last of four holes. "Perfect timing, Andy, and nice lookin' poles. How in the world did you get those loaded by yourself?"

Dad winked at us. "Couldn't have done it without my boys, but I wouldn't mind your help setting them in place."

Dad held the poles upright while Mr. Stein packed gravel around the bases, and I giggled when I noticed Mr. Stein, who wasn't wearing gloves, pulling his sticky fingers apart.

Mr. Stein stepped back. "I'll pick up the block-and-tackle. Anything else we'll need?"

"Yeah, four-foot-long pipes and short lengths of chain with hooks." Dad turned to us. "Come on, boys, let's get these posts tamped down and run some guy ropes while Mr. Stein's getting the gear. Like a circus tent, the guy ropes will keep the poles from falling down."

Using sawed-off two-by-fours, we helped Dad pound gravel around the bases. He retrieved a long coil of rope from the truck, leaned an extension ladder against a post, and tied the middle of the line to the tiptop. The ends he ran diagonally down to hefty wooden stakes, which we had helped him drive just inside the foundation, and another rope ran diagonally out from the corner.

"Done." The post looked like a circus tent pole. He clasped it with both hands and shook, but nothing wiggled. "Now, let's fasten guys on the other three posts."

By the time we finished, Mr. Stein was fishing a spaghetti mess of ropes and pulleys from his trunk. "Triple block-and-tackle, Andy. We can lift just about anything with these."

I was puzzled. "How are we supposed to pick up a log with that floppy thing?"

"Gimme a minute, and I'll show you." Dad climbed a ladder, bored a hole near the top of a pole, and slipped a metal pipe through the hole. After hanging a double looped chain on the post just above the pipe, he suspended the block-and-tackle from the chain with a hook. "This upper block," he said, touching a thick wooden disk, "holds three pulleys." He climbed down. "See, the lower block is identical. The rope runs around the pulleys six times and divides the weight of the load into six parts. It lets even a little guy like me lift over eight hundred pounds." With a wink, he flexed like Popeye. "That's more than enough to raise these logs."

Mr. Stein tugged on the lower block. "Andy, you may not be the biggest man I know, but you are one of the smartest."

"Necessity is the mother of invention, Wilson."

"Can I try?" James begged.

"Sure." Dad held out the loose end of the rope. "Think you can pick me up?" James hauled while Dad gripped the hook attached to the bottom block. The pulleys creaked, and the block rose until Dad dangled by his arms.

"No fair! My turn." I tried to grab the line.

Dad laughed. "You'll have to let me down first." We released the rope, the pulleys whirred, and he eased onto the mud.

Grinning, he snatched my brother up with one hand and caught hold of the hook with the other. "Now, Roy, let's see if you can lift us both." I heaved and strained until I felt I was climbing with my hands. Slowly and steadily, Dad's boots levitated off the ground, muscles knotting as the two of them dangled by his one hand. My arms ached, I released my grip, and they floated back down.

"I'm Supermaaaan!" I showed off my biceps.

My brother jumped out of Dad's arm to shove me aside. "I wanna be Superman."

Mr. Stein stepped forward. "How would you feel about directing your superpowers toward something more useful? Andy, what's the plan?"

"Sorry," Dad said. "Sometimes, I confuse work with play. Anyway, the first thing we'll do is lay long planks over the concrete all the way around to give us a smooth, level base. We'll have to drill each one so it will fit over the rebar." He pointed to the steel rods sprouting like oversized thorns from the top of the foundation. "Then, we'll have to drill through the first layer of logs so that we can fit them over the rebar as well."

Mr. Stein hooked his thumbs in the straps of his overalls. "Wow! This is sounding like a huge job."

A huge job? My jaw hung open. He was just back from vacation and was complaining already? Where was he while we worked our hands raw digging the footings and shoveling and hauling tons of rock and sand to fill this enormous pit? I kicked the concrete. "Ow!"

Without a word, Dad strode to a stack of boards, hefted a two-by-twelve plank, laying it across a pair of sawhorses. "As they say, work ain't gonna do itself. James, can you and Roy each grab an end of this board and steady it while I drill holes?" He fished in his pocket for a folding wooden measuring stick and stretched it along the foundation. "Fourteen and three-quarter inches to the first rebar." He reached behind his ear for a carpenter's pencil and marked the plank before retrieving a brace and bit from the truck. Ramming the bit into the wood, he rotated the handle. "I'll sure be thankful when they run power lines down this street."

"Amen to that," Mr. Stein said. "They did promise us electricity by fall." He strode to his car for another brace and bit and arranged a plank on the second pair of sawhorses. "Can one of you boys help me with this board?" I limped over to grasp the plank, my big toe still throbbing from kicking the concrete.

The men drilled and hand-sawed the planks until time to go home and cook dinner. As they stored their tools in the shed, Dad said, "Guaranteed, tomorrow we'll lay the first log."

That night at dinner, Mom asked, "So, what did my menfolk do all day while I was at work?"

"Rrar!" My brother roared like a chainsaw. "We cut down trees, and our fingers stuck together. Then we built towers, and I lifted Dad up the tower."

"And I lifted Dad *and* James up the tower," I boasted. "An' then I helped Mr. Stein make holes in boards."

Mom raised her eyebrows, but Dad laughed. "I suppose from the boys' perspective, that pretty much sums up our day. And they have been great helpers. By tomorrow, we'll start seeing walls go up."

"Well, very exciting." She smiled brightly. "Maybe you'll have a church to pastor after all."

The next morning, we stopped by the hardware store and bought caulking guns and caulk. On our approach to the worksite, I stood on the seat. "Hey! The posts make it look like a real building."

Dad shut off the engine and opened his door. "Yep. Once we finish the foundation, things change fast."

Mr. Stein stood by the log pile. "What's next, Andy?"

"First, we'll lay a double bead of caulk around the foundation. The boards sit on that, giving us a watertight seal. We'll also caulk between every row of logs as we go."

The men ran white beads of caulk around the top of the concrete wall and settled the first board on the foundation, rebar poking up through the holes. Dad cupped his chin. "The planks will need tamping. I don't suppose anyone here knows how to jump up and down?"

"I do!" We boys waved, and he lifted us to the plank.

"Woo-hoo!" we laughed, chasing each other back and forth, vaulting rusty rebar, and slapping the board with our boots. The men set the remaining planks in place, and we jumped and hopped until they no longer wobbled.

"Now, the real work begins," Dad said. Panting, we flopped on the muddy ground and stretched out as the men rammed peaveys into one of the longer logs. "These logs are tough to roll because they've been milled flat on three sides. Let's coax this one over to the foundation and drill holes for the rebar."

As they started drilling, James squatted beside Dad. "Can I try?"

"Me too!" I crowded in.

Dad wiped the sweat from his eyes. "Sure. You boys can take turns finishing this hole while I run caulk along the plank."

James seized the brace and whirled the handle around.

"Not fair," I complained. "My turn!"

Surprisingly, he let go after only a few rotations. "Here you go, Roy." He wandered off and sat on a log.

The brace, a thick metal rod with a flat wooden spindle at the top and a chuck for holding a drill bit at the bottom, was fashioned into a horizontal *U* in the middle with a free-wheeling wooden grip at the center. With the spindle in my left hand, I curled my right hand on the grip. Around and around and around I cranked. Despite the cool breeze, sweat trickled down my neck. Shavings rose from the bit, and I backed it out and peeked in. Nothing had changed. This job would take forever. My shoulder ached, and the only spot on my palm not covered with calluses had sprouted a new blister.

Standing back, I held out my wounded hand, fishing for a little sympathy, but Mr. Stein focused on his drilling while Dad bent over the foundation. If they could do this, I could too. I shook out my hand.

A few more turns and the bit popped through the other side of the log. "I did one!" I yelled. "I drilled a hole."

Dad looked up and smiled. "Thanks, Roy. You're a huge help." My chest swelled.

"I helped too," James whined.

"You're both a big help," Dad added. "Let me show you where to drill next."

Other than grunts and pants and songbirds chirping, the only sound was the soft *shush* of drill bits in wood. With everyone working, it didn't take long before the holes in the log matched the rebar. Mr. Stein ran a red paisley handkerchief across his broad forehead. "So, are we finally ready to set the first log in place?"

"Almost." Dad straightened and rubbed his lower back. "But, first, we need to cut splines and kerfs."

"Splines and kerfs?" Mr. Stein shook his head. "What are you talking about now, Andy?"

"It's a common method of joining two pieces of wood. Kerfs are matching slots lined up to face each other where two logs meet. The spline is a board, driven like a tab into both slots. We'll glue the splines in place. And that makes for a solid joint."

Mr. Stein slapped a mosquito on his arm. "Andy, why couldn't you have explained this to start with? We could have avoided that whole flap over which method to use."

"Sorry, Wilson, I should've. Louela's always telling me I need to work on my communication skills. Would you mind giving me a hand lifting this?"

The men hoisted one end of the log onto another one, and using a handsaw, Dad made two vertical cuts near the end. He chiseled the wood between to create a slot and checked to make sure the spline fit. "We'll cut a matching kerf into the end of the next log that butts against this one."

He attached a short chain to the hook on one of the lower blocks, ran it around the log, and backed up. Mr. Stein affixed one on the other end. Straining until their faces flushed, the men hauled on the ropes. Inch by inch, the unwieldy load creaked up the concrete foundation until it swung free above the rebar.

My stomach knotted, and I retreated backward, but Dad looked our way. "James, can you and Roy hold this while I position the log?" I shuffled over and helped James keep tension on the pulley rope. We hung on as Dad shoved the log, now suspended in midair. The holes aligned with the rebar. "Start letting down both ends, real slow."

What if the rope slipped out of our hands? My imagination filled the details. Broken bones. Crushed fingers. James cracked his eyes, which had squeezed shut from the strain. Lips pressed tight, he nodded, and hand over hand, we let out the line. The rope passed up, around, and through the pulleys, and around again. The massive load crept down.

The veins in Dad's neck bulged. He grunted, "Okay, Wilson, a little more down on your end. There. Perfect. Keep both ends coming." The log groaned and settled into place with the round peeled side to the exterior. Dad stepped back, wiped the sweat from his face, and beamed. "Great job, everyone."

Mr. Stein raised his hands in the air. "Hallelujah! The first log is laid! This deserves a special treat." He retrieved two thermoses and a paper sack of sugar-dusted donuts from his car. "Jay made these last night."

"Oooh." I dug into the bag. "Thank you, Mr. Stein."

Astraddle a log, James soon sported a powdered sugar and cocoa mustache. "Building stuff sure is a lotta work. I'm not gonna work this hard when I grow up. I'm just gonna hunt and fish."

Mr. Stein blew on his steaming cup of coffee and laughed. "If anybody can pull that off, it's you, James. A chip off the old block." Mr. Stein shook his head. "Andy, I can't recall ever meeting anyone who can make hard work seem like fun the way you do. I would love to know your secret."

Dad paused before replying. "Some secrets are best left that way. I'll just say that though my father taught me a lot of lessons I wish I could unlearn, this isn't one of them."

As I paused before we walked away that afternoon to admire that beautiful first log, a warmth swelled in my chest. We were building the church!

It took us all the next day to complete the first round of logs, the front and back ones trimmed so that they butted up against the side logs, all locked together by kerfs and splines.

"In the morning," Dad said, "we'll build the door bucks and true them up."

"Bucks?" James asked. "You mean papa deer?"

"Not this kind," Dad answered. "It's what we call the structure around the doorframe. Once the bucks are in place, true and square, we'll run the logs up to them, leaving openings in the walls for window frames. If it all goes without a hitch, we'll be ready to start on the roof by the time the volunteers come up from Seattle." Mr. Stein had informed us that a dozen Free Methodist men from Seattle, after hearing about our project, had volunteered to pay their own expenses to fly up in the fall and help us finish.

The next day we erected the front door buck out of short logs and began the second row on the walls by running a double bead of caulk on a bottom log. We hoisted a short log atop the first layer, which butted against the buck, the other end sticking out past the corner.

"Now, we'll start seeing something resembling a wall." Dad handed a brace and bit to Mr. Stein and took one himself. "Just like before, we'll drill through the top log every four feet. You boys want to help?"

"We have to drill all of them?" Arms outstretched, James collapsed to the ground. "We'll never finish!"

"Oh, yes, we will." Dad started bits for us boys. While the three of us drilled holes, he cut pieces of rebar with a bolt cutter and tapped them in. "Now, for the fun part." He raised a sledgehammer. *Whang!*

I held my hands over my ears as the metal rang, and the rebar pierced the lower log until it was flush with the upper. Dad picked up another piece, but before positioning it, he locked eyes with Mr. Stein. "Solid enough for you, Wilson?"

Mr. Stein raised hands in surrender. "If I had understood the whole process, I would never have questioned you, Andy. Between the rebar, caulk, and splines, this wall isn't going anywhere."

We turned the corner, cutting kerfs and splines, drilling holes, and spiking logs together. "Hey, this is goin' fast!" exclaimed James.

"Yes," said Dad. "I told you the walls would go pretty quick. The tricky part is when the logs' height doesn't match the tops of the door and window bucks. Then we'll have to rip them thinner with the chainsaw."

Over the next few weeks, in fair weather and foul, sometimes with extra help, but mostly without, log by log, row by row, the walls crept skyward while the pile dwindled to scraps. Window openings appeared partway up, three on each sidewall and a pair flanking the front door.

I admired our handiwork. Walls rose higher than Dad could reach on all four sides. Twenty-two layers of logs, he said. But could we close it before the first snow?

16.
STEALING FROM GOD

The next week, Dad parked the truck in front of the house at Mile 13, and my brother leaned over the dash. "Where're the boards? They're all gone."

Dad switched off the ignition and stared, open-mouthed. "The lumber was right there a month ago."

The stack had vanished. All the lumber Aunt Louise had donated to finish the church was gone. And the canvas tarp.

I held up my hands. "What are we gonna do?"

"I don't know." Dad's whisper was hoarse.

James scanned the clearing. "Where did it go? Did Aunt Louise take it?"

"No, I just talked to her yesterday to let her know we'd be picking it up. I have no idea what happened." Dad stepped out, and we followed him around behind the house, but there was no trace of the lumber.

"Did someone steal it?" my brother asked.

I turned to Dad. "If someone took the boards, we can't finish the church."

James scrunched up his mouth. "Who would steal from God?"

"And from orphans," Dad muttered, wiping a hand down his face. He took a deep breath. "I don't know, but if God wants us to get it back, He'll make it happen. And if not, we'll trust Him to show us another way."

My brother reached up for Dad's hand. "Can we pray about it?"

"Sure, son, let's do that now." He took our hands, and we knelt together on a bed of damp spruce needles. Dad lifted his face to the sullen sky. "Father, sometimes we think we have everything figured out, and then we're reminded that we're not the ones in control. You alone are sovereign. We don't know what happened to this lumber, but You do. Please, Lord, give us wisdom and provide the materials we need to complete Your house. In Your Son's holy name, Amen."

On the way back, James jabbered about the thief, but I was too sad to talk. How could something so unfair happen, especially to God? What was the point of working so hard to serve Him if bad men could undo everything?

Dad drove right past our house and swung left on McKinley Street. He passed Gilson's Mercantile and the bank. James glanced up. "Where we goin'?"

"I've got an idea." He parked beside the boardwalk and opened his door. We scooted across the seat, but he waved us back. "You boys stay here. I won't be gone long."

To our astonishment, Dad strode through the doors of the glass-fronted Pinzon Bar. Noses pasted to the driver's window, we gaped as he was swallowed up by that dark and smoky den of iniquity. James gasped. Dad was a minister. He didn't go into bars. My brother reached across me for the door handle. "I think we better tell Mom."

"No!" I grabbed his hand. "Dad told us to stay here!"

"He went into a saloon!" Brown freckles stood out on his pale face, and the whites showed around his amber eyes. "What if he doesn't come back?"

"He will." He had to. "If he comes out, and we're not here, we'll be in big trouble."

"Okay." James sat down, then popped up, and started jumping on the seat. "He better come back pretty soon, or I'm gonna tell Mom."

I huddled against the passenger door and bit my lip. "Do you gotta jump so much? You're makin' me crazy."

"I can't help it." He hopped off the seat to the floorboards. "I wish he would hurry."

The bar's door swung open a couple of times, and we sat up, but the men who came out were strangers, and I slumped back. What was Dad doing? What was taking so long?

James yipped, "I see him!"

Dad slid in behind the wheel. I stood to ask him what happened but sat back down at his grim expression. "Remember our friend Jim who took us fishing?" he said.

We nodded.

"I found him in the bar, although it seems a little early in the day for whiskey."

James blanched. "You drank whiskey?"

Dad's eyes widened, then he tousled James's hair. "Of course not. I ordered a ginger ale."

"So, why did you go to a bar?" I asked.

"As a young soldier, I spent enough time in bars to understand they're a prime place to fish for information, particularly about shady dealings. Jim told me that a ne'er-do-well won a homesite a couple of miles west of town in a poker game, but he had no money to build on it. Somehow, he found out about the lumber the orphanage had stored at Mile 13, and he just took it."

"What are we gonna do?" asked James. "Can we take it back?"

Dad frowned. "Maybe, if he hasn't already used it for building, but I don't want to cause any trouble."

"Why not? He's the one who started it!"

"I understand, but what did Jesus teach us to do when someone mistreats us?"

James pouted. "Turn the other cheek, but that doesn't feel right. I think he should pay!"

"So do I. Only following Jesus means we give up our right to do whatever we want. Either we follow Him whole hog or not at all, and if He wants us to turn the other cheek when someone wrongs us, then that's what we'll do."

James flung out his arms. "But Jesus wants us to finish the church."

"I'm certain He does." Dad sat back, one finger pressed to his lips. "And we will. Although, at the moment, I'm not sure how." He punched the ignition. "I have an idea." Making a U-turn, he headed northwest on McKinley. "Let's drive out to the thief's homesite. Jim told me how to find it, and we'll see if, by any chance, we can recover the lumber."

I panicked. "What if the robber's home? He might have a gun. He could shoot us."

Dad continued past the airport, the last sign of civilization. "Well, he is a robber, and he almost certainly owns a gun. Far as I can tell, everyone in Alaska does. That doesn't mean he's going to shoot us, though. I just don't want to leave any stone unturned."

"I thought we were looking for lumber?"

"It's an old saying. It means we want to check out every possibility before we give up."

Near the west end of the valley, he turned off the deserted road and followed a pair of muddy ruts winding a short way up a hill through dense woods. When the tracks narrowed to a footpath, he parked the truck. "Looks like we walk from here, boys."

He stepped out and reached up to catch us. James jumped down, but I hesitated. "I think I'll wait in the cab."

"Come along, Roy," Dad urged. "You'll be safer with us than here by yourself."

He was right, and I accepted his hand. Why did we ever leave Cincinnati? Here we kept ending up in scary places. Although, to be honest, there were parts of Cincinnati that were just as scary. Still, I missed it.

I trotted to catch Dad before he disappeared up the trail, but James called from beside the truck. "Dad, you left your shotgun behind the seat."

Dad shook his head. "Packing a gun is the last thing we need. We're here to make peace, not trouble. Now, come along."

After winding a quarter mile up the hill, the path opened onto a sloping meadow with a panoramic view of the mountains across Valdez Bay. Over the morning, the clouds had scattered, and heather and low-bush blueberries carpeted the sunlit slope beneath our feet in vivid patches of red, orange, purple, and yellow. In the center, beside a gurgling creek, nestled a small one-story cabin, the roof and walls wrapped in tarpaper. A tiny window peeked out the side, and a larger one next to the homemade plank door allowed a view of the bay. No smoke rose from the metal chimney.

Dad cupped his hand to his mouth and called, "Hullo!" No one answered. "Hullo!" He turned. "Appears no one's home. Let's take a gander around back."

Bad idea. "Can't we just leave?" I whined. "What if the robber's hiding out back?"

My brother scooted around the cabin. "Hey, I found some boards!"

Dad towed me along to where James balanced on one foot atop a wobbly pile of short remnants. Nearby lay wadded up brown canvas. "That's the tarp from our lumber pile." Dad shook his head. "Well, I guess that answers our question." He flipped a remnant with his toe. "The only thing left are these scraps." He ran his hand down his face. "It's only a week until the volunteers come."

I threw my arms out. "This isn't fair!"

"You're right. It's not." Dad paused and took in the spectacular view belonging to the robber. "Life is often not fair, which means we have to trust that God will make things right in His time." As he turned to go, his lips thinned. "Oh Lord, how long shall the wicked triumph?"

On the trail back down the hill, my brother threw sticks at squirrels and birds while I tiptoed as stealthily as an Indian. No way did I want to attract the attention of the robber.

Dad stopped by the Steins' house on our way home and delivered the bad news. Mr. Stein said he would invite everyone over that evening to discuss our calamity.

When Mom arrived from work, dinner was ready. Sitting around the table, we bowed our heads.

"Dear Father," Dad prayed, "ruler of Heaven and earth, forgive us our trespasses as we forgive those who trespass against us." I peeked between my fingers, and his hands were raised toward Heaven. "Lord, we ask for a miracle so that we may finish Your house, but more importantly, we ask for forgiveness in our hearts for the thief. Amen."

Mom looked around. "So how *was* your day? What in the world happened?"

"Dad went in the saloon and left us alone," James shrilled, "but he didn't drink whiskey."

Mom's eyebrows rose. "Pardon me?"

"Yeah," I piped up, "and we found the robber's house, but nobody got shot."

"Dad went in a saloon and left you boys all alone with an armed robber?" She turned to Dad. "Perhaps you need to fill me in."

Dad's mouth twisted. "I'll tell you the whole story later. The gist of it is that someone stole the boards from Mile 13, and now we have no lumber to finish the church."

Her hand rose to her throat. "What are we going to do?"

"Everyone's getting together at Steins' after dinner to discuss just that. We can only trust that God has the answer we need." Dad, who usually ate slowly, wolfed down his meal and excused himself. "I need to run a little errand, but I'll be back in time for the meeting."

An hour later, a dozen solemn parishioners gathered with their children in the Steins' living room. Dad stood and scanned the room. "Most of you already heard the unwelcome news that brings us together. All the lumber donated by Aunt Louise, which we planned to use for the roof and interior, has been stolen."

"Do we know who stole it?" one of the men asked.

"We do," answered Dad.

"Can we get it back?"

"I'm afraid we're too late for that. The thief used it all to construct a cabin on his homesite."

"What about the authorities?" a woman asked. "Won't they help us?"

"The troopers are spread too thin across the territory," someone answered. "Besides, we can't get the boards back without a lawsuit, and the nearest courts are in Anchorage."

"Even if we won a lawsuit," Mr. Stein chimed in, "we would have to tear down the house to recover the lumber. By then, our church would be covered in snow." He rubbed his cheeks. "Besides, I don't believe God brought us here to do anything like that."

Someone piped up, "Well, that leaves us needing a miracle if we're going to close the building by winter."

Let the thief go unpunished? That couldn't be right. How could that be okay with God?

Mrs. Stein opened the kitchen door, releasing a sumptuous smell. "Mind if I interrupt? This would be the first church committee I've known to accomplish anything without coffee." Grim expressions softened as she served coffee and passed around canned milk and sugar cubes. We kids went for the sugar cubes.

Mr. Stein blew steam off his cup, took a sip, and sat back. "We've poured all our resources into this project. We have nothing more to give, and the Free Methodist headquarters in Seattle allocated their budget toward starting a church in Anchorage."

Mom asked, "Wilson, what about the men flying up from Seattle next week?"

"I suppose I should send a telegram and let them know we might not be ready."

Dad cleared his throat. "Hold on. Just before coming here, I discussed our predicament with Pastor Rose at the Baptist Church. They just completed their log building, and he said they ended up with a surplus of lumber. He's checking with their board, but he's pretty sure they can help us out."

Mr. Stein's face relaxed a bit.

Aunt Louise leaned forward, a smile escaping her thin lips. "I almost forgot that we stored another stack of boards behind our home here in town. We planned to construct a dormitory, but we no longer need the space. I can't think of a better use for that lumber."

Miss Bortel set down her coffee. "Over the summer, I've watched how much you all sacrificed to make this church a reality, and you're an inspiration to me." She smoothed her dress. "Some of you know I recently purchased the house I'm in, so I'm strapped for cash at the moment, but God provided me with a teaching contract for this fall, and I'll receive my first paycheck soon." Thick lenses magnified her smiling brown eyes. "I'm going to step out in faith and pledge to buy the doors and windows."

Mr. Stein raised a hand. "Praise the Lord! Louise and Anna, I can't thank you enough."

Dad stepped to the center of the room, steel-gray eyes glistening with tears. "The Steins started this project with nothing but faith, and now the walls are up. A few hours ago, none of us had any idea how the church would be completed. Now, everything we lost has been replaced, plus some. I suppose that's what faith is, trusting God's leading, even when you can't see the way."

I was confused. How could we be sure of the right way if we couldn't see it?

Dad wiped his eyes and raised calloused palms in benediction. "O taste and see that the Lord is good. Blessed is the man that trusteth in Him."

Mrs. Stein appeared at the kitchen door. "Everyone, please stay. I baked a pineapple upside-down cake, confident this would be a celebration."

My mouth watered as she passed around saucers laden with steaming yellow cake. Eyes closed, I chewed slowly. The syrupy, fruity caramel lolled on my tongue, mellowed by a generous dollop of Alaskan style whipped cream—whipped sweetened condensed milk.

What did Dad say? "Taste and see that the Lord is good." Could the Lord's goodness be as yummy as pineapple upside-down cake? Heart full of gratitude, I leaned back and nodded. I had tasted grace.

17.
BLUEBERRIES AND BEARS

As James and Mom left for his first day in kindergarten, I trailed them as far as the street and waved until they passed out of sight beneath a crisp, clear sky. My chest filled with unexpected emptiness. James-and-Roy was one word. We had shared a crib. We worked together, played together, got into trouble together, had fun, and fought together. I couldn't remember a day or night in my whole life we hadn't been together.

Dad came out and lifted me to his shoulder. "You okay, son?"

I buried my face in his familiar flannel and breathed in Old Spice, Listerine, and a hint of sweat.

"It's chilly out here. Let's go back inside." He closed the door against the morning air. "How 'bout some hot cocoa?"

Dad set me at the kitchen table and heated canned milk in a saucepan. I hiccuped and rubbed my nose on my shirtsleeve.

"Today," he announced, "I'll teach you to tie your shoes, and then we'll memorize Psalm 100. Do you remember how it begins?"

I shook my head.

He poured hot milk into mugs and spooned in Hershey's cocoa powder. "Make a joyful noise unto the Lord, all ye lands," he quoted. "Can you say, Make a joyful noise?"

Steam rose from my mug. I tried a tiny sip and mumbled, "Make a joyful noise." The ache shrank a little. "Unto the Lord." My frown relaxed.

"Nice. Let's finish our cocoa so we can practice tying our shoes."

I had mastered counting to forty when Dad checked his new Timex. "Time to go get James."

My hand in Dad's, we ambled through mud-pocked gravel to the corner of Alaska and Sherman. Though the new grade school covered much of the block, the kindergartners met in the basement of an adjacent older building. Hopping on one foot, I watched Miss Bortel hug each child as they walked out the door. After telling her goodbye, James stopped and glanced around.

"James!" I yelled.

At first, he pretended not to see us, then his face broke into a grin, and he ran over and socked me on the shoulder. "Kindergarten was loads of fun. I made new friends, and we had milk and cookies."

I socked him back. "I don't care 'cause I had cocoa. And I have friends too. Ben at Sunday school is my friend." Side by side, we trailed Dad up Alaska Avenue. "But you're still my best friend."

"Yep." He took my hand. "You're my best friend too."

By now, the gable ends of the completed log walls swept skyward like arrows pointing toward Heaven. A single log beam spanned the center of the sanctuary at ceiling height from above the front door clear to the back, supported midway by a round post. Roofless as a ruined castle, the structure gaped at the blue sky.

Dad studied the open shell. "Thank goodness the volunteers come this weekend. We'd have a hard time finishing without them."

James jumped from the empty front doorframe to the coarse gravel. "Can Roy and I help make the roof?"

Dad shook his head. "I'm afraid not. Too many bodies to keep track of and too much chance of something falling on someone. Those of us on top will be almost twenty feet up, and we'll need to focus on what we're doing."

James pouted. "But I wanna help."

"You boys are going blueberry picking with Mom and Mrs. Stein on Saturday. If you come home with enough berries, Mom will fill a pantry shelf with jelly that should last us all year."

"Yay!" James leaped in circles. "I love berries."

I frowned. "Aren't the bears picking berries too?"

"I'm sure they are," Dad said. "But Mrs. Stein has lived here a couple of years and knows what she's doing. She won't take you anywhere near a bear."

On Friday morning, Mr. Stein accompanied Dad and me to the airport, where we met the half dozen men flying up from Seattle by way of Anchorage. The clouds that had cloaked Valdez earlier that morning, lifted long enough for the DC-3 passenger liner to slip over the Chugach Mountains, the same range we had driven through a few short months ago. Aluminum glinted in the sunlight as the plane, soft lines curving like molten metal, rumbled down the gravel runway in the center of our valley.

The men piled onto the back of our flatbed truck, and we dropped bags off at their host homes on our way to the building site. Mr. Stein pointed to the pole by the street. "After trying all summer, I finally managed to get electrical service a few days ago."

One of the men raised his eyebrows. "You did all this without electricity?"

Mr. Stein shrugged. "This isn't Seattle, you know. In Alaska, we do what we have to."

The oldest man, a grizzled white-haired carpenter, circled the log shell inside and out, not saying much. He pushed on logs and bent down, checking for cracks. He finally nodded and turned to Dad and Mr. Stein. "I don't know how long until the second coming of Christ, but I reckon this church will still be standing when He comes. Congratulations. An outstanding job."

"Thank you, sir." Dad flushed. "We built the way I was taught."

The carpenter gave a gap-toothed smile. "Then, you had exceptional teachers. Where did you learn?"

Dad glanced at Mr. Stein. "This is the way our family did things in the pine woods of Mississippi."

He nodded. "It will be my privilege to help you close it up."

The next morning, we arose before sunrise, the men keen to start on the roof. James and I couldn't wait for the berry picking adventure. Though rain had fallen during the night, the sun rose at six in a cloudless sky.

The old carpenter swallowed a bite of pancake. "Mrs. Taylor, I understand you ladies are taking the children blueberry picking on this gorgeous day. Where will you find berries?"

"Jay said we'll pick on the mountainside an hour's drive out of town," Mom answered. "She said she'd bring her .22 rifle."

Dad frowned. "Why would you ladies take a gun? A .22 won't make any difference with a bear, anyway."

The carpenter's eyes widened. He glanced at Dad and then at Mom. "Probably not," said Mom, "but Jay mentioned there might be ptarmigan or spruce chicken, and a little fresh meat is always welcome."

James eyed her. "Can I take a gun?"

"Not a chance, young man."

Dad set down his fork. "Does she even know how to aim that rifle?"

Mom's brown eyes narrowed. "These Alaskan women have skills you would never guess, Andrew Taylor."

With a sideways glance at Mom, our guest shook his head, muttering, "And apparently, they all wear jeans."

Mom pushed her chair back, hitched up her jeans, and clattered dishes in the sink. "Andrew, would you mind helping the boys brush their teeth while I fetch tin pails for picking? Jay and Anna will be here any minute."

Dad marshaled us through the bathroom before zipping our jackets. He straightened and locked eyes with Mom. "You ladies, be careful. You're on your own up there, you know."

She hugged him with her free arm and smiled. "Don't worry. We'll be fine. Now get that roof on."

The men were driving away when Miss Bortel pulled up in her green '51 Chevy, just ahead of Mrs. Stein in their new cornflower blue Ford sedan. Its grill mimicked the intake of a jet engine, and a sleek chrome airplane on the hood was still caked in Alcan dust. Clovis nodded drowsily in the front seat while three kids from the Children's Home squirmed in the back, Travis, my brother's age, and two slightly older girls.

After piling into Miss Bortel's car, we followed Mrs. Stein north on the gravel highway to arrow through dense spruce forest, splotched-green and yellow with alder and birch. From the depths of Keystone Canyon, the sky glowed like a ribbon of sapphire while waterfalls misted our windshields. Leaving the canyon, we traversed barren hills between snowcapped peaks. At Mile 23, we turned off to follow ill-defined tracks through stunted spruce for another mile and parked at the edge of a broad heather meadow. Orange and red splashed in ascending waves toward the blue sky.

Mrs. Stein popped open her trunk. "Everyone, grab a bucket, and I'll bring my rifle."

James and Travis jammed tin buckets on their heads like helmets. Yelling, they chased and rammed each other, clanking and clattering around the parking area.

"Will you boys cut out that awful racket?" Mom complained.

"The truth is," Mrs. Stein said, "noise is a good thing. If any bears are in the vicinity, they'll hear us and leave. Black bears are not normally aggressive unless they feel threatened."

"What about grizzlies?" asked Mom.

"We rarely see a grizzly around here."

"Watch out!" I tipped my bucket over my head and charged the girls, who shrieked and scattered across the meadow.

"Hey, kids, come back here," Mom ordered. "We all stick together. Now, let's find those blueberries."

It wasn't long before Miss Bortel called, "I found 'em. Big, juicy berries. Very ripe and sweet." She stuck out a blue tongue.

Converging like a flock of ravens, we squatted beside her at the edge of a football field sized mat of knee-high shrubs thick with dark berries, some fatter than my thumbnail. Berries plunked into her pail as her long fingers moved quickly among the branches and orange leaves.

In his excitement, my brother shoved me aside, and I tripped and fell in the berry bushes. "Mom," I complained, "James shmushed blueberries all over my jacket."

"I'll tell you what," Mom said. "Roy, you and the girls stick with me while James and Travis pick with Miss Bortel. Clovis can follow his mom."

Mrs. Stein rested the rifle on her shoulder. "Louela, if you wouldn't mind watching Clovis, I'd like to check over the next hill for ptarmigan."

"Sounds fair. We gather berries while you hunt fresh game." Mom took the two-year-old by the hand. "I doubt that we'll meander far." She motioned across the blue-speckled orange expanse. "Our buckets will be full before we even make a dent in this patch." Mrs. Stein climbed the springy carpet of heather and blueberries to vanish over the ridge.

I stuffed blueberries in my mouth by the handful. At first, I couldn't pick them fast enough, but at some point, my stomach said stop, and I began filling my bucket. The late summer sun warmed the meadow. I unzipped my jacket. My eyelids grew heavy, and I lay back on a prickly bed of blueberry bushes. Cross-eyed, I gazed up the colorful slope. A dark shadow moved through the trees beyond the clearing. I blinked, and it was gone.

"Huh." I sat up and shaded my eyes. "Mom, I think I saw an animal in the woods, somethin' huge."

She smiled. "You alright, sweetie? How's your bucket coming?" She turned back to her own bucket.

"Mom, I really did see somethin'."

"Don't worry. We're with people who know all about the dangers here."

"Okay." I settled back, eyelids warmed by the sun.

"Bearrr!" Mrs. Stein flew over the nearby hilltop, hollering and waving her arms.

Mom turned to Miss Bortel. "What did she say?"

By this time, we could make out Mrs. Stein's white face. "Run for the cars! There's a bear!"

We froze in place.

"GRIZZLY!" Mrs. Stein yelled as she approached. "Anna, you and Louela grab the kids and take them to the cars right now. I'll follow with the gun."

Miss Bortel jumped up, spilling half her berries on the ground. She waved her long arms, herding young children down the slope.

"Hurry!" Mrs. Stein gasped, snatching Clovis, tucking him under one arm, and clutching her rifle in the other hand. Her eyes jerked back and forth from the crestline to the safety of the distant cars.

Fleeing a grizzly across a heather meadow was a nightmare in slow motion. My foot sank deep with every step before springing up. My toe caught, and down I tumbled, plunging my face into scratchy stems.

Where *was* that bear? My back prickled. I could feel hot carnivore breath. Was that my heart pounding or the paws of the grizzly? The muscles in the small of my back twitched. Cowering, I snatched a backward glimpse.

With a desperate effort, I scrambled to my feet, only to trip and tumble again. And again. And again. Why had we wandered so far from the cars?

By the final sprint, not a single berry remained in anyone's bucket. Mrs. Stein tossed Clovis onto the front seat and slammed the door. Mom ripped open the back door, and James and I tumbled in. She threw herself in the passenger seat. Miss Bortel hurried Travis and the two girls into the back of her car.

"Lock your doors," Mrs. Stein panted, cranking the starter. Tires spun on loose gravel, and both sedans whirled and raced down the winding tracks.

As we turned onto the highway, Mom asked, "Did you actually see the bear?"

"Not really," Mrs. Stein confessed. "A covey of ptarmigan flushed ahead of me. I followed them into the bushes only to step in a fresh paw print bigger than both of my boots together. That's when I heard the snarl."

Mom began laughing. "At least nobody got hurt," she spluttered. She laughed and laughed, great, gasping belly laughs.

I leaned over to James. "There she goes." He nodded and rolled his eyes. Mrs. Stein smiled uncomfortably in the rearview mirror, unclear what was funny.

Mom finally took off her glasses and wiped her eyes with a handkerchief. "Sorry, Jay. You know I do that when I'm frightened. I've never seen a grizzly up close, and I don't ever want to. Just knowing one was around scared me out of my wits."

"Me too," Mrs. Stein said. "I love so many things about Alaska, but I wonder if I will ever feel at home up here."

Mom cleared her throat. "I know what you mean. One would think that growing up in the swamps of Louisiana during the Depression would have prepared me for anything, but I'm not so sure." She scanned the breathtaking scenery. "It sometimes feels like Alaska's an alien world. But here we are, and here we intend to stay."

Mrs. Stein turned toward Mom. "In Valdez?"

"I suppose, as long as Andrew pastors the church. I've dreamed of being a pastor's wife since I was a girl, though, to be honest, I imagined it being in a place a bit more civilized."

There was a long pause. Mrs. Stein flicked on the headlights, and we entered the dark tunnel. "Louela, you know you're one of my closest friends." She swallowed. "I wish I knew how to make this easy. Both Wilson and Andrew have bachelor of theology degrees, but neither is ordained. We came up here to build the church, never intending to stay."

Mom nodded. "I'm aware that Andrew needs a little more training before ordination, but I assumed that wouldn't be an issue on the frontier."

Mrs. Stein took a deep breath. "I'm deeply sorry, but I'm afraid it is. Wilson received a letter from the conference superintendent last week and said he would talk to Andrew about it. Apparently, he chickened out which really annoys me, but here it is. They plan on sending an ordained pastor up as soon as the church is finished."

Like a tire going flat, Mom's breath whooshed out. "What do you mean?"

"It means Andrew won't be pastoring here much longer."

"You're sure?"

"Yes. I'm sorry."

"Oh." Mom's shoulders shook, and her voice shrank. "I wonder what that means for me? For us?" The dark tunnel gave way to the perpetual gloom of the canyon.

Mrs. Stein placed a hand on Mom's shoulder. "I'm afraid I don't know. I'm not even sure what *we're* doing next. We've been exploring opportunities in the Lower 48—even Canada. Perhaps Andrew could go back for more schooling, or you can go back to Louisiana?"

"No." Mom shook her head. "I'll never go back there, and I know Andrew wants to stay in Alaska. Although it sounds crazy, I'm falling in love with this wild land. Who knows? Perhaps we are meant to be homesteaders. I just haven't been able to bring myself to admit that Andrew might not be cut out to be a preacher."

Mrs. Stein nodded. "I can only imagine how hard his hearing loss makes communication, but I'm humbled by his deep trust in God." She turned to Mom. "And I envy his natural gift of introducing others to Jesus. I know you both well enough to be confident you will continue ministering wherever you end up."

Mom ran the back of her hand over her eyes. "Oh Lord, why does life have to be so complicated?" She sighed and leaned her head against the window, and we passed in silence from the dreary canyon to the sunlit plain.

The morning was gone when we arrived home. Mom and Mrs. Stein joined several women from our fellowship who were taking lunch to the hungry crew. The log shell swarmed with workers, and rafters already spanned part of the opening. Men balanced heavy planks over their shoulders as they hurried up and down ladders. Now that we had electricity, circular saws screeched, and drills whined, while hammers rang. Balanced atop tall ladders, Dad and two other men wrestled a rafter into position against the long ridge board, which stretched end to end from the peaks of the gables. A nail clenched between his teeth, he spotted us and waved.

"Well," Mom observed, "at least somebody has something to show for their morning's effort."

While the men gathered for lunch, I wandered into the deserted church and leaned my head back. Rows of rafters soared across the flawless sky. Mom had shown us pictures and told us stories about Europe's grand cathedrals—how faithful men erected them, stone by stone, over hundreds of years. Here, rock by rock, log by log, board by board, we were raising the house of God. Filled with awe and dizzy from the scent of fresh spruce logs, I spread my arms and whirled in the gravel. I spun until my legs gave out.

Grabbing a sandwich, I sat on a log beside my brother. He was entertaining the lunch crowd with an animated and mostly fictional version of our morning's adventures. Everyone but Mom looked amused as he held out his arms like shooting a rifle. "Then Mrs. Stein chased the grizzly over the hill with her gun."

"What kind of gun?" one of the men wanted to know.

"A .22," James answered.

Mom rolled her eyes. "She did not chase the bear away with a .22. The truth is, we fled in a panic for the cars."

The crew roared with laughter. One man shook his head. "A city boy, myself, I can't even imagine going into the wild knowing I might meet a grizzly. Andy, you married a special kind of woman. I'm impressed."

Dad nodded. "The impressive thing is that she said, 'I do.' I'm a lucky man."

Mom stood and started gathering plates. "That you are, Andrew Taylor, and don't you ever forget it."

The next morning, over thirty of us crammed into the Steins' living room for Sunday service. How many more times would we have to do this before we could move into the new church? Dad preached from Nehemiah about how everyone pitched in to rebuild Jerusalem's walls, whole families like us. Only, my mind was back on the mountain, replaying our flight from the bear.

The ladies had planned a noon potluck at the Steins' house, and couples scurried home to pull scalloped potatoes, moose roasts, and breaded chicken from their ovens. They carried in enormous bowls of macaroni and potato salads, and whole cake pans of jiggling red Jell-O, mottled yellow and green by canned fruit cocktail, and lime Jell-O laden with peas and shredded carrots.

We kids stood on tiptoes to admire a long counter covered with blueberry and pumpkin pies, carrot cake, and banana cream pudding with vanilla wafers. After three rounds through the dessert line, fifteen shrieking, supercharged children were ejected into the yard.

My home lessons were placed on hold that week while Dad and I worked with the volunteers. James joined us in the afternoons, and he and I carried boards and nails, swept the floor, and brought water for the men. By midweek, tin covered the roof, and floor joists spanned the crawlspace. The old carpenter framed the windows and doors and even decorated the front door with a pointed arch he made from logs inset into the wall. It looked pretty fancy. The doors, windows, flooring, and Celotex for the ceiling were still on a steamship coming from Seattle. Though I had never heard of Celotex, Dad explained that it was a brittle, flimsy sheet of insulation which had been painted white and would make an attractive finish for the ceiling. It would not, he emphasized, support even a boy's weight.

Thursday afternoon, after nailing the last ceiling joist in place, the men packed their tools. James and I helped sweep sawdust and nails from the plywood subfloor, and everyone gathered in a circle.

Mr. Stein held out his hands. "I can't even begin to thank you all for what you've done here." He choked, pulled out his handkerchief, and dabbed his eyes. "Two years ago, I began this project with no idea what I was getting into, which was fortunate. Had I known, I would've never started." He paused while the men laughed, then raised his hands toward the crisscrossing joists and rafters. "Now, once again, God supplied what we needed—*you*—and we're sealed tight against the coming storms. Thank you. You're good people."

The sunny weather held, and the next morning we drove to the airport and bade goodbye to our construction crew friends. As the DC-3 rushed down the gravel runway and vanished over a pass in the mountains, I felt a loss. Maybe Dad did too because he hugged me hard before setting me on the truck seat. "I'm glad for what we got done," he said, "but I'm exhausted." He sighed. "And, I'll admit, pretty confused right now about our future. A little break from working on the church may help. Just happens, it's hunting season. There's nothing like a good hunt to take a man's mind off his troubles."

I nodded and settled on the vinyl seat. Whatever happened next, I trusted Mom and Dad to figure it out.

Hanging moose quarters from a later hunt

18.

AND MOOSE, OH MY!

On the drive home from the airport, Dad glanced my way. "Tomorrow, we're going moose hunting."

I straightened up. "Me too?"

"Yep, the whole family."

"I'm gonna shoot a moose?" My voice climbed an octave. "With a rifle?"

"Nope. You won't be shooting anything. Pastor Rose invited us to go hunting with him, and he's loaning me a 30-06. We're both hoping to bag our first moose."

"What do you need us for?"

"Because the law says we can't shoot a moose within sight of the highway. As far as I can tell, the moose spend their free time studying the Fish and Wildlife brochure, because during hunting season, every bull moose in Alaska lines up along the roads at first light. They graze in the ditches and grin as the hunters drive by. Your job will be to chase the moose away from the road while Pastor Rose and I wait in the woods with guns."

I gulped. "I'm s'posed to chase a moose?"

"It can't be much different from chasing a cow."

"Um. I never did that either."

"You run and yell and wave your arms. Just pretend you're chasing your friends on a playground. Next thing you know, the moose will be in our sights. *Ka-bam.* We got us our winter's meat."

"Aren't moose dangerous?"

He tipped his head to the side. "Well, to be honest, somebody told me that moose kill more people in Alaska than bears and wolves together. I'm sure, though, that most are from collisions with cars, and the rest are cow moose protecting their young. Since this will be a bull, you'll have nothing to worry about."

A bull moose! The ones I had seen were enormous! My chest tightened. Why couldn't Dad ever see danger? Everything to him was another adventure.

That night, Dad cleaned and oiled the borrowed rifle. The next morning, Mom shook us boys awake—far too early for my stomach to face breakfast. The mid-September sun wouldn't rise for another hour, and as soon as Pastor Rose arrived, all five of us crowded into the cab of our truck.

Our headlights stabbed at fog as thick as tapioca pudding, and I dozed in Mom's lap until the engine fell silent. Peering into the darkness, I rubbed my eyes. All I could tell was that we were above the fog but below the snow line which the Sourdoughs said had been dropping early this year. They predicted a fierce winter.

Mom helped me out of the cozy cab, and I shivered. A gray glimmer outlined treetops on the left beyond a small stream that burbled through the high mountain valley. The rocky ground on the right rose into shadow.

I yawned and stretched. "Why's it so dark?"

"Because the sun's not up yet," Mom replied.

"Then, why did we have to get up so early?"

"'Cause the moose are stirring," Dad answered.

"Where are they?" My brother threw a rock. A startled family of spruce grouse thrummed in the shadows. My heart skipped a beat.

"Shhh." Mom turned to James, finger on her lips. "We don't want to spook the moose until the men are in place."

Pastor Rose pointed up the highway and whispered, "While scouting yesterday, I spotted a real fine bull nearby, and I doubt that he's moved much by now. Andy and I are going to ease a couple hundred yards into the trees up that-a-way." He gestured to the right. "Give us about fifteen minutes to find a good place to wait, then walk on up the road. Soon as you find that fat moose, you know what to do. We'll be ready."

Mom frowned. "Are you sure this is safe?"

"Nothing to worry about," Dad assured her. "The moose are way more afraid of us than we are of them."

Adults always say dumb stuff when they know better. Who do they think they're fooling?

The men lifted rifles from behind the truck seat. Bolts rasped back and forward as they each shifted a shell into the chamber and checked their safety. Swinging leather straps over their shoulders, they melted into the shadows, leaving a defenseless mother and two children to search for the moose.

Loose gravel crunched as we trudged along the shoulder of the road. Mom hissed, "You boys, stay close." We trotted to catch up. *Please, Lord, please, not another adventure.* Trailing James and Mom at what I calculated to be a safe distance, I was dozing on my feet when I bumped into my brother.

"Hey," he started. Mom shushed him, then pointed to our right. In the shadows, barely a dozen paces away on the uphill side, a black silhouette stirred. My heart thudded. James gaped. I whimpered.

Mom patted my head and pried my fingers off her jeans. "It's okay, Roy," she whispered. "Go stand in the middle of the road."

I tiptoed to the center of the gravel highway, trying to look as small as possible. The van-sized shadow snorted and moved again. By now, there was no doubt. We had found our moose. But it sure didn't show any signs of running away.

"Shoo!" Mom waved her arms.

"Ewaaah!" the behemoth bellowed, and I stumbled backward and fell. At that moment, the sun peeped over the mountain range behind us, illuminating a full rack of flat, bony antlers, armored on the front

by sharp tines the length of my forearms. The antlers swept our way, and the snorting nightmare ambled across the ditch, snot flying as the massive head swung back and forth.

Mom retreated, and I crawled on all fours behind her. "What do we do now?" I squealed.

"I don't know." Her face glowed crimson in the sunrise. "Moose are supposed to be scared of us. Only I'm the one who's terrified."

"Aaah-yaaah!" James jumped up and down and flailed his arms.

The bull moose stretched his neck and studied my brother as though puzzled by how such a tiny creature could make so much noise. The spiked antlers swayed mere feet from the five-year-old, who blanched and grabbed Mom's hand.

An icicle slid up my spine. This was nuts. A young mom, unarmed, and a pair of little kids facing down an enormous wild beast. One that kills more people than bears and wolves do. And Dad was nowhere in sight. I tried to stand, but my legs shook too hard. I don't think I could have run if there had been anywhere to hide. Which there wasn't.

Time froze.

The monster sauntered onto the highway and huffed. Its moist breath wrapped us in a fetid shroud.

We froze.

The tangy odor of fur tickled my nostrils. The wet snout extended ridiculously far from between amber eyes, and a long beard quivered from his outstretched chin. He snuffled and pawed the gravel. Saliva dripped. Hackles rose and fell.

We were going to die. We should never have come to this wilderness. Now fate would smite my parents with the cruelest lesson as I was torn limb from limb. A martyr, I would be a gruesome example, an admonition to all those foolish parents with a yen for adventure. Today, the world would finally learn that you can't take your kids to Alaska.

Without warning, the bull snorted, swiveled, and shuffled back to the edge of the forest. *Crash*! The massive rack pummeled a young spruce. Squirrels chittered as limbs and needles showered the ground.

Crash! The tree shook again. *"Ewaaah!"* the bull bugled. Satisfied he had made his point, he wheeled with a snort and bolted up the steep slope, thrashing through low branches and scattered underbrush.

Our breath whooshed out, and I inhaled, perhaps for the first time since the moose had stepped out of the ditch. For a handful of heartbeats, we gawked at the empty forest. Mom's brown eyes were huge behind her thick, wire-rim glasses as she reached down to help me up. "Well, I sure hope the men shoot that thing because I'm never doing this again."

Boom! Boom! Rifle shots echoed across the valley.

"Can we go find Dad?" James grabbed Mom's hand. "I wanna see the moose!"

"Nope." Brooking no argument, she took our hands and dragged us down the road. "We'll wait in the truck. If they shot the moose, they'll come to retrieve their equipment to dress it."

We trotted a quarter-mile downhill to the truck. Mom tossed us inside, climbed in, and locked the door. I snuggled up beside her, but my brother gripped the steering wheel and jumped on the seat. "Mom, where are they?"

"Patience. They'll be here soon."

I awoke to voices and peeked out the window to see Mom and James standing with the men.

Pastor Rose laughed. "I don't know what you guys did to scare that moose, but he flew past us. It was like trying to shoot down a fighter plane with a rifle."

"What were the two shots we heard?" she asked.

"We both fired," Dad said, "but didn't come close to hitting that bull. We tracked him up the mountainside, but the way he was running, he's probably over the next range by now."

"So, what's next?" Mom asked. "I'm done hunting."

"I suppose we're out of luck for today. With the gunshots and daylight, there's no way we'll find another bull standing by the road waiting for us."

"What's more," she added, "you won't talk me into chasing a moose ever again."

"Why?" Dad asked. "You did well."

She turned and faced him, hands on her hips. "I've never been so terrified in my entire life. Just because nobody got hurt doesn't mean your family couldn't have died. The only reason we survived was that the monster decided not to charge."

Thank you, Mom. At least one of my parents was showing a glimmer of sense.

"Oh." Dad looked stunned. "I had no idea." He emptied the chamber of his rifle, put a hand on Mom's shoulder, and looked her in the eye. "I truly am sorry, hon. In hindsight, I suppose that was a foolish thing to ask of you." He turned to Pastor Rose. "Jimmy, would you mind loaning me this 30-06 a little longer? Bear season is still open, and I'd like to try bagging a tasty yearling."

"Of course," answered Pastor Rose. "Maybe you'll have better luck with a bear."

Mom climbed into the truck and slammed the door.

Though the men chatted on the hour-long, jolting ride down the mountain, Mom remained unusually quiet. Maybe she was recalling the story Dad told about his mother. During one of his father's long absences, a hawk started stealing their chickens. She found his 12-gauge shotgun which she had never fired. Resting the barrel on a fence rail, she lined up the sights, the butt of the gun against her mouth. She killed the hawk but was missing her four front teeth for the rest of her life. Only with time would I appreciate how Mom had intuitively internalized the teaching of Sun Tzu: "He will win who knows when to fight and when not to fight."

The fog lifted, and blue sky met yellow fall foliage by the time we left Keystone Canyon. We were driving the straight stretch of road across the valley when James stood and leaned forward. "Look, Dad. A policeman." A red light revolved atop a white cruiser parked in front of a sedan.

Dad pulled over and stepped out, returning a few minutes later with Aunt Pedo. "You're not gonna believe this," he said, "but a motorist killed a fine cow moose here this morning, and the patrolman is giving it to the Children's Home."

Aunt Pedo greeted us with a grin, her wild red hair backlit by the rising sun. "Andy tells me you have everything you need to dress a moose, and I happen to have a moose. I'd love to share the meat with both of you pastors if you wouldn't mind helping me. We'll need to field-dress it right away."

Pastor Rose hopped out of the truck. "God moves in mysterious ways. Looks like He supplied us with meat after all!"

In the shallow ditch, a dark brown carcass sprawled among brushy alder. Aunt Pedo turned to the patrolman. "Thank you very much. We can take it from here." He tipped his blue campaign hat, the gold badge on the front glinting in the sunlight and drove away.

Dad and Pastor Rose gathered around the carcass. James tugged on its goatee. I hung back with Mom on the safe side of the ditch. Even from there, my nose recoiled at the pungent odor. Aunt Pedo joined the men and grabbed a forefoot. "We need to roll this thing on its back so we can gut it," she said.

I followed Mom, who held one of the moose's hind legs up in the air while Pastor Rose braced the other. James and I together grappled a foreleg off the ground, the long snout and dark eyes inches from my face. I looked away as Dad unsheathed his six-inch hunting knife and sliced open the belly, only to choke on bile as hot, steaming guts spilled out. He slit the chest down to the breastbone and divided the bone using a wide-bladed saw with a wire loop handle.

Aunt Pedo held out a canvas sack in one hand. "You can drop the heart, liver, and tongue in here."

Dad nodded. "I wouldn't think of wasting the prize parts." He spread the ribs, cut out the heart and liver, and plopped them in the sack. He separated the contents of the chest from the neck, ribs, and backbone. Careful not to nick the bowels, he continued along the spine all the way to the tail. The entire innards of the moose spilled out in a squirming heap. The procedure took less time than walking James two blocks to school. My legs wobbled, and I sat down.

Mom turned. "You okay, Roy? You're looking a bit pale."

"Yeah, I'm okay." I couldn't appear weak now, not with my brother running the guts through his hands. Sidling over, I touched the intestines with one finger, never imagining that one day I would be a surgeon.

Dad cut out the tongue and added it to the bag, then severed the neck. He wiped his hands on a rag and stood back. "Now, all we need to do is quarter it and skin the pieces."

Aunt Pedo surveyed the carcass. "This isn't your first kill."

"Nope." Dad rolled his shoulders. "Turns out moose aren't much different from beef, pigs, or deer, and I've dressed more than my share of all those."

"I haven't known you long, Andrew, but I think you might have been born for the frontier."

"Apparently." Mom's smile didn't reach her eyes. "Here I thought I was marrying a pastor, only to find myself hitched to a frontier cowboy."

Dad didn't even look up, just kept cutting through both sides between the last two ribs before sawing through the backbone from the neck to the tail. He wiped his knife and saw with a rag. "Let's hang these quarters so we can skin and wrap them with cheesecloth."

My queasiness had settled, and I helped drag the bloody slabs to a nearby spruce tree. Pastor Rose and both women strained to hoist each hindquarter in the air while Dad tied the legs to branches with ropes. A few minutes later, the hide was off, and the quarters wrapped. We boys helped haul them to the back of our truck. I had never seen or imagined so much meat in one place—a mountain of red flesh.

Dad squatted and washed his knife and hands in a trickle of water running through the ditch. "I wonder how much meat we'll put away from one cow moose?"

Aunt Pedo looked up from scrubbing her hands. "I'd estimate about four hundred pounds. I forgot to ask. Did you folks even see a moose this morning?"

Mom coughed, and her face flushed. "I'm afraid we did."

"You didn't kill it?"

There was a pause as Dad shrugged back into his jacket. He avoided eye contact with Mom. "Well, to be honest, we men sent Louela and the boys to scare a big bull off the highway so we could shoot it." He scratched his neck. "Seemed like a clever idea at the time. In retrospect, maybe that wasn't so smart." He took a deep breath. "And I'm sorry."

Aunt Pedo's eyes widened, and her forehead crinkled. "You sent Louela with your two little boys, unarmed and unprotected, to face down a three-quarter-ton bull moose in rutting season? You might consider addressing your apology to them, not me."

Dad seemed to shrink as he turned to Mom. "Sorry." He took a deep breath. "I've hunted a lot. Only hunting in Alaska is a whole different sport. I promise not to ask you to do that again." He fanned his face.

"*Cheechakos!*" Aunt Pedo raised her eyes to the sky. "God must have appointed a special guardian angel just for Cheechakos." Shaking her red curls, she strode to her car.

19.

DAD AND MAMA BEAR

Boom!

Dad jerked as he lay face down in a gravel pit on the edge of town. A few steps behind him, I flinched and shoved my fingertips deeper into my ears. The bolt on the 30-06 rasped back and forward, and he lowered his eye to the scope. James and I squirmed.

Boom!

I gripped my ears tighter. "Are you done yet?"

Twisting, Dad pulled out earplugs. "What?"

"Are you done yet?" I yelled, my ears ringing. It never occurred to any of us that maybe we boys should have worn earplugs too.

He shook his head and held up a finger. "One more shot. Then we'll go check the pattern."

Boom!

The borrowed rifle bucked again. This time Dad flipped the safety on, scrambled to his feet, and waved us forward. We walked downrange to inspect the homemade cardboard target—concentric circles drawn with black crayon. Three half-inch punctures pierced the center in a pattern the size of my hand. He turned the square over, smiling. "Not bad. A few more shots, and I'll have this zeroed in."

James snatched the target and stuck three fingers through the holes. "I wanna shoot!"

Dad shook his head. "This rifle would knock a five-year-old head over heels. Maybe next spring I'll teach you to shoot a .22."

"I'm already five and a half. You said you hunted when you were five."

"Well, that was different. With twelve kids in our family and an absent father, it was either hunt or starve." Dad's green-flecked eyes focused far away. "Harsh times," he grunted. "Best forgotten." His gaze lingered on the horizon.

"Dad?" James waved the target in front of Dad's face.

"Yes?"

"Who taught you to shoot?"

"Guy, my older brother. He taught me so well I qualified as an expert marksman in the Army. On my first day in rifle training, the instructor asked if my name was Daniel Boone." His hand squeezed James's shoulder. "Don't worry. I'll teach you everything you need to know when you're ready."

My brother pulled himself up to his full height, about even with my nose, and huffed, "I'll need a real rifle if I'm gonna hunt a bear."

"Sorry, I'm not taking a five-year-old bear hunting, and that's that. I'm in deep enough water as it is. Now, come along. I want to try a pattern at three hundred yards."

I was tired of loud bangs by the time we left for home, but my brother's face told a different story. He was ready to hunt.

After dinner, we sat at the kitchen table, watching Dad disassemble the rifle. He cleaned the barrel, oiled the moving parts, and put it all back together. Lifting the stock to his shoulder, he peered through the scope at the dark window.

"Can I look?" begged James.

"Sure." Dad pulled him up on his lap. "Put one eye to the eyepiece. Tell me what you see."

My brother's face lit up, and his voice was reverent, as though he had just glimpsed the sacred. "Lights and a cross." Perhaps, in a way I would never understand, hunting to him was akin to worship.

I grabbed the gun barrel. "My turn!"

"You boys take it easy." Dad lowered James to the floor, and I climbed on his lap. "This isn't a toy."

My right eye pressed against the soft rubber flange on the end of the black cylinder, and I passed into another world. Amazing! All the way down Alaska Avenue, clear to the waterfront, I peeked into lighted windows of stores and houses. "What's the big black cross?"

"Those are the crosshairs," Dad said. "I don't know if they make them out of hair, but where they cross is where your bullet will go if the scope is zeroed in like we did today. You still need to estimate the target's distance to correct the barrel's angle and allow for wind. That's why I shot targets at a hundred, two hundred, and three hundred yards. Now, I know where to aim at those distances with one of these bullets." He held up a shiny brass shell, the tip dark and lethal.

"When you goin' huntin'?" James asked.

Dad slid back the bolt, checked again that the rifle was unloaded, and leaned it inside the hall closet. "I'll drive up the foothills tomorrow afternoon and do some scouting while it's still light. If I sleep up there, I can be hunting by the crack of dawn."

My brother grinned ear to ear. "I can help you scout and make camp."

Mom broke in. "Enough. You boys brush your teeth and find your bed."

"Aww." James followed me into the bathroom. "Why do I always hafta wait? Nobody ever lets me do anything fun."

"You're nuts. A bear would eat you for lunch."

He stuck out his tongue. "He'd eat you before he ate me because you're a fraidy-cat, and bears love fraidy-cats. Admit it. You're too afraid to have any fun."

"Am not." I led the way up the stairs to our bedroom. "I'm just not stupid."

Mom came to tuck us in. "What are you boys squabbling about now?"

"James called me a fraidy-cat," I tattled.

"Well, he's always scared. And he's a snitch!"

She sat on the side of the bed and tucked the heavy quilt under our chins. "God made you brothers very different, but that doesn't mean one of you is better than the other, and it certainly doesn't give you the right to call each other names." She palmed our shoulders and closed her eyes. "Father, thank You for these two wonderfully unique boys. For James, my exuberant extrovert. For Roy, as cautious as a sage. For my husband, Father, who loves you wholeheartedly, and I know, loves us like himself. Please bless us with rest tonight and take care of Dad on tomorrow's hunt. Amen."

On Friday, Mom took off work by midafternoon to be home with us before Dad left to go hunting. Likely, also, to make sure we boys didn't end up slipping away with him. Dad checked that he had an extra box of shells, strapped the scabbard with his hunting knife on his belt, packed spare clothes and a sleeping bag. Mom loaded the knapsack with food, and he tossed a saw and packboard into the back of the truck, which he had covered with the green canvas for winter. "Almost forgot." Stepping inside, he came out stuffing a couple of Almond Joy candy bars into his coat pocket.

James clung to his pant leg. "Are you gonna kill a monster bear?"

Dad pulled him up in a hug. "Nope. The grown-up bears' meat is tough and tastes of old fish. I want a yearling who's fattened on nothing but mother's milk and berries. People say they're tasty as pork." He set James down. "And the hide will make a rug just the right size for you boys."

Mom gripped him for a long time. "You be careful." She held him at arm's length. "You're on your own out there, you know." He hugged her and climbed into the driver's seat while she checked the cab one last time for stowaways. Flanked by brilliant stands of yellow birch and golden aspen, the truck passed through patches of pale October sunlight. We waved until it rumbled out of sight.

Mom threw her shoulders back. "I'm in the mood for penuche. Who wants to help?"

"Me!" I beat her to the kitchen. Never a huge fan of fudge, penuche was my weakness.

She pulled her *Betty Crocker's Cookbook* off the shelf above the stove. "I love this book. More great recipes than I'll ever have time to cook." Mom rambled as though filling the empty space with something other than her fear of becoming a widow at age twenty-nine. "I know I should've paid more attention when my mother tried teaching me to cook, but I was too much of a tomboy." She spread the red-and-white book flat on the counter. "Here we are. Who wants to fetch a can of evaporated milk?"

James raced for the pantry.

"Roy, can you bring me white and brown sugar, please?"

She simmered milk while stirring in sugar and corn syrup until a dribble of the liquid formed a squishy ball when dropped into ice-cold water. Turning off the burner, she cut two pats of butter into the pot. "Roy, you can stir this now." I climbed on a chair and made yellow swirls in the creamy brown mixture with a large wooden spoon.

"What story should I read to you while we wait for the candy to cool?"

"'Billy Goats Gruff,'" James said.

"No! 'Scuffy the Tugboat,'" I insisted.

Mom added vanilla and spread the mixture in a cake pan. We had plenty of time to finish both stories by the time it cooled enough to slice, and she cut a square for each of us. The soft, grainy candy melted in my mouth, and heavenly sweetness drooled down my chin, but no amount of begging earned us a second piece before dinner. I would later learn that cultures around the world simmer butter, brown sugar, and milk, yielding irresistible flavors of caramelized molasses.

We helped Mom clean up the dishes, and she read more stories. Every time she turned a page, she glanced at the front door. The evening dragged on.

Sometime before sunrise I slipped out of bed and picked my way down the steep stairs to the bathroom. On my way back, I heard mumbling from the living room and peeked in. Mom knelt at her floral upholstered chair, head bowed, hands held palms up. "Father, why does my man have to take so many risks? I think I jumped out of the frying pan of that Southern swamp just to land in the fire of adventure. I married him, after all. But what about me?" Pausing to wipe her eyes, she took a shuddering breath. "I doubt. I fear." A long sigh. "Lord, give me hope. Help me to act on that hope and believe your promises." While she blew her nose with her handkerchief, I crept up the stairs to bed.

In the morning, we found Mom sipping coffee at the table, eyes rimmed pink behind her glasses.

"When's Dad comin' home?" James asked.

"Soon as he gets a bear," she answered. "Until then, we'll learn to practice patience."

Following a quiet breakfast, James and I built cabins with Lincoln Logs, played pick-up sticks, and flicked Tiddlywinks at each other across the kitchen floor. The morning hours crawled, and still no sign of Dad.

While Mom fixed lunch, we moved to the front yard and built roads in the dirt. Scraps of discarded lumber served as cars and trucks. We were chasing each other with rusty rebar when James's head snapped up. "Dad!" He beat me to the street as our truck pulled up. Dad popped out of the cab door and hefted a boy in each arm.

"Where's the bear?" James squirmed.

"Come see." Dad carried us around to the back of the canvas-covered flatbed and dropped us into the shadowy cavern. I gagged at the rank stench and backed against the wooden side of the truck. When my eyes adjusted to the darkness, I made out a headless body the size of a small man wrapped in cheesecloth like a mummy. Alongside the carcass lay a pile of black fur.

One finger extended, James touched the long hair. "What is it?"

Dad's smile grew. "A black bear. Whadda ya think?"

"Neat." James ran his fingers through the silky fur.

I hesitated. "Is it dead?"

Dad laughed. "Of course. It's a yearling cub, just like I promised." He reached around and grabbed Mom by the waist.

She held him tight for a moment, then gazed into his eyes. "Everything go okay?"

"Yep. But there *is* a story." He dropped the tailgate. "Let's hang this thing, and I'll tell you over lunch. Can you boys help Mom take the hide out back? I'll bring the carcass." He handed the pelt down to Mom, who wrapped her arms around the smelly skin. The eyeless head bobbed a foot from my face, fangs bared in a savage grin. I backed away so fast I sat in the gravel. Dad laughed. "Be careful of those sharp teeth. I skinned the head but left the jaws in, and the claws are still attached." Razor-tipped claws parted my hair as I scrabbled away like a crab.

James, who had wrapped his arms around one hairy leg, giggled. "Roy, you gonna help?" I stood, grabbed a leg, and stumbled alongside them to the backyard.

We returned in time to see Dad dragging the body to the edge of the tailgate. Pulling it across his shoulders in a fireman's carry, he toted the carcass around to the shed in the back. After sticking the pointed ends of a yard-long sharpened stake through the bear's rear heels, he looped a rope around each end of the stake and hung the skinned bear upside down from a rafter in the shed. Bloody fluid oozed and dripped on the rough wood floor.

I stretched out my arms. "It looks nearly as big as you."

"Well, this is its second season, so it was about a hundred pounds whole. I probably packed around seventy pounds, including the hide, a half-mile down the mountain, and we'll end up with at least fifty pounds of meat."

Mom asked, "How'd you tote it out?"

"Strapped to a packboard, leaving my hands free to carry the rifle."

"You packed half your weight down the mountain?" Mom raised her eyebrows.

"I am a Taylor." He shrugged. "Even at noon, this October air has a frosty edge. So long as it stays under forty degrees, the meat will be fine hanging here a couple days, but we'll need to take care of the hide after lunch. Right now, I'm hungry enough I could eat a bear all by myself."

Mom herded us boys toward the front door. "Come in and wash up. I've got moose chili simmering on the stove."

Tantalizing steam wafted from our green Melmac bowls as we waited for Dad's prayer. "Thank You, Father, for this food." He paused. "And your unrelenting care for us. Amen."

"So." Mom passed around cob-shaped cornpone. "I'm dying to hear your story."

Dad winced. "Maybe not the best choice of words, hon, but here goes." He buttered a piece of cornpone. "I followed a logging road deep into the mountains and parked beside a small stream below a wide avalanche clearing. My goal was to scout in the evening for a sow with cubs so that I could hunt at first light. A few minutes scanning the steep mountainside with binoculars, and I spotted a mama black bear with twins in a clearing."

"How big was she?" James asked around a full mouth.

"Really huge. As things turned out, almost too big." He blew on his chili and took a bite. "I lit a fire by the creek and fried Spam and hash browns. After scrubbing the skillet clean with sand, I sipped tea until the sun dropped below the mountains. The fire had died to embers, and the air was getting nippy, so I stretched out on the truck bed in my Army surplus bag between layers of blankets."

"Where was the bear?" James urged.

"We'll get there. Anyway, by the middle of the night, the chill had seeped through the covers and into my bones. I was so cold I shivered like a leaf and didn't think I would make it 'til daybreak."

"What did you do?" Mom asked.

"Before the sun came up, I pulled on my long heavy hunting coat and stamped around in the pitch dark until I could feel my legs again. Not wanting to take a chance on spooking the bears with fire, I ate a breakfast of biscuits with peanut butter and drank cold water instead of making coffee. Except for a candy bar, that's been my only meal so far today." He shook his head. "It seems ages ago."

He bit off the end of a cornpone and spooned in a few bites of chili. "Hoping the bears would still be up in that clearing, munching blueberries for breakfast, I strapped on my packboard and slung the 30-06 over my shoulder. Scrambling through the dark, I was careful to go straight up the mountainside." He swallowed a few more bites. "The ground was slick with frost and so steep I had to grab alder branches to climb. The air was calm, and fog still covered the clearing when I sneaked out of the woods at the first hint of dawn. That gave me time to set up."

"But, what about the bears?" I asked.

"I still hadn't seen them, so I worked my way along the edge of the trees to the downwind side of the clearing."

James's forehead creased. "If it was calm, how'd you know the downwind side?"

Dad buttered another piece of corn pone. "It isn't easy without much wind, but I wet a finger in my mouth and held it up. The side that cools first is upwind."

Mom poured more milk into our glasses. "Would you boys please stop interrupting so Dad can tell his story?"

"That's okay," he said. "I needed a break to enjoy a few more bites of this wonderful chili." He swallowed before continuing. "So, I set up behind a chest-high granite boulder, which gave me a view of the whole clearing. Feelin' kinda hungry, I was reaching in my pocket for an Almond Joy when I saw movement."

"The bear?" James's eyes widened.

"At first, I wasn't sure," Dad continued. "I could tell something was out there, so I eased the rifle up and scanned the edge of the woods with the scope."

I couldn't take it. "Wha'd you see?"

He smiled. "Nothing at first. Then something dark moved. I froze and waited an eternity before this *e-nor-r-r-mous* mama bear ambled out. High on her hind legs, she raised her nose and sniffed. I hardly dared breathe." He set his spoon down. "Somehow, she signaled her cubs, and out they came from the trees." He chuckled. "They chased each other in circles and were fun to watch. I felt a little guilty about wanting to shoot one."

"But you did!" said James.

Dad nodded. "With a swat, their mother led the way to a patch of low bush blueberries. All three bears set to work, stripping sweet berries into their mouths with their long claws, acting as hungry as I am now." He got up and dished another bowl of chili.

"Where was the daddy bear?" I asked.

"Being a daddy," Mom interjected, "probably off having an adventure of his own."

Dad smiled as he returned to his chair.

"Is that when you shot the cub?" James swayed back and forth in his seat.

"Well, I took my time since they didn't act like they were goin' anywhere soon. I waited for the sun to come up. When the first sunbeam peeped over the ridge, I slipped off the safety and rested the crosshairs on the nearest cub."

"How far away was it?" James breathed.

"I figured a hundred and fifty yards and adjusted for that distance and the freezing air."

"Why?"

"Cold air is denser than warm air and slows the bullet down, so I raised the crosshairs a smidge. I let out my breath and, between heartbeats, squeezed the trigger. Boom! The rifle kicked up, but I had the scope pulled back down by the time the crack echoed off the cliffs."

James scrambled to his knees and leaned forward. "Did you get 'im?"

"The cub I shot lay still. The sow roared, and she filled the whole viewfinder. Boy, did she look huge." He put down his spoon and raised his arms in the air. "She stretched up on her hind legs and bellowed again. Her nose twitched all over the place, tryin' to find me."

James looked pale. So did Mom, who whispered, "What did you do?"

He dropped his arms. "I hoped the mama bear would just run off with the other cub, but it didn't appear that was going to happen. Figuring I'd better have a live shell in the chamber, I slid back the bolt. The instant the empty cartridge clicked out, she dropped to the ground and charged straight at me."

Mom paled.

My brother's mouth fell open.

My insides knotted. "Wha . . . what did you do?" I asked.

"I rammed the bolt forward. Only it refused to go. The next shell had jammed in the chamber. Frantic, I beat on the bolt, but it was stuck."

He drank from his milk glass and wiped his lips.

Mom blanched as white as the refrigerator.

James finally croaked, "What happened?"

"I once read that a black bear runs over thirty miles an hour and from a standing start can cover a hundred and fifty yards in ten seconds." He ran his hand through his hair. "Which she did." He wiped his mouth with his napkin. "She came for me, roaring like a freight train, fangs bared and spittle flying." He paused.

My heart pounded like a jackhammer.

"I jerked and beat on the bolt but knew it was the end of me." He held up a finger. "My one chance was that she wouldn't see me. So I hunched behind those boulders, quiet as I could, trembling and waiting to die."

He looked around the table. "My only thought was how much I loved my family."

Mom's hand rose to her throat. "And then?" she squeaked.

Dad leaned back. "That monster sow thundered right on past, less than ten yards away, and kept on going into the woods. Her lone cub scrambled to keep up." He shook his head. "They disappeared, and the only sound was the thud of my heart."

James gripped the edge of the table. "What did you do next?"

"I fell on all fours and retched. When I could move again, I leaned back against one of the boulders and picked up that useless rifle. It took me a half hour to stop shaking enough to slip a hand in my pocket and retrieve my knife. I pried out the jammed cartridge and vowed I would never again hunt with a borrowed gun."

James sat back down. "Why did the bear run past you?"

Dad grimaced. "It's a mystery, one I puzzled on all the way home." He sat back in his chair. "The only explanation I came up with, other than a miracle, is that bears are nearsighted. They have keen hearing and smell, and she homed in on me by the click of the bolt. But I was downwind on purpose, so she couldn't locate my scent. She ran on past without ever seeing me."

Mom let out her breath. "I'm going with a miracle."

Dad smiled. "After that, I guess she didn't want to risk losing her other cub, so she kept on running."

"Did she come back?" Mom asked.

"Naw," he assured her. "But I didn't know it at the time. So, I sat with the loaded gun until I was pretty sure she wouldn't show up. And I still didn't lay that rifle out of arm's reach, even while field dressing and skinning that yearling."

A blush of color returned to Mom's cheeks. "So, that's the end of your hunting?"

Dad shook his head. "I didn't say I would stop hunting. I said I wouldn't hunt again with a borrowed gun."

Mom leaned back. "Though nobody got hurt this time, I have no intention of being a wilderness widow." She crossed her arms. "How will we survive up here if you're dead?"

He flinched. "God called us to this wilderness. He'll take care of us."

"Just because God called us here doesn't give you license to embrace every dangerous opportunity Alaska offers. God also expects you to take care of your family. Maybe it's time to choose—husband and father or reckless outdoorsman?"

Dad wiped a hand down his face. "It wasn't my fault. The gun jammed."

Mom rose. "Bigamy is illegal, even in Alaska." She began clearing dishes. "I can't be married to two men at the same time. So, which one is it?"

Dad's mouth pursed, but no words came out.

"I want the bearskin!" James interrupted.

Dad let out his breath. "You boys can have it, but you'll have to help me stretch and clean it. In fact, this would be an excellent time." He carried his empty bowl to the sink. "Thanks for the chili, hon."

Mom didn't even turn around.

For the rest of their lives, for almost five more decades of marriage, Mom and Dad would each tell their own version of the bear story. Mom's a warning. Dad's a promise.

James and I trailed Dad to the backyard and held the skin against the outside wall of our storage shed while he nailed it on, stretching the hide as he went. A thin layer of white fibers and red meat streaked the inner surface, which faced out. Including the head, the bearskin was taller than me, and the arm span was wider than I could stretch. "This has to be cleaned," Dad said, loosening the deer antler handle of his hunting knife. "You boys go ask Mom for table knives. I'll cut all the fatty scraps off the hide, and you can help scrape it."

For an hour, we scraped and scraped until the inside of the hide was white, and Dad nodded his satisfaction.

James flipped his knife and tried to catch it, but it bounced on the ground. He stooped to pick it up. "What now?"

Dad rummaged in the shed for a large washtub. "We need to rub salt on the hide so it won't rot. Roy, would you mind asking Mom for a bag of her pickling salt?"

By the time I returned, the bearskin was folded in a tub. Dad poured in the whole bag, and we rubbed salt all over both sides before draping it across two sawhorses. "We'll leave it here to dry for a few days before preserving it with borax and alum," he explained while we washed blood and salt off our wrinkled hands.

We returned to the kitchen, where Mom was kneading dough on the counter. "Mom," James announced, "we cleaned the hide."

She didn't respond. Dad circled an arm around her waist, and she stiffened. He hesitated, then turned to us and nodded toward the door. "Come along, boys. I think we need to check on the church."

Jimmy from the orphanage, Dad, James, and Roy are enthused about the bear skin

20.
BEARSKIN RUG

The sun was settling below the mountains on Monday when Mom cleared dinner dishes and covered the kitchen table with our blue-checked oilcloth. Dad stepped in, clutching the white-shrouded bear carcass in both arms.

Mom cocked her head. "Dancing with a corpse?"

He chuckled, lowered the stiff body to the table, and peeled off the cheesecloth. "I threw away the heart and liver because of the risk of trichinosis."

James looked befuddled. "Bears have tricky noses?"

"Trichinosis is an infection," Mom explained. "A tiny worm, too small to see, can live in bear's meat, and eating it can make you sick."

My brother stuck out his tongue. "Yuck, worms. I'm not eatin' no bear."

"*Any bear*," she corrected. "But don't worry, it's not a problem as long as the meat is frozen and then cooked properly. Folks say bear is delicious."

"Maybe those folks don't have nothin' better to eat," James replied. Mom just shook her head.

The skinned carcass, all red muscle and white tendons, sprawled across the table. Mom dropped rags on the red paisley linoleum to catch pools of bloody fluid dripping off the edge. I wondered if meat that might make you sick was worth all this trouble.

The *shush, shush* of Dad's whetstone ceased, followed by the whisper of steel on his leather razor strop. He examined his favorite butcher knife, the blade the size of a small machete and the wooden handle wrapped in twine. The gleaming edge passed lightly across the back of his hand, and hair fell off, leaving a patch of bare skin. He smiled, stood back, wiped the blade on his white apron, and studied the bear. "Looks like a long skinny pig to me, and I know how to butcher a pig, so let's start with the front legs."

He separated the shoulder joints with practiced skill, set the forelegs aside, and removed the hind legs. Exchanging the knife for a hand saw, he cut the ribs off, divided the backbone into three parts, and sliced along the rear section. "Tenderloin. I wouldn't be surprised if we eat it first." He held out the long strip of meat to James. "Mind carrying this to Mom?"

At the counter, Mom wielded a sharp, thin-bladed knife to debone the shoulders and hams on our scarred cutting board. I climbed on a chair to observe. "Can I help?"

"Of course." She moved aside. "I have just the job for you. You can wrap the pieces. Let me show you."

She cut a square of brown freezer paper off a roll, dropped the tenderloin on the center, and brought opposite corners together over the meat. After folding both ends and then the sides toward the middle, she placed the wrapped package upside down on another square of paper, repeated the procedure, and taped it shut.

She tilted her head. "Can you do that?"

"I think so."

Mom offered me a roast. The red meat sagged over my hands. Raw muscle. On my bare skin. Butterflies fluttered in my stomach. The limp, bloody mass quivered and slithered across my palms. I plopped it on the freezer paper.

"You okay, Roy?"

I nodded, swallowed, and grabbed two corners, bringing them together, then the other two. I held them with a finger while Mom folded both ends and the sides. She helped me flip this over on the next piece of paper for a double wrap.

"That wasn't so hard, was it?"

"Only kinda hard."

She nodded. "It's not quite so hard if you do it a little bit at a time." Smiling, she held out another roast. "Ready?"

"Yep." I wrapped the next one like a pro.

James brought over a chunk of meat. "Can I wrap too?"

She rinsed her hands and picked up a black wax pencil. "Sure, do what your brother's doing. With both of you wrapping, I can trim, tape, and label."

Dad carved and sawed, Mom deboned and trimmed, and James and I wrapped. In no time, a tall stack of tan paper packages, fastened with masking tape and labeled with Mom's neat print, filled one end of the counter.

She washed and dried her hands. "Need to freeze these right away. The sooner they're frozen, the better they'll keep." She lifted the lid of the chest freezer in the back room. "I'll spread the packages in the wire trays, so they'll freeze faster. In the morning, I can rearrange everything, one end for bear meat, moose in the middle, and the other end reserved for berries."

The next afternoon, we helped Dad rinse the bearskin several times in a galvanized steel washtub in the yard. He dissolved borax in warm water and poured it into the tub, adding cold water until the solution covered the fur. "If we were tanning the skin, we would need a tanning solution," Dad explained, "but we're only preserving it for a rug." His forearms rippled as he folded and squeezed the stiff pelt.

We boys knelt beside him, immersing our hands in the cold liquid, grabbing the hair, bending, and working the stiff leather. My arms ached to my shoulders. The hide softened, and so did my fingers until they were numb and wrinkled. Dad stood and shook droplets from his hands. "We'll leave this to soak overnight. Right now, I want to get dinner started before your mom comes home."

He fried tenderloin bear steaks for dinner with mashed potatoes and boiled greens. The steaks, tastier than pork and tender enough for a baby to chew, made as excellent a meal as I could remember.

The next morning, Dad and I lingered at the kitchen table after Mom and James left. Tipping his white Army surplus mug, he swallowed the last dregs of coffee and shook his head. "Still tryin' to clear the cobwebs. Been off schedule for too long. Soon we'll be back on routine, but first, let's take care of that bear hide."

We lifted the pelt out of the borax water, stretched and nailed it to an inside wall, fur side against the wood. "Can you bring me the borax and alum?" he asked, reaching for a bucket hanging on a hook.

I nodded and found the red-lettered box and the bag of alum he had left on the floor of the shed. Mom used borax for washing clothes, and she had been clear that we weren't to put it in our mouths. But she had mentioned that alum made crisp pickles. Perhaps it tasted like pickles. When Dad turned his back, I stuck a finger in the bag and then in my mouth. *Aaagh!* That white powder had to be the bitterest thing ever.

Dad must have heard me cough and glanced my way. "Tried the alum, eh?" He smiled. "Puckered you right up. Looks like you're waiting for your first kiss."

I spat and rubbed my tongue. If kissing tasted that bad, why did people do it?

After mixing the borax and alum with water, he used a wooden spoon to smear the paste over the fleshy side of the bearskin, and we rubbed the white goo in with our fingers. "We'll do this a few more times to preserve the pelt. Otherwise, it will rot, and the hair will fall out. Come on inside, and we'll rinse our hands."

That morning, I memorized another line of Psalm 100, repeating after Dad, "Serve the Lord with gladness. Come before His presence with singing." A happy Psalm. I hoped there would be more like this. We moved on to math, and my head still spun with sums when we met James at school.

Since it wasn't raining, we spent the afternoon rubbing linseed oil on the outside of the church. Dad climbed high on a ladder while we boys worked on the lower logs, the sharp, nutty scent permeating our clothing and trailing us home. On rainy days, we oiled the inside of the walls.

Early Saturday morning, we picked up Aunt Pedo and several children for a second try at blueberry picking. Aunt Pedo stepped out, toting her 30-06. "Pedo," Dad said, "You won't need a gun. I still have Pastor Rose's rifle."

She threw her head back and laughed. "No offense, but given your history with that rifle, I'll feel better bringing mine along for backup." She tucked it behind the seat.

With adults in the cab and six kids loose in the back, Dad drove twenty-three miles out of town and turned onto the ruts that took us to the high meadow. Late fall foliage flamed orange and maroon, more vivid even than on the previous outing when we fled from the grizzly.

Dad and Aunt Pedo led the way, each carrying a rifle in one hand and a bucket in the other. Aunt Pedo swept her arm up the blue-tinged hillside. "Everyone stays together. The berries are so thick we won't have any trouble filling our pails." She was right. The bushes were blue with berries the size of small marbles and bursting with a sweet, earthy flavor. After stuffing myself, I filled my bucket. Best of all, no one saw a bear, and we drove away with three five-gallon buckets heaped with blueberries.

We kids steadied the buckets while the truck jounced back to the highway and down the mountain to where the Lowe River spread wide and shallow. Gulls clamored overhead, the crisp air ripe with autumn.

As far along the gravel bank as I could see, a tall hedge of wild rosebushes painted a scarlet ribbon. Their delicate pink blossoms had long since fallen, leaving yellow leaves and bright red, pregnant-looking rosehips the size of acorns. Aunt Pedo had said they were loaded with vitamin C and would help prevent scurvy since we didn't have fresh fruit in Alaska.

"Careful about the tips," she warned as we piled out of the truck. "The points will prick your fingers." We were careful, and with nine of us picking, we soon filled two five-gallon buckets.

We dropped Aunt Pedo and the children off with their bounty and headed home. While we boys helped Mom wash blueberries and rosehips in the sink, Dad peeled and sliced chilled moose tongue he had boiled the day before with bay leaves, cloves, onion, and celery. Starting with thick slices of Mom's home-baked rye bread, he constructed jaw-popping sandwiches for lunch. Mayonnaise and mustard oozed around cheddar cheese, onion, leaf lettuce, and moose tongue.

A cloud of flour rose from the counter where Mom was rolling dough. "I want to get a couple blueberry pies in the oven. You all go ahead and eat."

After giving thanks, Dad handed a moose tongue sandwich to each of us boys. I held mine at arm's length. The last time I had seen this tongue, it dangled from the dead moose's mouth at the roadside, bloody drool dripping to the ground. No way would I stick that in my mouth. I glanced at James, surprised to see him wolfing his down. Well, if he could eat this, so could I. Holding my breath, I nipped off the smallest bite I could manage and was taken aback by the texture of tongue-on-tongue. Determinedly, I chewed until the meat, as tender as filet mignon, released a flavor rich like gravy. I was hooked on another Alaskan delight.

Mom divided the rosehips into kettles, added water, and set them on the stove. "I heard somewhere that cooking destroys the vitamin C, but Aunt Pedo scoffed and said that's an old wives' tale." While the rosehips boiled, she transferred trays of blueberries to the freezer. She mashed the steaming rosehips through a colander lined with cheesecloth, ending up with over a gallon of bright pink liquid. When the juice reached a boil, she added sugar and pectin and poured the jelly into hot sterilized pint jars.

The irresistible aroma of browned crust and caramelized blueberries drifted through the house. Mom shooed us away as she pulled pies out of the oven and set them to cool on the stovetop, purple syrup bubbling up through golden lattice.

My mouth watered. "I want pie," I whined.

She sighed. "You just ate an entire sandwich. Better let these cool a bit." She sat, wiped a handkerchief across her forehead, and cleaned her steamy glasses. "Time for a break before we make blueberry jelly." Along the counter, jars of pink rosehip jelly popped softly as they sealed. "You know, we still have a lot to learn, but I think we might make it after all."

Dad nodded. "I hope you're right, dear, although we have yet to survive an Alaskan winter. The old-timers claim this'll be a hard one." I recalled the falling snow line on the mountains and shivered.

For three days in a row, James and I helped Dad scrape off borax and alum paste and apply fresh coats to the still stiff but darkening bear hide. The final time, we left the paste on over the weekend. On Monday afternoon, we watched while he pulled nails and folded the semi-stiff pelt into the galvanized tub. We squeezed and worked the hide with several rinses, then draped it over a sawhorse. "The hide has to dry before we oil it," Dad said. After the skin stopped dripping, we stretched and nailed it to the inside of the shed for the last time, the fleshy side now dark brown.

A week later, he announced, "Your rug is ready for the last step, boys. All we have left is to soften and preserve the leather with this." He held out a round, orange can.

"What is it?" I asked.

"Neatsfoot oil." He dribbled a little on his palm. "They render this out of cow hooves. Since it stays liquid at room temperature, it works well for softening leather and will keep your bear rug from getting brittle."

We followed him out to the shed, where he poured neatsfoot oil on our hands. We massaged the softening skin, at the same time softening our hard-earned calluses, and repeated the process for several days in a row.

The day finally came when our whole family paraded to the

backyard. Using a claw hammer, Dad pulled the nails for the last time and with a broad smile, draped the heavy pelt over our arms. "One bearskin rug. All yours, boys." He beamed. "You earned your prize."

"Wow!" James ran his cheek across the soft black fur. "I love it!"

Stroking the silky pelt, I couldn't help but remember that the bear had given his life to give us a rug. I would treasure it.

While I contemplated how complicated life can be, Mom stood back, chin in hand. "You know, boys, what this bearskin cost. Nearly your father's life."

He wiped a hand down his face. "You don't need to remind me. I could have been a bear's meal instead of the other way around. I learned my lesson." Mom rolled her eyes.

Why did everything worthwhile have to cost somebody something?

The rug was magnificent. Though the bearskin wasn't entirely supple, it flexed enough to lie flat on the floor beside our bed. That night, an aura of tangy leather drifted up, the aroma of a saddle on a bear. Enfolding us like a blanket. Exotic but comforting. And, like everything else in this land, it became our new normal.

By the time I stirred the next morning, James's side of the bed was empty. Eyes squeezed shut, I slid out from under the quilts and dropped barefoot to the floor. Scrunching my toes deep in the dense fur, I glided my feet back and forth through the long silky pile. *Aaah*. A warm tingle crept up my legs. Weeks of effort. So worth it.

I sighed and looked out the window. My mouth hung open. Giant snowflakes flew past, so thick I couldn't see the street. The Sourdoughs had frightened us with tales of Valdez winters, stories of houses buried under snowdrifts, people freezing to death in the mountain passes. They even claimed this valley was the one place the Natives had always refused to live because the snow fell so deep. The worst part was we knew they weren't lying.

Now winter had arrived. My nightmares were about to become real. What were we in for? Feet still immersed in the luxurious pelt, I glanced down at the bear's snarling fangs and vicious claws. "Ha," I sneered at the storm. "Ol' Man Winter, you don't scare me none." My toes wriggled in the soft fur. "We're ready for you now. Come and get us."

Ol' Man Winter must have heard me gloat. He took up the challenge.

Aunt Pedo takes a turn shoveling the trailer out of a snowdrift

21.

OL' MAN WINTER

We hadn't even finished Halloween costumes when Ol' Man Winter banged on the door. The blizzard howled. I shuddered and stepped barefoot off the plush bearskin rug to the cold linoleum. How would Mom and James make it to town through this storm? I stumbled downstairs in my pajamas and threadbare robe.

"Roy, come look!" My brother scraped a dirty fingernail across lacy frost on the inside of the kitchen window. "There's a ton of snow already, and it's blowin' all over the place."

Mom flipped pancakes. "There won't be school today, and I'm not going to work either. Nobody in their right mind will see Dr. Spencer in this storm. Emergencies can go to the hospital."

I glanced around the kitchen. "Where's Dad?"

"Remember Jim, the man who took you fishing last summer? He stopped by earlier and asked if Dad wanted a job shoveling snow off the oil tanks at the harbor." Mom smiled. "For a change, it's my turn to stay home and be lazy."

"What about the missionaries?" I asked.

"What do you mean?" She loaded steaming pancakes onto our plates.

"Maybe they're trapped in the trailer," I said.

A missionary couple was visiting from Seattle for a month to help finish the new church. They stayed in the fifteen-foot travel trailer beside the Steins' house—the one we had lived in our first few weeks in Valdez. Dad had impressed us that we had to move out before the snow came or risk being trapped inside and suffocating.

Mom's brow furrowed as she drizzled syrup over our pancakes. "The Steins are away in Anchorage. We better check on them. Hurry, boys, eat, and dress."

We gulped breakfast and raced for the front door in our pajamas to greet our first Alaskan snow.

"Wait!" she shouted. Too late. James released the latch, and a gust of wind slammed the door open. I gasped. Yesterday it hadn't even been freezing. Now, frigid arctic air sucked the oxygen right out of my lungs. Ice crystals stung my face.

Mom lunged past us and shoved the door shut. I wiped the snow off my face and shook it out of my hair. "*Brrr.* Do we hafta go out there? They're prob'ly dead now anyway."

"Really, Roy! Must you always be a pessimist? Come upstairs, and I'll dig out some warm clothes." Once we dressed, Mom opened the hall closet and pulled out parkas and snow pants she had recently ordered from Sears, Roebuck & Co. She ripped off tags. "Now hurry." Holding out a pair of blue snow pants, she motioned me over. The legs were so thick and stiff that I half expected them to stand up and walk away. "Roy, please hold still." She struggled to stuff my stockinged foot into the first leg.

By the time she bundled us from head to toe, mittens on our hands, eyes peeking through a slit between scarf and parka hood, everyone was sweating. "Ready?" Mom checked us over, and we nodded. "How in the world does a genteel Southern girl find herself in a fix like this?" She reached for the door handle. "I hope love is enough." The front door flew open, and like an assault from the North Pole, a drift of snow cascaded into the vestibule and whistled up the walls. I sucked in single-digit air, and my throat spasmed despite a double layer of scarf covering my mouth. On the way out, she passed kid-sized snow shovels to each of us and grabbed a big one for herself.

With grim determination, we lowered our heads and marched into the savage gale. "Stay close." Her muffled shout sailed south on the icy blast. Leading our brave little troupe along the street, Mom plowed through fluffy, knee-high snow a half-block to the Steins'. She motioned us forward, and, advancing into the storm, we powered behind her into the side yard through swirling curtains of white.

I could barely hear James over the shrieking wind. "Where's the trailer?"

"I think over there. Oh no, it's completely buried!" Head down, Mom tromped toward a smoking chimney protruding from the highest snowdrift. "Hurry, boys, before they run out of air!"

It turns out that shoveling snow is a wonderful way to warm up, especially in a blizzard. For every fluffy shovelful of powder we flung downwind, a gust would whine over the trailer and refill the hole. By the time we found the bottom of the door, I was perspiring, which did nothing to make me more comfortable.

Mom knocked. "Hello! Are you okay?"

Nothing.

What if we were too late? What if they *were* dead? I panicked. I'd never seen a human corpse.

The door thumped open. "Good morning!" The tall gentleman waved us in. "Come in out of the storm. Coffee's hot."

Mom pulled us out of the blizzard. We filled the cramped space and stomped a circle of snow on the floor. She unwrapped her scarf. "Didn't you worry about running out of oxygen?"

The lady smiled and poured coffee for Mom. "We figured eventually someone would remember we were here and come dig us out. I guess it never occurred to us we might run out of air."

"Cheechakos," Mom muttered.

Winter storms rolled out of the north as regular as railroad cars. A few days break, a rare day of sunshine, and then the world blanched white again. By late November, the snow had drifted to the eaves, and all that showed of Valdez were rooflines bordering deep canyons of streets. Vehicles left parked for more than a couple of days disappeared beneath high banks thrown up by the snowplows. Fences vanished as did heating oil tanks even though they rested on head-high frames. Anything forgotten outside was lost until spring.

The day before Thanksgiving, Mom came home from work and shook herself in the vestibule. "I'm not sure I'll ever thaw out again." She hung her coat on a peg and held out a short, well-used sled by the frayed cotton rope attached to its handle. "Sarah at work sent this sled for you boys to enjoy, since their kids have outgrown it."

The varnish had long since worn off the graying wood, and the rails were rusting. But a sled was a sled. My brother stroked the weathered boards. "Can it be mine?" he begged. "It looks my size."

I grabbed the rope. "But I want a sled."

Her mouth twisted. "Okay, James, we'll call it yours, but you'll have to share it with Roy."

"No fair!" I tugged. "Why can't I have it?"

"Because your brother is older. Remember, Christmas is coming, and . . ." she raised one eyebrow, "who knows . . . if you're good, Santa might bring you a sled."

"I don't wanna sled for Christmas. I wanna sled now."

"Well, patience builds character. It's already too dark to sled today, but tomorrow's Thanksgiving. If we get a break in the weather, you can try it then."

I stomped off. Who needed character, whatever that was?

The next day, the Steins joined us at noon for Thanksgiving dinner. Stuffed with turkey and dressing, the adults shifted to soft chairs in the living room, and Clovis nodded off in his mother's lap. The wind had let up, and the sun sneaked out between high clouds. "Mom," James begged. "Can we try the sled?"

She glanced out the window. "I suppose, but you'll need to put on your snow gear. The thermometer's near zero again. It's not even Christmas, and I long for spring."

Bundled against the cold, James and I carried his sled outside, where he scrabbled up the bank along the path from the front door to the street. I handed him the sled and followed to the wind-crusted snow, our breath puffballs of white in the still air. Sunlight sparkled from a million crystals, and I shaded my eyes and squinted across the brilliant landscape. Smudges of smoke rose from houses, a hundred white mushrooms hunkered in tidy rows.

"Where we gonna sled?" I asked. "There aren't any hills here." The nearest slope was miles away.

James turned a complete circle. "The drifts. They go clear to the roofs. Come on. We can slide right off our roof."

Kicking into the crust, I pushed while he pulled the sled up the ten-foot drift to the snow-caked shingles and from there to the roof peak, where we turned it around. He clutched the rope and sat in front with me behind, gripping his waist. Our heels dug into the snow. From sixteen feet up, we could see all the way to the bay, where waves glimmered and churned the blue-green porcelain water. Ice heaped along the shoreline like fractured emeralds. On every side, steep-flanked mountains thrust chiseled peaks nearly a mile into blue sky, an icebound stockade imprisoning our valley.

Peering over his shoulder down the pitched roof, I sucked in a breath. We might as well have been on the top of Mount McKinley. "James," I wheezed, "is this safe?"

"Safe? Pick up your feet. *Whooeee!*"

The sled plummeted between the eave and the snowbank, the gap swallowing us whole, my stomach still on the roof. Like sugarcoated gingerbread boys, we crawled out, coughing and choking. He dug snow out of his hood. "*Uff!* That didn't work. The snow's not hard enough to hold us both. We better take turns. You go first while I fill the gap."

I climbed back up, pointed the sled down, lay flat, and closed my eyes. My toes came up, and the runners screamed down the roof, shot over the small cleft, and flew over the crust. I shrieked the whole way across our yard, my face so frozen I was afraid my grin might crack my cheeks. James took the next turn. Trailing a rooster-tail, he streaked clear into the neighbor's yard.

We improved the run with each pass, adding snow to dips and building small jumps. After an hour, I couldn't feel anything through my knitted wool mittens. "James," I panted, "my fingers are numb."

"Mine too." He giggled. "Your nose looks like Rudolph. One more ride, and we'll go in."

"Boys," Mom called, her head appearing over the snowbank. "You okay?"

James waved. "Yeah, Mom. Be there in a minute."

"All right. Don't be long. The sun is going down, and the Steins will be leaving soon."

Cheeks rosy from the cold, we climbed back to the roofline. The fiery sun traced a horizon as jagged as ripped parchment and blazed across the valley floor, now shimmering like a lake of molten metal. I swiveled around. As though their hearts were on fire, the mountains across the bay glowed lustrous rose quartz —something I had heard Mom call alpenglow. Bedazzled by the miracle of the sunset, we leaned into each other for warmth, content to catch our breath. The brilliance faded to orange, pink, and mauve and receded to icy sapphire.

By the time we slid down the roof and dropped to the dark pathway, I couldn't feel my fingers or toes. It took three tries to grip the doorknob with ice-encrusted mittens, and we tumbled into the foyer. James's nose went up. "Hot cider," he croaked.

Like miniature snow trolls, we charged along the hall and into the kitchen. Mom took one look. "Get back to the vestibule until I can brush you boys off," she ordered. "You're dropping snow like a winter storm. And please close the front door."

After the Steins left, Mom washed dishes while we sat at the kitchen table and licked sweet cider off our lips. I rubbed my frozen nose with numb fingers. "Mom." I attempted to sound casual. "I need my own sled."

"Want me to help you write to Santa?" She dried her hands and sat across from me at the table, pencil poised above a tablet of blue-lined paper.

"Dear Santa," I dictated. I chewed my lower lip. I had one chance to get this right. "I want—no, I need—a Flexible Flyer sled for Christmas. I've been very good this year."

Mom lifted the pencil and tilted her head. "Are you sure you want to say that? Santa already knows if we've been naughty or nice."

"All right. Change it to . . . I'm trying to be good. Thank you, Roy."

My friend Ben from church owned a Flexible Flyer, four feet of fire-engine red steel runners supporting a wooden slat deck tastefully emblazoned with a flying duck and a long red arrow. Even at rest, it looked as fast as lightning, easily the coolest sled in the world.

I focused back on Mom. "How long 'til my letter gets to the North Pole?"

She folded the paper and stuffed it into an envelope. "I'll mail it Monday. He'll receive it well before Christmas."

"Does Santa know we don't live in Cincinnati anymore?"

"He knows where every boy and girl lives." As improbable as Mom's statement was, I willingly believed it.

Afternoons, while James and I shared his sled, I fantasized about my Flexible Flyer. At night I dreamed of mad descents down sheer mountainsides, snow erupting in twin tails, townspeople pointing in awe. The days inched toward Christmas, and I tried my best to behave but had to bank on more than a little grace from Santa.

The first Saturday in December, Dad announced at breakfast, "Today we hunt our Christmas tree."

"Hooray!" James bounced on his chair until Mom pushed him

back on his seat.

"Are you sure?" I asked. "The snow is really deep."

Dad laughed. "We're Alaskans now. We won't let a little snow, or even a lot of snow, slow us down."

After breakfast, Dad stepped out to warm up the truck while Mom helped us boys tug on our snow gear. While Dad scraped ice off the windshield, James and I climbed onto the front seat vinyl, brittle from the cold, despite lukewarm air roaring from the defroster.

Dad hopped in and cleared a bit of windshield with the sleeve of his coat. Though I wasn't sure how much snow had already fallen, the sheer snowbanks along each side of the street rose higher than the truck. Unable to spot crossing vehicles before entering intersections, motorists learned to aim for the banks when a quick stop was needed.

The frozen transmission complained as Dad depressed the clutch and wiggled the long floor-mounted shifter. A couple of jerks, and we clanked down the street, tire chains banging. Dad kept his nose plastered to the windshield. I hoped he could see the road better than the rest of us since I couldn't make out anything beyond the frosty cab windows.

Mom glanced Dad's way. "You doing okay, Andrew?"

"No problem," he reassured her, his breath fogging the peephole. He rubbed it again. "At least we won't have far to go to find a tree. How about a Christmas song, everybody? Dashing through the snow . . ." He started in a key too high.

Mom picked up the melody at a lower pitch. James and I yelled along. "Jingle bells, jingle bells, jingle all the waaay . . ." I felt warmer.

The defroster sort of cleared the windows by the time Dad parked beside the snow berm lining the highway. "There's our Christmas tree, right there." He waved a glove toward the desolate landscape of endless snow-covered hills.

James stood on the seat. "Where?"

"We'll have to go find it."

No matter which direction I looked, snow phantoms darted before a brisk breeze. Thick clouds brushed the treetops, and the ground melded into the sky. In this featureless scene, distances became impossible to gauge.

Mom helped us out of the cab, and Dad grabbed the handsaw. He took James's hand, she took mine, and we scrambled over the berm and sallied forth in search of the perfect Christmas tree. On the second step, our parents plunged through the crusted snow up to their waists, pulling us down with them.

"Aaugh!" Mom let go of my hand and thrashed, making the hole bigger. "What are we doing here, Andrew? I didn't follow you to Alaska to wallow in snow to my neck."

"It's okay, hon."

Mom flailed again. "It's not okay. You're so lucky I'm not a quitter."

Dad turned toward the closest patch of spruce, about a half-block away. "I'll break a trail. Fall in behind me."

"Like I have a choice," Mom muttered, wiping snow off her face.

My brother skittered ahead across the crust and called, "I found one!"

Racing to catch up, I shook my head. "But it's not the perfect tree."

Mom slogged up beside us. "It will be," she panted. "Cut it down Andrew before my fingers freeze off."

Shoot! Why settle for less than perfect? Sure, my face felt like an icicle, and I couldn't feel my fingers or toes, but why the big rush? If only we kept looking, the perfect tree would reveal itself.

Dad quickly felled the not-quite-perfect tree, and uncertain how I was doing on Santa's balance sheet, I pulled in my pout and helped drag our tree back to the truck. I even joined in singing carols on the way home.

We helped Dad carry the tree inside and secure the base in a stand centered on the front picture window. After he wired limbs on a few bare spots at the back, the tree filled the entire corner of the small living room. As much as I hated to admit it, James's tree looked pretty good. Maybe not perfect, but okay.

Mom spread a sheet under the branches and held up an angel with a white satin robe. "Andrew, could you stick this on the very top?"

He pulled up a chair, stood on tiptoes, and balanced the angel on the highest sprig. She gave him the end of the silver garland, which he wrapped around the tree in a smooth spiral.

"I wanna help!" James scraped a chair in from the kitchen, scrambled to the seat, jumped for the garland, and lost his balance. "Whoops." He tumbled into the tree.

"Whoa!" Dropping the garland, Dad steadied the trunk. Mom grabbed James. I backed away.

She stood my brother back on the chair and lifted me to another. "You boys settle down and let me help you." Starting from the top, she showed us how to wrap the garland around in a silver spiral. We ran a gold garland in the opposite direction, so they crisscrossed. It looked pretty neat.

Digging through a box of ornaments we brought up the Alcan, she pulled out a tangle of red, green, blue, and white Christmas lights and shook the snarled mess. "I'm convinced a mischievous elf sneaks into our ornament box every year. I can hear him cackling as he ties our lights into knots."

I giggled. "Can I help?"

"Why not? Andrew, would you mind putting together some sandwiches, and maybe James can help you set the table for lunch." She handed me the plug end of the twisted green cord. "Okay, Roy, you hold this while I try sorting out this knot."

I draped the recalcitrant ball of lights from my fingers. "This is impossible."

Mom straightened a loop. "Then we'll just buckle down and do the impossible, which is pretty much how things work in Alaska." With a last twist, she stretched out the string. "*Hallelujah!* Now, let's see if by some miracle this lights up."

It didn't, and after lunch, we tried a new bulb in every socket before the string lit. We boys clambered onto chairs, and Mom and Dad helped us wrap the lights around and around the tree. Dusk was falling by the time Dad plugged the cord into the baseboard outlet and turned off the room light.

"Wow." My brother and I stood side by side, mouths open.

"We're not done yet." Mom switched on the fluorescent ceiling fixture and pulled out a box of blue glass balls. "Can you boys be careful with these?" We nodded. She passed us the ornaments and demonstrated how to hook the little wires over the branches. Dad lifted us in his arms so we could reach the higher limbs.

Next, she opened a package of long, stringy strips of floppy tinsel. "Now for the fun part. Throw handfuls as hard as you can all over the tree." She draped several pieces on each of our hands.

"Yay!" James flung a wad, and I followed. For the next few minutes, a silver blizzard settled on the branches in glittering uneven swatches. It no longer seemed important whether the tree was perfect. We had the most beautiful Christmas tree in the entire world.

Dad pulled leftovers out of the refrigerator to reheat for dinner. While we waited, Mom thumbed through *Betty Crocker's Cookbook*. I sidled over and stood on my tiptoes at the counter. "What're you makin'?"

Her eyes twinkled. "My favorite, peanut brittle."

I tugged at her blue-checked apron. "Can I help?"

"Of course." She pulled a chair up and held out a stick of butter. "Just smear this all over these two cookie sheets."

By the time we sat down to eat, the scent of nutty caramel had infused the warm room. After dinner, Mom retrieved the pans of peanut brittle cooling in a snowbank beside the house, and my brother and I pulled chairs to the counter. She smoothed a clean dish towel over the candy and handed us a small ball-peen hammer. "You boys take turns cracking the peanut brittle." While Dad heated water for cocoa, we hammered.

With the houselights off, the four of us squeezed together on the couch and marveled at our magical Christmas tree. Colored lights reflected off the front window and illuminated snowflakes as they drifted past. When I squinted through my lashes, the red, green, and blue lights blurred and sparkled. I licked cocoa and melted marshmallow from my lips and breathed in the aroma of chocolate, caramel, and nose-tickling resinous spruce.

Dad snaked an arm around Mom's shoulders, and she leaned into his embrace. "We *will* make this work," she murmured.

He smiled and pulled her close. "We have to."

She began to hum, and Dad fished his harmonica from a shirt pocket. His hand fluttered, and Mom's contralto joined the harmonica's warble.

"I heard the bells on Christmas day,
their old familiar carols play."

The melody swirled down the hallway, up the stairs, and into the darkest corners of our small house.

"Then pealed the bells more loud and deep:
'God is not dead, nor doth he sleep.'"

The harmonica quavered to silence, and Mom finished a cappella.

"The wrong shall fail, the right prevail,
with peace on earth, good will to men."

I crunched a bite of sharp-edged peanut brittle. Our family didn't have much, but that night I felt rich.

Celebrating in the new sanctuary

22.

HAPPY BIRTHDAY

Mom picked me up and hugged me on her way out the front door. "Have a wonderful birthday, Roy. I'll see you at dinner time."

My threadbare bathrobe hardly cut the chill from the door, and I shivered as I pattered back to the kitchen, pondering, how is five different from four? Dad turned from stacking dirty dishes in the sink. "Hey, birthday boy. Sorry to work on your special day, but we have to get the sanctuary ready for tonight's Christmas pageant. Why don't you dress while I finish here, and we'll be on our way?"

Now only two days before Christmas, a bone-numbing freeze had settled over the entire Territory of Alaska. Dad bundled me in snow pants, parka, mittens, and sturdy leather boots, a wool scarf wrapped twice around my face until I could barely see. Flipping on his flashlight, he led me out into the frozen world, the snow so cold it squeaked with every step. Over the bay, the moon hung like a golden scimitar against a glittering backdrop of stars. Although my birthday didn't fall exactly on the shortest day of the year, the nights felt thirty hours long, and the winter sun had yet to sulk from behind the high mountain bowl. My eyes were the only part of me uncovered, and by the time we reached the church, I wondered if eyeballs could freeze.

Light streamed from the windows as we neared the log building, and Dad pulled me along. "Looks like Wilson beat us. Let's hope the place is warm."

We stomped through the door, and Mr. Stein glanced up from adjusting the oil stove, a brown metal box against the right wall of the sanctuary. "Andy, am I glad to see you two." He checked his watch and looked around. An entire corner of the rough subfloor still needed planking, and the windows lacked trim, but at least it was snug and warm. "I can't believe how much is left to do before the program tonight."

Dad unwrapped his scarf, tugged his mittens off with his teeth, hung up his long canvas overcoat, and kicked the snow off his boots. "Well, then, better get started."

I picked up a broom to sweep sawdust, but Dad pried open a can and held it out. "Roy, think you can varnish these window trim boards?" Dropping the broom, I found a brush. As sick as I was of varnishing, I couldn't say no, not this close to the finish.

Every afternoon in December, James and I had traipsed through the snow behind Dad and helped put the final touches on the new church. Day after day, we oiled, then varnished, the flat interior surface of the logs. Thank goodness, we had finished oiling the outside by the first snowfall. The men had built a Sunday school room behind the back wall, which opened into the sanctuary. Wires had been run through the attic, light fixtures and switches mounted, insulation stapled to rafters and ceiling joists, and doors varnished and hung.

Circular saws whined, and hammers banged as Dad and Mr. Stein edge-nailed plank flooring over the subfloor. Following a break to pick up James from school and a quick lunch at home, we rejoined Mr. Stein. By four o'clock, the world outside had grown dark, and we still had a section of unfinished floor.

Dad stood and stretched. "What time is the program again, Wilson?"

"Eight, but we still have to go home, eat supper, and clean up." Mr. Stein swiped a hand across his flushed forehead. "We'll need a miracle to finish in time."

Miracle or not, there would be no time for my birthday. I attacked the floor with the broom. Why did God have to make my birthday so close to Christmas? Jesus's birthday got all the attention. Sure, I couldn't turn water into wine and raise people from the dead, but Mom said I was special. Sawdust flew into a pile. It just wasn't fair.

Cold air rushed in with Mom and Mrs. Stein, their arms loaded with paper bags and boxes. "Looks nice in here and feels as hot as Louisiana." Mom peeled off her scarf and wiped frost from her glasses. "We didn't know how much longer you'd be working, so we thought we'd bring your dinner."

"Bless you." Dad rested his hammer on a sawhorse. "You might be just the miracle we need."

The women dished slices of ham, green bean casserole, and cornbread onto paper plates. Dad asked the blessing, and we ate sitting on folding chairs. Nobody mentioned my birthday. A tear trickled down my cheek. How could everyone forget, even Mom?

While Mrs. Stein cleaned up, Mom reached for a box. "Roy, were you afraid we had forgotten something?"

I nodded.

She smiled and drew out a white frosted birthday cake shaped like Pluto, my favorite stuffed animal. She struck a match and lit five blue candles, my favorite color.

I rubbed my cheeks. "Thanks, Mom."

"Sure, son." She held up the lighted cake, and everyone joined in. "Happy birthday to you, happy birthday to you . . ."

The moist yellow cake, laced with shredded coconut and slathered with white coconut frosting, was my favorite. I stuffed myself with Pluto's whole head, sorry that I had ever doubted Mom.

After we ate, she pulled out a small, wrapped package. "I don't know what I was thinking, letting Dad buy this for you, but he claimed no Alaskan boy could live without it." Dad's smile revealed his crooked teeth as I ripped off ribbons and paper and tore open the present.

I gasped. Not even James had one. In the box rested a single-blade pocketknife. I caressed the smooth, fake mother-of-pearl handle, admiring the subtle gray ripples. As tenderly as a mother with a newborn, I lifted the exquisite treasure from its soft bed of cotton. My thumbnail slid into the notch, and, flipping the knife open, I brandished the polished blade for all to admire.

Mom frowned. "You know that's not a toy. You be careful, Roy. Now close that thing before you cut yourself."

The slim knife slid easily into my front jeans pocket, but nothing could wipe away my grin. I could tell James was jealous. It seemed unfair since he was older, but his birthday was only three weeks away, and until then, we were the same age. I pulled my prize out. "Wanna see?"

"Sure." Still frowning, my brother turned my knife over in his hands, opened and closed the blade, and handed it back without a word. A little stab twisted in my chest. I wished his birthday had come first.

The ladies packed the food, and we boys helped them sweep, dust, and set up chairs. Dad drove the final nail in the last floorboard, slid his hammer into a belt loop, straightened, and rubbed the small of his back. "Seven o'clock. Hallelujah! We did it! Now we better dash home and clean up."

We hurried home by flashlight and dropped our coats, hats, mittens, and scarves in the vestibule. Mom guided us boys down the hallway. "I set your clothes out on your bed. Dress and brush your teeth before we bundle back up. Can you believe it? Our first service in our new sanctuary!" She paused, her smile slipping. "Ours for now, anyway."

Dad looked like he was going to say something, but his lips just twisted into a half-smile.

Thirty minutes later, we stepped out into the frigid blackness. Just beyond my reach above the canyon of snow, the Milky Way floated like a jeweled necklace tossed across a velvet sky. Dad carried Mom's accordion case under one arm and his Bible under the other. The cold bit off my first breath, and I gasped. Valdez lacked streetlights, and like a school of fish, we clustered around the yellow puddle cast by Mom's flashlight.

A line of parishioners was filing into the church when we arrived, kicking snow off their boots at the front steps and shedding parkas and hats on a coat rack beside the door. The men shook hands with Dad and Mr. Stein.

"The sanctuary is beautiful."

"Praise the Lord. The church is finished."

"Amazing accomplishment."

The long labor had paid off, caulking every chink in the walls and insulating the roof and ceiling. The warm space smelled of heating oil, spruce, and varnish. Four fluorescent fixtures reflected brilliant white circles off the Celotex ceiling, while the varnished log walls glowed like amber. A beam running overhead from front to back marked the center aisle between five rows of gray metal folding chairs. Parishioners, friends, and well-wishers streamed in until forty adults and children packed the room. The men sported suits and ties and the ladies wore wool dresses, several with hats. Kids squirmed and bounced on the contoured metal seats. No more sitting on the Steins' linoleum. Compared to their living room, the sanctuary felt vast, beautiful, and sacred. I loved it.

Eyes closed and face glowing, Dad raised his hands toward Heaven. "Our Father," he prayed, "bless this, Your house, and thank You for the labor of love invested by so many here. We ask that You meet us in this place. Bless this congregation tonight as we celebrate Your gift, the Advent of Your Son. Amen."

Mom stepped to the front and ran her arms through the straps of her accordion. "Please stand for the first song to be sung in this sanctuary. A celebration of the birth of our Lord Jesus." Her fingers found keys and buttons, and the bellows expanded.

"Joy to the world," we proclaimed, "the Lord is come! Let earth receive her King." Our jubilation reverberated from the thick log walls. Adults dabbed their eyes. I relived the months I had sweated and struggled alongside some of these people. For half of my fifth year, I had anticipated this day. Now, here we stood, shoulder to shoulder—in my case, shoulder to hip—proclaiming our joy while celebrating Jesus's birthday.

My mind drifted to my birthday and the new knife in the dresser drawer at home. As fine a surprise as that had been, this moment in our new log church was my best birthday present. A memory I would always keep.

While Dad announced the program, Miss Bortel herded the young kids into a wiggly line across the front. Stricken by sudden shyness, we mouthed the words of "Away in a Manger." Everyone that is, except two girls with decent voices and my brother, who proved loudly to everyone's amusement that he was incapable of finding the right key.

Amid generous applause, we scampered to the Sunday school rooms to ready our costumes for the nativity scene, the highlight of the evening. I held out my secondhand bile-green chenille bathrobe, which no longer even reached my knees. Why couldn't I at least don my dad's robe like the bigger kids? And why did I have to be one more shepherd while James got to be a wise man wearing a red cape covered in sequins? Even with a gold crown, though, he must have been the shortest king in the history of the world.

A tiny angel bumped me off my feet.

"Sorry," she chirped, straightening her wings as she twirled away.

Scrambling to my feet in the crowded room, I belted my ugly bathrobe around my white shirt and black corduroy pants. I hefted the warped stick Mom imagined would pass for a shepherd's crook. I'll admit it did cheer me a little to see the sheep, cow, and donkey wrestle ridiculous costumes over their heads. Things could be worse.

Through the open door, I watched Dad. Standing to one side near the front, he opened his worn, leather-bound Bible, and the sanctuary quieted. Without looking down, he recited, "And it came to pass in those days that there went out a decree from Caesar Augustus that all the world should be taxed . . ." When he reached, "she brought forth her firstborn son and wrapped him in swaddling clothes and laid him in a manger," Mary stepped out of the backroom, golden tresses leaking from beneath a blue headscarf. Dwarfed by dark-skinned Joseph, she arranged the blond, blue-eyed doll in the wooden manger. They gazed down with rehearsed adoration, though Joseph kept pushing his thick glasses back up. The cow, donkey, and sheep—mooing, braying, and baaing—ambled in on all fours to snickers from the crowd.

Dad continued. "And there were in the same country shepherds abiding in the field, keeping watch over their flock by night." Our cue. My heart raced. Miss Bortel rounded up the half dozen shepherds and squeezed us out the door to the stage where the bigger kids were tripping on their parents' bathrobes as we fidgeted into place behind the animals.

"And, lo," Dad quoted, "the angel of the Lord came upon them, and the glory of the Lord shone round about them, and they were sore afraid." I wasn't sore, but I sure was afraid. So afraid I thought I might throw up.

"Fear not!" Fifth-grade Connie strode forward, adorned in a sheet, a halo of gold garland atop her long, flaxen hair. "For, behold, I bring you good tidings of great joy." She flashed a toothy smile at the audience.

Dad raised his hand. "And suddenly there was with the angel a multitude of the Heavenly host praising God, and saying, 'Glory to God in the highest, and on earth peace, goodwill toward men.'" Six more angels appeared, followed by the wise men who strode in and laid foil-wrapped gifts before the manger. Things were getting pretty crowded. I felt hot. My head swam.

To my relief, Dad reached the conclusion. "Mary kept all these things and pondered them in her heart."

We scattered to a standing ovation. I wasted no time ripping off the embarrassing robe and stuffing it under my seat. Mom strode to the front with her accordion, and we concluded the service, singing, *"What child is this, who laid to rest, on Mary's lap is sleeping?"*

Now came the best part, the necessary element of every Christmas program—cookies and Kool-Aid. Not just any cookies. Sugar cookies—bells and stars and angels—slathered with green, red, and white frosting and glittering with sprinkles. The noise level in the sanctuary rose with each pass through the food line. Mom snagged James the next time he darted by. "It's too cold to go outside, but why don't you boys play in the Sunday school room."

"Okay!" He led the way through the door behind the stage. "Whadda you wanna do?"

My friend Ben looked around. "Hey! A ladder." He pointed at a homemade wooden ladder leaning against a rectangular opening in the ceiling. A few months older than me, he was taller and huskier. A sandy crew cut topped his round face, and though he had inherited his mother's hooded blue eyes, his elfin ears and thin lips gave him an impish look. His family had settled in Valdez several years prior, and I deferred to him as an expert on everything Alaskan.

Still, I shook my head. "Dad told us not to play in the attic. It's too dangerous."

Ben ran a hand through his blond crew cut. "What can go wrong?"

"Dad said we might fall through the ceiling." I crossed my arms.

He started up the ladder. "You're just chicken."

A challenge? Whoa! What to do?

As I wavered, James followed Ben up the ladder. Then two more giggling boys disappeared into the dark maw of temptation.

I'm not sure how my foot found the first rung, then the next, and the next. Stomach clenched, I peeked over the edge. Yelling boys chased each other through the semi-darkness that stretched the length and width of the church. Enough light leaked around the fixtures and through the ladder opening to see the long planks Dad had laid at intervals across the joists. I recalled Dad's warning not to step on the Celotex, a brittle, porous membrane nailed on the underside of the ceiling joists.

"Chicken, chicken," Ben jeered from one of the nearby planks. "You just gonna stand there, lookin'?"

The angel's words echoed like an Old Testament prophecy. *Fear not!*

Taking a deep breath, I pulled myself up and tried a timid first step on the nearest plank. It wiggled a little, but nothing terrible happened. Boys shrieked and chased each other in every direction, the conversation downstairs loud enough to drown their footsteps. I lingered a moment longer, still cautious, waiting for an adult to show up. Ben was right. What could possibly go wrong?

With a burst of daring, I sprinted along the walkway after Ben, who turned a corner and circled to the far side of the dim space. "Ha," I crowed. "You can't get away from me." Without hesitating to engage my brain, I leaped off the plank and dropped so suddenly that if my arms hadn't already been outstretched, I would have crashed to the floor eight feet below.

"Aiee!" I shrieked, my legs kicking fiercely while my fingers clung to adjacent ceiling joists. Like flipping a switch, the sanctuary fell instantly silent. The boys scrambled down the ladder and merged quietly into the crowd.

"What?" a voice floated up from below. Then laughter erupted. Not giggles or cackles, but enormous, bent-over, Alaska-sized belly laughs. This-is-the-funniest-thing-I've-seen-in-my-whole-life laughs.

"Santa came early this year," someone guffawed.

"He must've started in the Pinzon Bar, 'cause he clear missed the chimney," hooted another. Even the ceiling shook with mirth.

"Hang on." Mr. Stein's welcome baritone rose from directly below, his hands steadying my frenzied feet. "Andy, can you go up in the attic and retrieve whoever these black corduroy pants belong to? I'll keep watch down here."

Dad thumped up the ladder and paused at the opening. "Who's there?"

My arms, spread-eagled across two ceiling joists, were falling asleep. "Roy," I whimpered. "Help."

"Roy? What are *you* doing up here?"

Shame burned my face. Like Adam and Eve in the Garden of Eden, there was no hiding my guilt. I wanted to blame Ben, only I was the one dangling through the ceiling.

Dad knelt beside me, slid strong hands under my arms, and lifted me gently out of danger. "Are you alright, Roy?"

I nodded and choked. "I'm sorry."

He hugged me tight against his chest and carried me down the ladder. "Maybe you learned your lesson."

I wiped my nose on my sleeve. "But what about the Celotex?"

He stood me on the floor and took a deep breath. "I'll take care of it tomorrow. I'm relieved you're not hurt."

By the time we emerged, parents were bundling kids in snow clothes. Except for a few winks, it was like nothing had happened. That is if you ignored insulation dangling through a boy-sized hole in the ceiling.

That night, Mom came up and sat on the side of our bed. "You boys brushed your teeth?"

We nodded.

"So, Roy, did you have a happy birthday?" She stroked my cheek. "At least you didn't hurt yourself."

I reflected on this strange birthday. It was bad enough to compete with Jesus's birthday. Then we worked on the church all day, barely squeezing my party into a break. I didn't have time to try my new knife. I had to trot out in front of the whole congregation in my threadbare bathrobe. And that was all before nearly breaking my legs and destroying the house of God while suffering public humiliation in front of everyone I knew.

On the other hand, our church was finally complete, I had a pocketknife, and I was now five years old. What did happy mean, anyway?

"Yup," I mumbled.

"Good." She kissed us each on the cheek. "Sleep well, my two amazing five-year-olds."

Her head disappeared down the stairwell, and James punched me on the shoulder. "Don't forget, twerp. You'll always be my little brother."

The log church wrapped in snow for Christmas

23.

BITTERSWEET

Predawn light teased reluctant eyelids apart. I rolled over to check if James was awake. As usual, his rumpled pillow lay empty. With a yawn, I settled back. Whoa! My eyes popped open. The day before Christmas. The day after my birthday. I had a pocketknife!

Wrestling back the heavy quilts, I dropped barefoot to the bearskin rug's deep pile and pulled open the top dresser drawer. On tiptoes, I peeked in. There it lay, weapon and tool, menacing and beautiful. I flipped out the blade and lovingly stroked the edge. A bright red line sprang across the pad of my thumb. "Ow!" I should have known. Dad hated a dull knife. I stuck the stinging digit in my mouth and snapped the blade shut against my pajama leg. Drawn by the aroma of cinnamon oatmeal, I pulled on my bathrobe and slippers and headed downstairs.

"Hey, big guy," Mom called from the stove. "Hungry?"

"Roy." James scrambled off his chair. "That your new knife? Can I see it?"

I held my thumb tight against my leg so no one would notice the slash. "Sure." I offered him the dangerous device. "Careful."

Dad raised his head from reading his Bible, a morning discipline. "Oh, Roy, I should have told you, I sharpened your new knife. Be careful."

"Yeah, thanks," I mumbled and ambled off to wash.

After breakfast, Dad pushed his chair back. "I'm off to the church to fix that ceiling."

"Need help?" I offered. Though I wanted to play with my new knife, I was the one who broke through the Celotex.

He smiled. "Thanks, Roy, but I'll be okay."

Relieved, I tugged Mom's robe. "Can I please show Ben my new knife? He's already got one, and he said he wants to see mine."

She glanced out the window. "I suppose. It's cold but not snowing. Do you need me to walk you to his house since the sun's not up?"

I shook my head and ran upstairs to change into warm clothes. Mom helped me with my parka, snow pants, boots, and mittens, which she had tied together on a long yarn passing up my sleeves and across the back of my neck. Ben's family lived a block and a half toward downtown, and I puffed marshmallow clouds with every breath by the time I knocked on his door.

His mom answered in a pretty blue dress. Mom had mumbled once that she couldn't figure out how Ben's mom dressed in the latest styles in this forsaken land. Blond ringlets glinting in the sunlight, her baby blue eyes lit her angelic face. "Roy," she lilted, "Merry Christmas Eve. Are you by yourself?" Whenever she noticed me, my heart raced, and my tongue froze. I stood gawking until she motioned me in. Nodding mutely, I shuffled inside. She smiled. "Happy birthday, by the way. Ben's in his room."

"Hey, Roy," Ben yelled. "Did you bring your knife? Come show me."

I started down the hall backward, still staring at his mom, grateful she hadn't mentioned my fall through the ceiling. She frowned. "Please, Roy, drop your snow clothes here in the foyer."

Embarrassed, I peeled off my boots, parka, and snow pants.

"You boys, be careful," she called.

"Sure, Mom." Ben shoved the door shut with one foot and reached out. "Lemme see."

I drew the most prized possession of my life out of my jeans pocket and offered it up for inspection. Streaming sunlight pulled subtle colors from the handle. Nodding his approval, he retrieved his knife from his pocket and held the two out, side by side. His was a tad longer and heavier, although I preferred my faux mother-of-pearl to his bone handle. He flicked open the blades on both knives and arranged them on the floor. On our hands and knees, we squinted and scrutinized. His blade, concave on the back edge, ended in a wicked point while mine was technically a penknife with a semi-rounded tip.

"Have you tried doin' anything with it yet?" he asked.

"Not really." I wasn't about to admit I had already cut myself. "The blade is sharp, though."

He grasped the blade expertly between thumb and forefinger, waggling it up and down. "Is it a good throwin' knife?"

The thought had never occurred to me. "S'pose so."

He eyed me and returned my knife, handle first. "Ever play stick?"

Pinching the bare metal between my thumb and forefinger, I waved the knife up and down as he had done. "Naw. How do you play stick?"

He picked up his knife by the stiletto point. "Easy. We start side by side. One of us throws his knife, and if the tip sticks, the other player has to stretch out and touch the blade with his right foot before he throws his knife, but if you move your left foot, you lose." Ben ran his hand through his crew cut and broke into a toothy smile. "Wanna try?"

"Uh." I studied the hardwood floor. "Won't your mom be mad if we throw knives in the house?"

"She'll never know. She's busy gettin' ready for Christmas." He backed up against the wall and motioned to his left. "Stand right here."

I glanced at the bedroom door, still latched tight. Dishes rattled in the kitchen.

"C'mon." He sounded so sure of himself, my doubts dissolved, and I lined up. Raising his knife by the blade, he flung it toward the floor, where it skittered and clattered across the room. "Shoot." He recovered his weapon and returned to stand by me. "Your turn."

I checked the door once more. Dishes clanked. My insides cringed. "Here goes!" Trembling, I raised the knife by the blade and flipped it toward the center of the room. *Thwang*. I stared dumbfounded. Against all odds, the tip had stabbed a floorboard. The knife quivered. As did I.

Bang! The door flew open. In strode his mom. "What are you boys up to?" Her blue eyes landed on my knife, stuck fast in her wood flooring, the handle pointing like a finger at the guilty party. Teeth bared, and her voice colder than a glacier, she asked, "You do realize this is a house, not a barn?" Golden curls bouncing, she extracted the incriminating evidence from her floor, flipped the blade closed, and held my knife out on her open palm. "I would have thought after last night you might've learned something."

My face burned. I wanted to shrink into a dust mote and float away. Head down, I stuffed the knife in my pocket. Dang! Why did I have to get caught every single time I did something stupid?

She turned and glared at her son. "Do you ever actually use your brain?"

"Sorry, Mom." Ben folded his knife and slipped it into his pocket.

"What you boys need is exercise and fresh air." She glanced out the window. "The thermometer's not much above zero, but the sun's shining. Why don't you go play outside?" She herded us to the vestibule, stuffed us into our snow clothes, and guided us out the door.

The center of the backyard was trampled gray, and high snowbanks lined the fence. Ben squinted at the late morning sun, skimming the southern peaks like a hot air balloon low on fuel. "I know!" He tugged one mitten off with his teeth, dug under his parka and snow pants, and extracted his knife. "We can play stick out here."

"But won't we lose our knives in the snow?"

He gave me his you-can-trust-me-I'm-your-best-friend grin and flipped open his blade. "Naw. This snow is hardpacked." He tilted his head. "Chicken?"

I was but refused to admit it. Pulling off a mitten, which dangled by its yarn from my sleeve, I reached under my parka and squirmed to find the pocket of my jeans. With two fingers, I fished out my knife, wondering why I was doing this.

He motioned with his head. "C'mon, Roy." I edged over beside him, paused, and planted my left foot. My thumbnail found the notch, and with a snap, the blade flipped open.

His condescending smile egged me on. "You go first this time, Roy."

I grasped the icy steel with numb fingers, wound up like a baseball pitcher, and before I could chicken out, released my arm. The blade slipped from my grip and flew end-over-end, flashing like a semaphore in the sunlight. Frozen with horror, I gaped as the white-handled knife soared across the yard until, with a final dive, my most cherished possession vanished into a snowbank higher than my head.

"Nooo!" I sprinted across the yard and floundered on all fours to the spot where my knife disappeared. Panicked and bare-fingered, I clawed the bottomless snow.

Ben tromped over and joined me. "Sorry, Roy."

"Help me, please. I hafta find my knife."

We dug and dug until, in desperation, I clapped numb hands together and raised my head, lips moving in supplication. "Please, Jesus, help me find my knife. I'll do anything You ask. I'll be a missionary in Africa. Just help me find my knife." The blue sky stared back, cold, silent, unmoved.

Our hands were red and chapped when Ben's Mom called from the back door, "Boys, lunchtime. Why don't you come in now and warm up? Are you digging a snow fort?"

Ben stuck his head up out of the pit. "Roy lost his new pocketknife, and we gotta find it."

I wiped frozen snot off my face with a numb hand. "My knife, I can't find my knife! Can you help us, please?"

She grabbed some mittens and joined the search. We churned the snow like a rototiller for another fruitless half hour. Finally, she clapped her mittens together. "I'm so sorry, Roy, but I don't think we have a chance of finding your knife today. We'll keep an eye out for it when the snow melts in the spring."

Spring? No knife until spring? Eyes blurring, I turned toward the street to hide my tears. "I'm goin' home."

She hugged me. "Sure, you don't want lunch first?"

An empty ache filled my chest. "I'm not hungry." On the trudge back up Alaska Avenue, tears froze to my cheeks. What if my knife *was* gone forever? I couldn't bear to face Mom and Dad. They had given me the best birthday present of my life. How could I explain that I threw away their gift?

A warm holiday fragrance greeted me at our front door. Dad and James were playing pick-up sticks by the Christmas tree, but I continued straight into the kitchen where Mom was loading fresh cookies into a gallon jar. "Hi, Roy, how'd it go with Ben?" When I didn't answer, she turned and pulled a handkerchief from her apron pocket. "Come here, son." She squatted and reached out her arms. My tears flowed. Wiping my nose, she folded me in a tight embrace. "What happened? Are you okay?"

I sobbed. "My knife."

"What about your knife?" She stroked my dark hair.

My whole body shook with my confession. "I threw it in a snowbank, and we couldn't find it!"

She pulled back. "You threw your new knife into a snowbank? Why would you do that?"

I caught my breath. "Ben wanted to play stick, and his mom made us go outside," I sobbed. "And then we played stick in the backyard."

James wandered into the kitchen. "You played stick in the snow with a white knife?"

I nodded. He rolled his eyes and retreated into the living room.

"Can I get another knife?" I sniveled, my face buried in the lavender perfume of Mom's dark hair.

She hesitated, then sighed. "No, sweetie, not this year. Perhaps next year you'll be ready for a knife. At least you didn't hurt yourself."

"Next year!?" I wailed. "I can't wait 'til next year! That's forever!"

"Alaska is teaching us all hard lessons." She reached for a fresh oatmeal raisin cookie. "Here. Taste this and tell me what you think."

Why bother? I was resigned to dying from grief, however long that would take. She held the cookie under my nose, and I sniffed. Maybe I wouldn't die. I nibbled a crumb. A couple of sobs, a hiccup, and I forced down a tiny bit. Moist, crunchy sweetness made me salivate, and I licked currant jelly from the center. Perhaps life could go on.

"Good?" She unzipped my parka. "Now, how about getting out of these snow clothes while I make you a sandwich."

After lunch, I joined my brother in the living room while Mom and Dad cleaned the kitchen. I stared into space, puzzled by how I could have been so stupid. James kicked the pile of pick-up sticks. "Hey, Roy, I'm bored! Let's play Lincoln Logs. Wanna get 'em while I pick these up?"

"Okay." I opened the hall closet door and reached up to the game shelf. High above, a flash of red caught my eye. Backing away, I stretched on tiptoes and gasped, the missing pocketknife forgotten. On the top shelf lay a long cardboard box emblazoned with a picture of a sled. Not just any sled—a Flexible Flyer! How could that be? Santa was going to bring my sled, and Christmas was still a day away. What was my Flexible Flyer doing in our closet?

Leaving the door open, I backed into the living room. "James," I hissed. "There's a Flexible Flyer in the closet."

He dropped the last of the pick-up sticks into the cardboard cylinder and snapped on the lid. "Uh-huh."

"But I saw it," I whispered louder, turning to face him. "It's not even Christmas yet. Why would Santa hide my sled in our closet?"

"He wouldn't." He stood and crossed his arms. "Santa keeps our presents at the North Pole until Christmas Eve. Then he loads them on his sleigh and flies around the world behind his reindeer."

"I know," I grated. "But it's gotta be my Santa present. So, who put it in the closet?"

"You're nuts!" His forehead furrowed. "If Mom and Dad hid your sled in the closet, then what about Santa?"

If Santa wasn't real, then what about God? Like Humpty Dumpty, my faith teetered on edge. My brain churned. Could I trust anything? "Come on!" I rasped. "I'll show you."

My brother followed me into the hall. Someone had closed the closet door, so I pulled it open and pointed. No sled.

I blinked—just an empty shelf.

James shrugged his shoulders. "See? You're crazy." He retrieved the can of Lincoln Logs and returned to the living room.

I trotted after him. "No, I promise, my sled was up there. Cross my heart and hope to die."

He dumped the green and brown pieces in a pile in front of the tree. "If you don't stop making up stories, Santa's for sure not gonna bring you anything but coal. You wanna play or not?"

I took a deep breath and traipsed into the kitchen where Mom stood alone at the stove. Maybe she had answers.

"Mom, James called me a liar."

She lifted a spoon from a steaming saucepan. Thick white liquid dripped off, and a heavenly scent wafted by. "Did you tell a lie?"

"No." My stockinged toe traced a circle on the linoleum. "At least, I don't think so." I looked up. "Did you ever think you could see something that no one else saw?"

Her spoon paused. "What exactly do you think you saw?"

"Um." I stalled, not sure where this conversation might go. No way could I risk spoiling Christmas. The celestial aroma made my stomach growl, and I hugged her leg. "What are you doin'?"

Mom let out her breath. "Making divinity." She pushed her cookbook out of the way. "Want to help?"

I nodded. "Where's Dad?"

"He had a little chore to take care of." Cracking two eggs on the rim of a ceramic bowl, she coaxed the edges apart. The whites oozed into the bowl, leaving the yolks trapped in the shells. "How would you like to whip these egg whites?"

I nodded, dragged a chair from the table, and climbed up, grateful for the change of topic.

She handed me our hand-crank mixer. I gripped the handle with my left hand and twirled the crank with my right. The cogwheel at the top spun.

Mom touched my hand. "Wait to spin the beaters until they're completely in the liquid. Otherwise, you'll spray egg white all over the kitchen. Don't ask how I know that."

Careful to lower the beaters into the bowl, I cranked until they blurred, knowing exactly what those whites must feel like. My whole life felt like a blur in a beater since we came to Alaska. I missed Cincinnati.

"That's enough, Roy." She lifted the mixer, and the whites formed sharp little peaks, a surprising outcome considering how they started. "Nice. Can you keep beating, but a little slower?"

I cranked while she poured a stream of steaming liquid from the kettle into my stiff egg whites. The mixture thickened, and my muscles burned. She took the mixer and raised it for inspection. "Perfect."

White stalactites dangled from the beaters. I wiped one off and stuck my finger in my mouth. Oooh! How could slimy egg whites turn into something this amazing. Was that what God was doing? Changing me in ways I never could have dreamed of?

She stirred in vanilla and broken pieces of nuts. "Bless my brother for mailing these pecans. A little taste of Louisiana. Fresh nuts are hard to find up here, and so expensive."

"Whatcha makin'?" James had sneaked in and stood behind us.

"Divinity. I took advantage of the sunny day because divinity won't set up in cloudy weather. Want to lick the beaters?" She handed him the mixer.

My brother grabbed the beater, and his tongue flicked out.

"Hey!" I complained. "Not fair. I did the work."

Mom dropped the last dollops of divinity onto wax paper. "Don't worry, Roy. You can scrape the bowl and lick the spoon. Only, don't make yourself sick on Christmas Eve."

"Humph," I grumped. After a day like this, why should I care? I scraped the bowl and aimed the spoon at Mom. "Know what I'm gonna do when I grow up?"

She tipped her head and peered over her glasses. "No, but I suppose you're going to inform me."

"I'm gonna eat as much candy as I want, whenever I want. And I won't have no rules."

"*Any rules.*" She untied her apron and hung it on a hook. Bending, she squeezed me tight. "We'll see. But first, you'll have to grow up."

Mom leads singing with Anna Bortel at the piano

24.

CHRISTMAS EVE

Mom slid the tray of divinity to the back of the counter to cool. "Would you boys like to walk downtown?"

"Yay!" We scrambled off the vinyl chairs and ran to the foyer, where we tangled with Dad coming in the front door.

Mom followed us down the hall. "Andrew, just in time. Care to join us on a walk downtown? I want to check our mail, and the sky is dark enough to enjoy Christmas lights."

He unwrapped his scarf and kissed her cheek. "Thanks, but my Christmas Eve devotional needs a touch more attention. Just don't let the clear sky fool you. That wind has a real nip."

We bundled until we could barely wiggle and waddled like ducklings behind Mom along the short path from our door to the street, which had been plowed wide enough for two cars to pass. On the flats, snow lay deeper than Mom was tall, and the banks thrown up by the snowplows formed a canyon twice as high. Wispy snow ghosts danced across the bleak landscape, stealing the last of the day's warmth.

James crawled onto a snow boulder left by the plows and tried making a snowball, but the fresh powder wouldn't stick with the temperature in single digits. His eyes glittered through a slit in his purple scarf. "Roy, c'mon."

Mom turned. "James, we have to keep moving or we'll freeze." He jumped off, and we trailed her down the center of the street.

The elementary school lay buried to the eaves, a foot of fresh snow blanketing its flat roof. Someone had stuck a cardboard sign in the snow with an arrow pointing left.

My brother held out a mitten. "What's that say?"

Mom read the hand-drawn words and laughed. "It says, 'Use side door.'"

James looked around. "Where's the front door?"

"Somewhere under that sign. Seems nobody's shoveling over Christmas break. It's scary how quickly the snow piles up around here."

Clank, clank, clank. She held up a hand. A car with tire chains eased through the intersection, and she peeked around the high bank. "Come on, the street's clear. Let's circle around Broadway."

We turned left for a block and then right, where James stopped and leaned back. "Wow, Mom! Why can't we go to this church?"

Designed in the shape of a cross, the building on our left emanated an aura of light, reverence, and purity. Arched windows, outlined in white lights, swept skyward in the deepening dusk. Three stories above, a bell tower crowned the steep gray roof, and at its pinnacle, a lighted cross pointed the way to Heaven. While we gazed, the wind died, and, one by one, stars twinkled to life in the purpling sky. *Silent night, holy night.* Mom hummed. *All is calm, all is bright.* She took James's hand. "The Episcopal Church *is* lovely. And good people worship here."

He waved a mitten at the ornate structure. "They must be a lot richer than us. All we have is a log church."

"Ours is beautiful in God's eyes. Remember what I've taught you? God loves each of us just the same, whether we're rich or poor." She turned away. "And in the end, it's a lot easier if we just accept what God has given us." She waved her arm. "Come along downtown."

A right turn took us onto McKinley Street where blue and green lights traced the pharmacy's windows. Bright bulbs winked around the windows of Egan's Valdez Supply, but between the bright lights of Egan's and the neon glow of the Pinzon Bar, the bank squatted in dour darkness. "Hey, Mom." I pointed. "How come the bank doesn't have any Christmas lights? Are they almost flat broke?"

She laughed. "I doubt it. It's just that not everyone celebrates Christmas."

At the next corner, blinking lights in Gilson's Mercantile highlighted scenes of Santa's elves painted on the insides of the broad panes, the garish display reflecting off the snow.

We stepped into the post office, and the mail clerk raised his head and smiled. "Mrs. Taylor, you have a package." He placed a box and a stack of envelopes on the counter and handed a candy cane to each of us boys. "Merry Christmas."

I looked up at Mom. "Can I eat my candy cane now?"

She scooped up the package and letters. "Why not? It *is* Christmas Eve."

With my scarf pulled below my chin, I slid the red-striped cane over my tongue. Nice. Real nice. The candy cane lasted all four blocks back up Alaska Avenue, and by the time we reached home, my red mitten was glued into a sticky peppermint fist.

Dad met us in the vestibule and flipped through the mail while we stomped snow off and shed our parkas and snow pants. He turned the package over and read the return address. "Hey, this is from your folks. It must be a Christmas present. Want to open it now or wait 'til tomorrow?"

Mom blew on her fingers and rummaged in a kitchen drawer for scissors. "Might be perishable. Better open it now." She cut the twine and slit the tape, and we gathered around as she tipped the box and released a foil-wrapped wheel. "Heavy," she said, hefting it in one hand. Her mouth quirked. "I think I know what it is."

"Open it!" James and I jittered around the kitchen.

She unwrapped the foil to pull out a darkly variegated cake. I drew back at the strong citrus odor. Dad laughed. "Fruitcake. How sweet of them." He turned to Mom and raised his eyebrows. "Your favorite?"

She shook her head. "I can't stand fruitcake."

"Neither can I." He took a sniff and frowned. "Why would they send us fruitcake if you don't like it?"

"My aunt made us a fruitcake every Christmas, and it was a big deal to her, so everyone ate a piece and told her how much we liked it. I guess I never set the record straight."

Perhaps I had sated myself on the peppermint stick. One mouthful of citrusy fruitcake proved almost too much. James spat his out in his hand and poked at gelatinous red, green, and yellow chunks. "What *is* this stuff?"

"Candied fruit and citrus peel." Mom giggled and washed his hand off in the sink.

I never saw the fruitcake again. I did check the closet for the sled, but the shelf remained as bare as Mother Hubbard's cupboard. My stomach tightened. Maybe I had been so naughty that the elves took the sled back. I really had tried to be nice, but how good was good enough? Or maybe there wasn't even a Santa Claus.

After a simple supper of potato soup, we bundled up and ventured forth. Subzero cold snapped us in the face, and we sealed our lips against the frigid air. Dad strapped his carbide lamp on his forehead, where it hissed, stank, and stabbed a yellow beam through the moonless night, the silence broken by the squeak and crunch of packed snow beneath our boots.

Christmas music spilled from the sanctuary door. Colored lights from the Christmas tree reflected off the donated piano where Miss Bortel sat. We kicked the snow off our boots and hung parkas on the coat rack. James and I greeted our friends from the orphanage before settling in the front row beside Mom.

Ben, already seated across the aisle, gave me a little wave. His mouth twitched, and one eyebrow went up. Deliberately turning away, I stared straight ahead. My stomach churned. I was mad at Ben about losing my knife. But it *was* Christmas Eve. If I didn't forgive now, would Santa still bring my sled? And how much forgiveness would be enough? I turned and waggled my hand in the tiniest wave I could manage, and his face lit up. I couldn't make myself smile back. It would have to do.

Miss Bortel stayed at the piano while Mom stepped to the front with her accordion and led us in Christmas carols. While Mr. and Mrs. Stein passed the offering plate, she set down her accordion, and Miss Bortel's fingers floated across the piano keys. As smooth as Grandpa Smith's sugar cane molasses, Mom's solo voice flowed through the sanctuary. *"O holy night, the stars are brightly shining, it is the night of our dear Savior's birth."*

I sat spellbound. It was a holy night.

Dad struck a match and lit a tall white candle on the lectern. "The people that walked in darkness have seen a great light," he quoted from the prophet Isaiah. "They that dwell in the land of the shadow of death, upon them hath the light shined. For unto us a child is born, unto us a son is given."

He nodded to Mr. and Mrs. Stein, who walked down the center aisle, passing out finger-sized candles until we each had our own. Dad raised his hand. "In the beginning, in His second act of creation, God said, 'Let there be light,' and there was light. And God saw the light that it was good." He smiled and described how light brings deliverance and hope. How the wise men followed the light. He talked about Jesus, who declared, "I am the light of the world. He that followeth Me shall not walk in darkness but shall have the light of life."

When Mr. Stein switched off the lights, the sanctuary was as black as night save for tremulous glimmers from the Christ candle on the lectern. Some of the younger children whimpered while Dad carried the candle down the aisle, lighting the first candle in every row. In turn, we offered the flame to our neighbor until, candle by candle, flickering yellow framed each face, and an otherworldly glow suffused the log walls.

Raising our lights, we sang "Silent Night" a cappella in four-part harmony. I shivered despite the warmth of the sanctuary. We had the most beautiful church in Valdez.

We bundled up, said our goodbyes, and turned for home. High above, Little Bear clung to the North Star while the myriad host of heaven circled in eternal pursuit. A twinkling reddish light made me pause. Rudolph's nose? Was Santa Claus on his way? Where in the world was my sled?

James stuck out his purple mitten. "Hey! A policeman." Flashing red lights lit shadowy figures on our snowy street.

"Andrew!" Mom picked up her pace. "That patrol car is in front of our house." We boys jogged after Mom and Dad.

A light blue late-model sedan had jammed its front end under the heavy-duty rear bumper of our truck, which was parked beside the high wall of snow in front of our house. A patrolman stood by the sedan and wrote in a small notebook while the driver, nose red as Rudolph's, leaned one elbow out the open window. He gazed up through his cracked windshield, apparently fascinated by the steel bumper of our truck.

Mom took our hands. "Drunks. Come on in the house, boys."

James hung back. "But Mom, I wanna know what happened."

She hurried us inside. "Nothing good, I'm sure, and you'll freeze out here. We need to get ready for Santa."

My heart leaped. *So, Santa is coming!*

She sent us upstairs to change into pajamas, and we raced back down as Dad came in. "The guy had too many drinks at the bar and lost control driving home. His car is too beat up to drive, so they'll leave it here tonight."

Mom shook her head. "I find it sad that people have nothing better to do on Christmas Eve but drink."

Dad tousled our hair. "Come on, boys. Let's get ready for Christmas."

We gathered in the living room. Presents spilled out under the tree—from friends and family as far away as Louisiana. Colored lights reflected off silver tinsel and shimmered across the walls. A fat candle glowed on the coffee table and scented the room with cinnamon and clove, a perfect complement to the aroma of cocoa simmering on the kitchen stove.

Mom set a tray of steaming white mugs and red and green frosted sugar cookies beside the candle. "Everyone, pick your Santa chair." Our family tradition required that each of us mark our Santa chair with our empty stocking. On Christmas morning, our main present—the Santa present—magically appeared unwrapped on our chosen seat, and our stocking bulged with gifts, one particular gift always in the toe.

Picking a Santa chair was first come, first served, and James and I raced for the couch. When it came to receiving, bigger was always better. Scrambling up to stand on a cushion, my brother declared, "I got here first."

"You cheated." I dragged him off, and we wrestled across the linoleum to the tree.

"Whoa, boys." Dad scooped us up, one under each arm, and planted us back on the couch. "There's plenty of room for both of you. No fighting on Christmas Eve."

Mentally measuring the couch, I debated whether the cushions were long enough for anything more than a Flexible Flyer. Or was I foolish to hope?

"Alright." I prodded James with my stockinged toe. "I'll share."

"Me too." He tickled my foot, and I jerked back.

Aside from the flickering candle, the Christmas tree cast the only light as Mom handed us mugs of cocoa topped with marshmallows. Leaning back in his overstuffed chair, Dad opened his Bible to the Gospel of Luke. He cleared his throat and began reciting from memory, "And it came to pass in those days, that there went out a decree from Caesar Augustus. . ."

I imagined Joseph, dressed in a bile-green bathrobe, riding a donkey for days and days with his "espoused" wife, whatever that meant. Arriving homeless and friendless in Bethlehem, they had their baby in a barn with the animals. If God was so poor, maybe it was okay that we didn't have much either. Except, I really wanted a Flexible Flyer.

Mom's turn came next. Settling between James and me, she lifted us to her lap and opened a large, illustrated book. "'Twas the night before Christmas and all through the house, not a creature was stirring, not even a mouse . . ."

Christmas sure was complicated: mice and reindeer, Jesus and Santa Claus, angels and elves, wise men, donkeys, candy canes, fruitcakes, Christmas trees, stars, presents with bows, colored lights, tinsel, and carols. What did it all mean? Which parts mattered?

Please, just let Santa come tonight.

Mom held out a small glass of milk and a saucer with a cookie. "Where shall we leave the Santa snack?"

"By the tree." James and I jumped off the couch.

"Okay, but Santa won't come until you boys are asleep. Go to the bathroom, and I'll be up in a minute to tuck you in."

The heat from the oil stove in the kitchen hardly registered in our upstairs bedroom, and we could see our breath as we crawled into our shared twin bed. Mom pulled the quilts under our chins, knelt, and said prayers before sitting on the side of the bed. *"O Little Town of Bethlehem,"* she sang softly, *"how still we see thee lie."* She kissed us each on the forehead. "Good night, boys." At the head of the stairs, she paused. "Remember, not a creature stirring 'til Dad plays 'Joy to the World' on his harmonica tomorrow morning."

My eyes had just closed when voices drifted up from the street. Our heads popped up like puppets. My heart did a flip.

"Maybe it's Santa," I whispered.

James nodded. "Let's check."

Tossing off the covers, we dropped to the bearskin rug and peered through frost-traced filigrees on the inside of the single-pane dormer window. The golden glow of our porch light extended onto the shadowy street where we could make out a small crowd gathered around the wrecked car.

James grabbed his bathrobe and slid on his slippers. "They're lookin' at the wreck. Let's go tell 'em what happened."

"Yeah, we better." I donned my bathrobe and fuzzy slippers and trotted after him down the stairs. Dishes clinked in the kitchen, but the living room was deserted. I tagged behind my brother out into the subzero night.

The front door banged behind us. "What are you boys doing?" Mom nabbed us each by the collar.

James wriggled in her grip. "We wanna tell the people about the wreck. They don't know what happened."

The onlookers tittered as she hustled us back inside and pulled the door firmly shut behind her. "I can tell you exactly what'll happen if you don't stay in bed. Santa will bring you nothing but coal." Scowling, she extended her arm toward the stairs like a traffic policeman. "Now, off to bed, and stay there."

I lay in the cold, semi-darkness. "James," I asked. "Do you think Santa Claus is real? Or did Mom and Dad make him up?"

"Does it matter?" he answered.

I considered for a moment. "I think so. I wanna believe in magic, and Santa's like magic. Hey, I hear someone. What if it's Santa, and we're not asleep?" We leaped from our bed and ran to the window. No Santa, only more onlookers inspecting the wreck.

"We oughta go talk to them." James pulled on his bathrobe and slippers.

I grabbed mine and followed. "But Mom said we'd get nothing but coal if we aren't asleep when Santa comes."

"You believe that? She made it up to scare us. Come on."

This time, our parents waited in the living room. Hands on her hips, Mom blocked the front door like a castle guard. "Did you boys hear what I told you last time? What are you doing down here?"

James smiled innocently. "We heard noises outside and figured we better check."

Mom glowered over the top of her glasses. "If you expect Santa to come, the only thing you better check on is your pillow. Now, both of you back in your bed and stay there!"

I tossed for a long time. Was there a Santa or not? If he was real, had I been good enough? How could I know? I drifted off, wondering what I had actually seen in the closet.

My brother's elbow jerked me awake. "Somebody's outside." He threw the covers off, climbed over me, and dropped to the bearskin rug.

Groaning, I rolled off the bed. By the golden glow of the porchlight, I could see James gaping out our window, face white, eyes as big as 'Nilla wafers. I stretched on tiptoes and followed his gaze. My heart sank to my knees.

Larger than life, Santa Claus himself stood on our street. Right outside our front door. Red coat. Black boots. Tasseled hat. Long white beard. And, when he laughed, his fat belly shook like a bowl full of jelly.

James turned to face me, his mouth a giant O. "What do we do now?" he rasped.

I could only whimper. We had wrecked Christmas! My brother got us into this mess; he had better get us out.

"Duck!" he screeched. Diving to the floor, we wriggled like GIs across the cold linoleum to the bearskin rug and hauled ourselves into bed. "Maybe he didn't see us." We tugged the quilts over our heads as Mom tiptoed up the creaky wooden steps. I held my breath and counted to ten, afraid she could hear my thumping heart.

Her footsteps padded back down. My breath whooshed out. "Whaddaya think? Is Santa still gonna come?"

My brother rolled away from me. "Don't be silly. Of course, he's coming! Now be quiet and go to sleep."

"Okay."

A tear trickled onto my pillow. The night stretched as black as coal. No matter what James said, we had ruined Christmas.

Christmas Day with the Steins

25.
CHRISTMAS UPS AND DOWNS

An avalanche of coal scraped and rumbled down the chute, cascaded across my bed, and crushed my lungs. Panicked, I struggled for breath. Red-suited Santa leered from the high cab of the dump truck. "Ho, ho, naughty boy. I saw you peeking out your window on Christmas Eve. Thought I wouldn't know you were out of bed? Ho, ho, ho. Let's see how you like coal for Christmas. Ho, ho."

"Ungh!" I grabbed at the sharp pain in my side.

"Roy," my brother hissed, poking me again with his finger. "Wake up. You're gonna miss Christmas! The snowplow just drove by."

So, that's what I heard! Thank goodness. Maybe Santa wasn't mad at me after all. Light from the porch lamp filtered through our bedroom window. "O-o-h." I pulled the heavy quilts over my head.

James prodded me again. "Get out of bed!"

"The snowplow goes by at four in the morning," I moaned. "I don't hear Dad's harmonica. Go back to sleep."

He tossed our covers aside. "We better go downstairs. We might miss it."

The crisp night air made me sneeze. "Are you crazy? It's way too early." I tugged the quilts back up. "You go if you want. I'm stayin' in bed."

"Suit yourself." He crawled over my prostrate form and dropped to the bearskin. "But if you miss Santa, I get dibs on your sled."

"Aaagh," I threw off the covers and sat up. "Wait for me." Retrieving bathrobe and slippers from the foot of the bed, I shuffled to the head of the stairway. The house lay dark and silent. Not a creature was stirring, not even a lemming, which was the closest thing Alaska had to a mouse. Probing with one foot, I felt for the stair. Step by cautious step, I descended the steep stairway and bumped into my brother at the bottom where he leaned against the closed hallway door. "What now?" The black night swallowed my whisper.

"We wait."

"I'm freezing. Why can't we wait in bed?"

"You wanna miss Christmas?"

"No," I whispered, "but Mom and Dad are still sleeping."

Whap! The door shook. *Whap!* He kicked it again. "They might be waking up right now."

"I don't hear nothin'. It's the middle of the night." I plunked down on the cold step, leaned against the wall, and drifted off.

"Joy to the World" jerked me awake. Dad's harmonica warbled from the far side of the door, now outlined in yellow incandescence.

The doorknob rattled. "Hooray!" James burst into the hallway. I staggered behind, blinking at the blazing ceiling light.

Cheeks dark with stubble, Dad grinned around his harmonica, plaid robe swaying as he dipped to the rhythm and tapped the beat.

"Merry Christmas," Mom croaked. Wrapped in her pink robe, she rubbed her eyes. "Let's see if Santa came."

She wasn't sure? Last night she seemed so confident. This might be the worst Christmas of my whole life.

Turning, she led the Taylor Christmas procession through the hall and into the living room. Dad, bringing up the rear, jigged to the last wavering notes of "heav'n and nature sing."

James sprinted for the couch. *"Woo-hoo!"*

I paused at the doorway, afraid to look. What if the couch was empty? Maybe I *was* getting coal. What if I hadn't been good enough? Or maybe Santa wasn't real after all.

With a pat on my shoulder, Dad nudged me through the door. "Roy, what did Santa bring you?"

In the subdued glow of Christmas tree lights and the dancing flame of the honey-colored candle, my eyes opened to the most beautiful sight in the world. Fire-engine red runners and varnished wood filled the back of the couch. The front end angled skyward, and up the center, a long red arrow vaulted into flight. *My Flexible Flyer*! I looked back at Dad, who bit his lip.

Mom beamed from beside the Christmas tree. "Roy, looks like Santa read your letter."

Of course Santa was real! Why had I worried so much? I strode to the couch, lowered the sled to the floor, and stretched out on its smooth surface. Eyes squeezed tight, I bared my teeth and slashed down treacherous mountain slopes.

"Wow! Look!"

I opened my eyes to James pumping one arm over his head, a bone-handled pocketknife clenched in his fist. His smile lit the room.

"Don't hurt yourself," Dad warned, though his grin matched my brother's. "That's not a toy. It's a Schrade."

A Schrade! Every boy in Valdez dreamed of owning a genuine Schrade pocketknife, an elite symbol, one that set you apart from the pack. Even the name was uttered with reverence. The only boy I had heard of who actually owned one was Butch, and he was a fourth grader. Glancing from my Flexible Flyer to James's knife, I felt a twinge of jealousy. But Santa brought me exactly what I asked for. And a sled, I reminded myself, would be hard to lose in a snowbank.

James inserted a thumbnail in the notch. *Click.* A long, wicked blade flipped out. He turned it over and over, colored tree lights reflecting off the carbon steel onto his amber eyes.

Dad asked. "So, Louela, what did Santa bring you?"

"Sorry, I got so caught up watching the boys I forgot to check." She turned, and her hand flew to her mouth. "Is this really what the box says?"

"Yep."

Mom slid out a black plastic case and snapped open the clasps, revealing a turntable. "I can't believe it, a phonograph! By any chance, did Santa bring me records?"

Dad nodded toward the pile under the tree. "Looks like he must have wrapped them."

Mom moved the candle, set her new record player on the coffee table, and plugged the cord into the outlet. "At least I can get this ready. Are you wondering what Santa brought you, hon?"

Dad raised his wrist, and Christmas lights sparkled off his Timex. "Christmas came early for me, and I'm not sure how good I've been. I didn't expect Santa to show up again, but let's take a look." He turned and lifted a gray-blue woolen scarf, cap, and mittens from his easy chair and wound the scarf around his neck. "Well, bless Mrs. Claus."

Mom kissed him on the cheek. "Who would have known Mrs. Claus could find yarn that matched your eyes. Now, kids, what's in your stockings?"

Like hogs turned loose on a food trough, we rooted through our stockings, flinging aside socks, mittens, pencils, Tootsie Rolls, and Whoppers. I shook the stocking out to be sure I hadn't missed something. An orange fell out of the toe and rolled across the linoleum.

Meanwhile, Dad set his stocking loot on the floor, still wrapped, and settled back in his chair. Crossing his feet on the ottoman, he retrieved his well-worn Schrade from a robe pocket. I watched him score the rind of his orange, wipe the blade on a handkerchief, and return it to his pocket. He peeled the orange and broke it as though it were the holy sacrament. Separating the wedges one by one, he chewed them with obvious relish, eyes focused on a scene only he could see.

I turned to Mom. "What's Dad doin'?"

"Eating his orange. Why?"

"Doesn't he wanna look at his stocking presents?"

She set her stocking aside and smiled fondly at Dad. "Your Dad and I grew up during the Great Depression. We both came from families without much money and a lot of mouths to feed. Some years there was no money for presents. Still, somehow his mama always found a way to make sure there was an orange in each of their stockings on Christmas morning, sometimes the only fresh orange they got all year. That orange seemed like a miracle to those kids."

Dad placed the peel on the floor. I walked over and leaned my elbows on the arm of his chair. "Were you hungry?"

"Too often."

"Do you think we'll go hungry?"

"No," he reassured me and spread his arms. "We live in Alaska, the land of opportunity." Dad gathered the spilled contents of his stocking. "Looky here. I got some new socks."

James brightened. "Somethin' smells good."

Mom sniffed. "Mmm. Smells like cinnamon rolls." She stretched. "Let's go see if they're ready. I'm hungry too."

Slurp, slurp. The coffee percolator greeted us as we filed into the toasty kitchen. While Dad poured mugs of coffee, Mom pulled a Postum tin off a shelf and mixed a cup for each of us boys. She lowered the oven door and slid out a pan of mountainous rolls, studded with pecans, golden caramel running like lava down their sides.

It seemed that Dad was hungry, too, because his prayer was quicker than usual. Ripping apart warm, airy rolls, I stuffed fist-sized chunks in my mouth and washed down the gooey confection with sips of Postum. The rich flavor of roasted grain and molasses tamed the sweet, nutty caramel. I sat back, sighed, burped, and licked sticky sweetness from my fingers and lips. How could Christmas get any better? Indeed, Alaska *was* the land of opportunity.

Dad glanced at our Big Ben on the counter. "Six o'clock." He eyed James. "Good thing *somebody* started Christmas at four o'clock. At least we'll have time to open the rest of our gifts before Steins come."

"If we can stay awake," Mom added. Fortified with caffeine, she and Dad followed us into the living room, where James and I sat side by side, beating a rhythm on the couch with our heels.

We took turns opening one gift at a time, starting with the youngest—me—and after a few rounds, wads of paper and curly ribbons carpeted the floor. We boys tossed aside the practical presents—jeans, shirts, and socks. But when I opened a brand-new, blue-striped bathrobe, I didn't waste a moment shedding my hand-me-down. Wrapping myself in the warm new robe, I snugged the belt around my waist and spun in a circle. Next year, I wouldn't even mind playing a shepherd in the Christmas pageant.

"Oh!" Mom finished tearing the paper off a flat present and pulled a record from its sleeve. Placing it on the turntable, she lowered the needle.

Low and mellow, a voice swirled through the room. *"I'm dreaming of a white Christmas."* Mom swayed to the beat. Her pink robe swished about her calves, and white skin flashed. I stole a peek at Dad, who tried to hide a smile. James gaped. We had never seen Mom dance. What was going on?

She noticed our stares and plopped into her chair. "Blame it on Bing Crosby," she giggled, and her eyes met Dad's. "Thank you, Santa. This may be my best Christmas ever." She shuffled through her stack of records. "And it looks like the Mormon Tabernacle Choir, Mantovani, and the Boston Pops will bring a little welcome relief through this long dark winter."

James and I both unwrapped Slinkys. Dad showed us how to step them down the stairs until they were tangled into a hopeless mess.

Mom scooped up the coils. "Time to get dressed, boys. Dad can sort this out after he delivers presents to the Children's Home."

"What are we giving them?" I asked.

"I knitted socks, mittens, and hats for all twelve of the kids."

"Can we go sledding after we get dressed?"

She checked the thermometer outside the kitchen window. "Sure. Just don't stay out too long. The temperature is a tad above zero."

After we dressed, Mom helped us with our snow clothes. I hefted my new sled with a grunt and followed James outside, where we waddled through fresh knee-high snow in our clumsy boots and puffy pants.

"Let's try the drifts by the house," he suggested, but towering banks of packed snow hemmed the path from our door to the street. I struggled to drag my sled to the crest. Snowflakes drifted from low clouds onto the white tabletop landscape, broken only by roofs and tips of trees. I paused atop the buried town to catch my breath. A thousand people lay hidden beneath this blanket of snow. I hoped they all had oxygen. Looking around, I could see nowhere to sled and dropped back down to the street. Taking turns, we plodded up and down our block, pulling each other on my sled, swerving to the side for clattering cars, and waving to the drivers. We were bushed by the time the Steins arrived, and Mom called us in to eat.

While shedding snow gear, I admired my long-anticipated Flyer. Its wooden slats and polished metal gleamed every bit as beautiful as I had hoped. But where were the thrills? Today, sledding had been more work than fun, like a racehorse straining against a loaded wagon. I sighed and followed the aroma of roast ham, sweet potatoes, green bean casserole, and pumpkin and pecan pies. At least Mom's cooking never let me down.

Our two families squeezed around the kitchen table with Clovis perched on a wobbly stack of *Encyclopedia Britannica*. Eyes closed, Dad lifted his face toward Heaven. "Thank You, Father, for this feast, and for," he paused, "grace. For safety despite our foolishness. For strength when we couldn't go on. Definitely for friends. Now we plead for wisdom to figure out what comes next. Amen."

Mom gave a little cough and after a deep breath, smiled. "Merry Christmas, everyone. Last year in Cincinnati, we never dreamed how much our lives would change, and to think it all started with your letter."

"Hear, hear!" Mr. Stein raised his water glass. "To good friends, to the goodness of the Lord." James and I tittered and tinkled our milk glasses together.

Dad lifted his tumbler. "And, to hard lessons learned the hard way."

The Steins chuckled. Mom winced and started the ham around. Conversation resumed. The silvery strains of Mantovani mixed with the clink of tableware.

While Mom cut my ham, I chewed on a cheesy green bean. When we moved to Valdez, I was only four and a half. Now, I was five. How could so much happen in just half a year? I looked up. "Mom, are we Sourdoughs yet?"

"I'm sure we're not. Why do you ask?"

"Just wonderin.' We've done a lot since we got here."

Mr. Stein nodded. "You certainly have. For one thing, the church would've never been finished without your long days of hard work." He looked around. "All of you."

"And" Mom added, "despite being complete Cheechakos, we managed to put a moose and bear in the freezer and make jelly. It's a comfort facing winter with a full larder. But look at that snow. Up to the eaves. You can't even see out the window, and winter's not half over."

Mrs. Stein touched Mom's arm. "I know how you feel, Louela, but trust me, you'll make it through your first winter just fine. Even in Alaska, spring will come."

"Andy," Mr. Stein said, "I know things didn't turn out the way you were expecting, but with a new pastor coming to fill the pulpit, what will you do next?"

Dad's mouth twisted. "You're right. Things didn't work out the way I expected." He leaned back. "To be honest, I've been making inquiries about homesteading."

I sat up straight. "What do you mean? We're already homesteading."

The adults chuckled, but James stared. "We live in a town, dummy."

"James," Mom reprimanded, "your brother is not dumb. He's just younger than you. Now apologize."

"Sorry," he mumbled.

Mom's eyes met mine. "Roy, you thought living in Valdez was homesteading?"

I nodded. "Everything's scary and hard. We're homesteaders, aren't we?"

"Homesteaders live way out in the woods with bears and moose," explained Mr. Stein, "and their closest neighbors are miles away."

"What?" My eyes blurred.

Mrs. Stein gave him a sharp look. "Wilson, you didn't have to scare the boy. Now you've made him cry."

I swallowed. "Would we have a house?"

Mom touched my tears with her napkin. "Probably a cabin at first."

"What about a bathroom?"

"An outhouse, I think. And it's unlikely we'd have electricity." She thumped her fork down and sat back. "We'd work our fingers to the bone and undoubtedly hurt ourselves if we didn't freeze to death or starve first." She raised an eyebrow at Dad.

"Oh, hon," Dad said, "it'll be our own warm, cozy place."

"Why can't we stay here?" I sniffed. "Or go back to Cincinnati?"

Mom patted my hand. "We just can't, but wherever we're together, we'll make it our home."

Mr. Stein cleared his throat. "Have you turned up anything, Andy? By now, most of the available land must be far out in the boonies."

"True," Dad answered, "but I ran across a unique opportunity. I'd rather wait until I know more before I talk about it, but if things work out, we might be homesteading by summer."

Mr. Stein smiled. "No surprise. Andy, one way or another, you'll figure out how to be a homesteader."

James bounced like a slinky. "I'll be one too."

"Obviously," Mr. Stein agreed. "Your mom and brother might take a little longer warming up to the idea, but having watched them, I know they'll do just fine."

"We will?" I squeaked.

Mom rumpled my hair. "Remember, Roy. We're on our way to being Sourdoughs, and Sourdoughs are fearless."

I nodded, but knew she was only trying to make me feel better.

After the Steins left, Mom suggested we go to bed early, and neither James nor I complained. High snowbanks reflected the porch light, casting soft shadows across the bedroom. Mom tugged the quilts under our chins. "Did you boys have a good Christmas?"

"Uh-huh." James yawned. "I love my pocketknife."

"How 'bout you, Roy?"

"It was good," I murmured. "I got my Flexible Flyer and a new robe."

"Are you glad we came to Alaska?" she asked.

"Yeah," James answered. "When can we homestead?"

She hesitated. "I don't know. Several things need to come together before that happens." She sat back. "Roy, I'm sorry you were surprised. I didn't realize you thought we were already homesteading."

"Then why'd we move here, anyway?"

She brushed my cheek. "To be honest, I'm not even sure I know anymore. Why do you ask?"

"I sorta wish we were back in Cincinnati."

James punched my shoulder. "How many kids in Cincinnati have a bearskin rug? I love Alaska. I'm gonna live here 'til I die."

Mom smiled and ran her fingers through his hair. "Valdez *is* very different from Cincinnati, and homesteading will be even more so."

"But everything here is new and scary. And now," my lip trembled, "now we're takin' off for the woods."

"But *you're* brave now too, Roy." James patted my shoulder. "Really brave."

"I am?" I turned to look at him. "I wanna be brave, but I don't like Dad's adventures."

"That makes two of us." Mom's gaze lingered on the frosted window. "Roy, do you really wish we hadn't come?"

I reflected on the past half year. The long trip. Terrifying adventures. Unending work. Learning to live off the land. Hard-earned courage.

"No," I whispered. "Alaska is our home now. But why can't we stay in Valdez?"

"Good question." Mom sat back, a finger on her lips. "I agreed to come to Alaska to be a pastor's wife, possibly in a frontier town, but in a *town*." She took a deep breath. "Now, everything's changed, and I don't doubt I'm more scared than you are."

I frowned, but she kissed our foreheads. "Sleep well, my little Alaskans. Whatever happens, I know we can count on God to take care of us."

As she disappeared down the stairs, I turned to James. "You really think I'm brave?"

"Almost brave. Not bad for a little kid."

"Do you get scared?"

"Sometimes." He yawned. "But I still don't wanna live anywhere else." He rolled over, and except for our breathing, the house lay quiet.

"G'night, Roy."

"G'night."

"Sleep tight."

I giggled. "Don't let the bedbugs bite."

"If they do, hit 'em with a shoe."

"Kill forty-two."

"I love you."

"I love you too."

The last I remember, my brother snored softly beside me.

ACKNOWLEDGEMENTS

The most surprising aspect of this project was the sheer number of people whose intellect, expertise, and insight were required to bring the book to print. The following list is undoubtedly incomplete.

First and foremost, thank you to my wife, Nancy, who gently propelled me out the door in 2012 when I tried to back out on my first writing class, Memory to Memoir. Over the next eleven years, she has, without complaint, acted as first reader and editor, miraculously transforming my often incomprehensible first drafts into good writing.

Laura Kalpakian, author, teacher, mentor, and friend, thank you. Your insights and painfully honest critiques have inspired a host of first-time authors to push through mediocrity and publish the stories we dreamed of writing.

Tale Spinners, my drafts would still be in a file drawer without you. Thank you, Joe, Linda, Cheryl, Kate, Victoria, Debbie and Laura, our leader. I am awed by the six years we shared meals, stories, laughter, and tears. Thank you also, Red Wheelbarrow Writers, for your unflagging applause and assurances.

I owe a considerable debt to the beta readers whose encouragement and honest critiques pushed me to rethink and rewrite everything. Thank you, Jenny, Janel, LL, Chuck, Chad, Betsy, Mary, Joseph, and Sean.

Obviously, no book comes to fruition without editors, and I am genuinely grateful despite the hard labor you asked of me. Robbi Sommers Bryant cleaned up a wagonload of grammatical errors before tactfully guiding the project back from the edge of the earth. Amber Qureshi winnowed out a cloud of chaff and injected the manuscript with new life thanks to her energetic imagination.

Finally, my thanks to Koehler Books for taking on this project, to acquisitions editor Greg Fields, who saw the potential for a book, to editor Joe Cocarro, who cheered me across the finish line while grooming the manuscript for printing, and to designer Lauren Sheldon, whose magic made the rest of us look good. Finally, thank you, John Koehler, for bringing this book into being.

COMING

Curious about what happens next to the young Taylor family as they homestead in the Alaskan Territory? Watch for the sequel to *The Road to Courage*.

www.ingramcontent.com/pod-product-compliance
Lightning Source LLC
LaVergne TN
LVHW091718070526
838199LV00050B/2449